D1453679

Digital Nomads

Dental Notes

DIGITAL NOMADS

In Search of Freedom, Community, and Meaningful Work in the New Economy

Rachael A. Woldoff and Robert C. Litchfield

OXFORD
UNIVERSITY PRESS

OXFORD
UNIVERSITY PRESS

Oxford University Press is a department of the University of Oxford. It furthers
the University's objective of excellence in research, scholarship, and education
by publishing worldwide. Oxford is a registered trade mark of Oxford University
Press in the UK and certain other countries.

Published in the United States of America by Oxford University Press
198 Madison Avenue, New York, NY 10016, United States of America.

© Oxford University Press 2021

All rights reserved. No part of this publication may be reproduced, stored in
a retrieval system, or transmitted, in any form or by any means, without the
prior permission in writing of Oxford University Press, or as expressly permitted
by law, by license, or under terms agreed with the appropriate reproduction
rights organization. Inquiries concerning reproduction outside the scope of the
above should be sent to the Rights Department, Oxford University Press, at the
address above.

You must not circulate this work in any other form
and you must impose this same condition on any acquirer.

Library of Congress Cataloging-in-Publication Data
Names: Woldoff, Rachael A., author. | Litchfield, Robert C., author.
Title: Digital nomads : in search of freedom, community, and meaningful work in
the new economy / Rachael A. Woldoff and Robert C. Litchfield.
Description: New York, NY : Oxford University Press, [2021] |
Includes bibliographical references and index.
Identifiers: LCCN 2020022225 (print) | LCCN 2020022226 (ebook) |
ISBN 9780190931780 (hardback) | ISBN 9780190931803 (epub) | ISBN 9780190931810
Subjects: LCSH: Knowledge workers. | Flexible work arrangements. |
Telecommuting. | Self-employed. | Alternative lifestyles.
Classification: LCC HD8039.K59 W65 2021 (print) |
LCC HD8039.K59 (ebook) | DDC 331.7—dc23
LC record available at https://lccn.loc.gov/2020022225
LC ebook record available at https://lccn.loc.gov/2020022226

9 8 7 6 5 4 3 2 1

Printed by Sheridan Books, Inc., United States of America

To Rosabel and Roscoe, our magical travel companions. Suksma.

CONTENTS

PREFACE

On March 11, 2020, the World Health Organization declared a global pandemic. Covid-19, a viral infection originating in China, had been spreading around the globe. Government officials scrambled to declare states of emergency. As cases spread and the death toll rose, governments issued directives that citizens must stay at home to slow the rate of infections and reduce the load on overwhelmed health care systems.

In the midst of this public health crisis, people quite naturally worried about work. News articles advised anxious people about how to tell their bosses that they wanted to work from home. These articles quickly became less relevant as working from home became the only option for all but those employed in essential jobs related to food, transportation, and health care. A class divide rapidly emerged between those whose jobs could be done remotely and others whose jobs required their physical presence. Individuals were confused about what their managers could and could not request of them. Managers struggled to deal with disruptions to business, with many feeling skeptical about remote work and distrustful of employees who were suddenly out of immediate reach. In some cases, workers themselves wanted to take the risk and come to the office, as their offices had never made any real effort to digitize their jobs, and they could not imagine another way. What about vacation time, layoffs, retaliation, micromanaging? How would this all go down?

As we write this in early April 2020, the Covid-19 pandemic has already killed tens of thousands of people worldwide and is expected to kill hundreds of thousands more. Yet efforts to suppress infection rates have also taught us many positive lessons about remote work. In the space of a few days, organizations learned that many traditional, in-person jobs could, in fact, be performed remotely. As managers contemplate a future in which it may be dangerous to unnecessarily gather employees in person for quite some time, the idea of granting individuals new locational freedoms at work cannot be dismissed as readily as it was only a few weeks before. For many jobs, it will no longer be possible to say that remote working "can't be done," and conversations will shift to focus on how to optimize it.

This book is, on one level, about a nomadic style of remote working that may mostly cease until the pandemic lightens. On another level, however, digital nomads' desires to choose their location, to work on their own terms, and to live in proximity to like-minded others are more relevant than ever. We cannot know how the pandemic will ultimately affect the global economy, international travel, or knowledge work, but we feel confident that workers will continue to seek both individual freedom and the support of like-minded community. We imagine a post-pandemic world in which many more employees, and even managers, will wonder why we ever forced people into full-day in-person schedules with others with whom they may have little in common other than the organizations that employ them. We hope that, by the time you read this, we are all living in such a world.

ACKNOWLEDGMENTS

To the digital nomads, in Bali and elsewhere, who have inspired us with your search for freedom, community, and meaningful work: thank you for sharing your stories and insights. Though we differ from you in many ways, we are inspired by your tendencies toward nonconformity and your spirit of self-determination. We are grateful that you spent so much time with us and trusted us with such intimate details of your life. You have taught us enough to write a dozen different books. We recognize your struggles and triumphs, and we appreciate your openness and generosity. We are especially grateful to those informants who helped us in the earliest stages of research and who were integral to the process of sampling, who invited us to events, and who provided enthusiastic triangulation.

The Balinese people we met during our fieldwork helped our very non-nomadic family acclimate. Since most nomads we interviewed did not have children, it was the very family-oriented Balinese people around us who helped us navigate childcare, sickness, and daily struggles living abroad as a family as we conducted our research. We are especially grateful to I Ketut Artono, who made sure that we did not drive a scooter anywhere and whose patient, calming, and kind smile was a source of comfort to us all as we muddled our way through Bali with a three-year-old and a seven-year-old. More than that, we are grateful to have lived among and interacted with the people of Bali for an extended period of time. This was the experience of a lifetime for our family. We will always treasure our memories of being surrounded by a beautiful group of people who continue to inspire us in their devotion to traditions and their philosophy of life. It was eye-opening and transformative in ways that are difficult to describe, but we hope to meet again.

James Cook, our editor, provided support for and thoughtful questions on the early formulations of our ideas and interpretations. We thank you for your analytical mind, your trust, your time, and especially, your interest. We also thank the anonymous reviewers for their many suggestions that significantly improved this book, and we thank others at Oxford University

Press, including Emily MacKenzie for her assistance. In addition, we thank the many participants in sessions of the Academy of Management, the American Sociological Association, the Creativity Collaboratorium, the Eastern Sociological Society, and the Urban Affairs Association who offered questions, suggestions, and lively dialogue as we presented portions of these ideas over the past few years.

Finally, we thank our many family members, friends, neighbors, and colleagues who talked to us about their own mobility decisions and work lives, offering comparisons that showed the similar struggles that many people have across generations and countries. In writing and thinking about the digital nomad community, we benefited greatly from their practical, challenging, curious, and clarifying questions.

We began this project after writing about the creative class, considering the rise of remote work, and hearing so many anecdotes from students who are frightened of the world of work. As we embarked on the writing process, many people around us told us that they hate their jobs and commutes and are desperate for more time and more meaning. While many current trends in employment policies and practices are undoubtedly harmful to individuals' well-being, we hope that the ideas in this book will spur others to consider adaptations that may restore autonomy and dignity to individuals' working lives and communities.

Introduction

Today, as always, men fall into two groups: slaves and free men. Whoever does not have two-thirds of his day for himself, is a slave, whatever he may be: a statesman, a businessman, an official, or a scholar.

Friedrich Nietzsche,[1] *as quoted by Nadine,[2] a forty-year-old entrepreneur and digital nomad*

Ellie had been working as a journalist in London for eight years when she arrived at the Indonesian island of Bali in 2014 to become a *digital nomad*. At thirty-three, her decision to leave London might have seemed impulsive or irrational, especially for a graduate of a prestigious university who was lucky enough to land her dream job. But Ellie told us that she has idealistic tendencies. For instance, she considers it an act of rebellion that she chose to enter the world of journalism at the inopportune moment when most of her peers and role models were sounding alarms about the industry's changing landscape and rapid decline in sustaining employment options. Most of her college friends moved to large cities to chase coveted jobs: "Everyone just moves to London. . . . A lot of them go into banking and law, but I didn't want to." Unfortunately, Ellie soon faced the harsh realities and disappointments of being a creative professional in the big city. She felt alone in her refusal to settle for unfulfilling work, uninspiring colleagues and role models, and a life that she believed was moving in a losing direction:

Actually, newspapers are just owned by big corporations, and they have their own agendas. And also, just the realities of ringing up hedge funds and trying to find out who's lost the most money in the first quarter of the year is just not terribly inspiring, really. And when you look around, your colleagues are much older than you, and you just have no desire to end up like that. I was like, "None of this works for me."

The solution? Ellie booked a flight to move almost 8,000 miles away in order to reinvent her life. She believed that in Bali's digital nomad scene she would have all she needed to pursue the freedom and community that she craved. She would begin living like others in that ecosystem: finding employment online, keeping her possessions to a minimum, traveling as she pleased, and working remotely from anywhere she wanted. Her only requirement would be a good internet connection. She explained that now, Bali feels like home to her. There, she has found a community of kindred spirits in search of another way of living: "Most [digital nomads] who end up in Bali are idealistic. They're people who are not prepared to accept the reality presented by everyone else."

A revolution is brewing in cubicles worldwide. Creative class jobs and cities, supposedly the bedrock of the new economy,[3] are failing to deliver the personal fulfillment that many ambitious younger professionals believe is essential to their lives. Unwilling to sacrifice their autonomy and values to strive for someone else's dream on someone else's terms, and excited by new options for personal mobility and online work, digital nomads have struck out on their own. As a starting point, they turn to online communities for opportunities to connect to like-minded others, but soon these driven but disaffected individualists need more. They leave their cities, jobs, friends, families, and countries in search of a face-to-face community of unconventional people who share their ideals and goals—what they call a *tribe*.[4] Usually, they find their community in low-cost global hubs in places like Indonesia, Thailand, the Philippines, Cambodia, Vietnam, Colombia, Mexico, or Portugal. There, united by an intense, shared commitment to personal reinvention, digital nomads are creating new paths to meaningful work. More surprisingly, they are also pioneering a new type of place-based community.

This book began with the goal to better understand why work-focused, creative professionals with promising careers would abandon not just their jobs but their home cities and countries, and move around the world in search of new working lives that are untethered to any particular location. Our immersion in the world of these digital nomads through fieldwork, interviews, and social media analysis yielded a wealth of description about why they left and how they crafted new lives and new communities. Collectively, these rich data provide a sense of how some individuals have responded to the transformation of creative class work into a routine commodity, and to the limitations of community in world-class cities.

Why study digital nomads? Digital nomads deserve systematic attention because they represent the vanguard of a growing rejection of the terms imposed on workers within the new economy. The failures of creative class cities and jobs have led many individuals to despair that they will not be able to realize their work and life goals through traditional employment. In creative class cities, the cost of living has outpaced wage growth. Although creative class professionals earn good wages by societal standards, many find that their wages do not go very far in the top-tier cities where their jobs are located. Moreover, their busy lives leave them little time to enjoy urban amenities, and the low vacancy rates in top-tier cities mean that individuals do not necessarily live in close proximity to others whom they view as like-minded. In terms of employment, some digital nomads have rejected the mainstream cultural norms of tolerating long hours of boredom and unnecessary face time at the office, where they do not have enough work to do and feel that they add little value. Others have felt overworked and powerless to control important aspects of their jobs, including the amount of work, the pace, the hours, the travel, and the quality of the end product. Whatever their varying circumstances, these individuals have in common that when they considered their futures and trajectories, they felt stifled and unable to be creative—to develop and produce work that would be rewarding and fulfilling.

In addition to their feelings about their own work and life outcomes, digital nomads view their decisions to leave home as a reaction to broader conditions in contemporary work and society. Many digital nomads believe that the cultural norms of creative class cities and workplaces resist change and spread fear, encouraging workers to be dispassionate and unquestioning robots. Digital nomads recognize that some people are content to go through the motions of their lives and jobs, but nomads are not; they believe this path will only lead to deeper dissatisfaction. Enacting their belief that "You can't change who you're with, but you can change *who you're with*," digital nomads have abandoned their efforts to change attitudes at home and moved in search of new communities that make sense to them, where like-minded people are building new lives and identities that return control over work, life, and the balance between them to each individual. This group of people has walked away from the jobs, locations, and lives that constitute the Promised Land of the new economy, but they have not done so in order to *avoid* working. Instead, they want to transform work from a dehumanizing experience into one that builds and sustains their sense of freedom and purpose.

In this book, we show how digital nomads' search for a new path to more freedom, more meaningful work, and a better quality of life has led to a new type of place-based community in Bali, one that is paradoxically characterized by simultaneously high levels of fluidity and intimacy. Nomads move around frequently, so their community is *fluid* in the sense that individuals are constantly coming and going. This fluidity defines the community, continuously stoking it with the energy of newcomers and returnees, while simultaneously draining it as nomads drop out of community life at their whim or leave it altogether. However, this fluidity does not result in social distance. Rather, their community is *intimate*. Living in a digital nomad hub means choosing to be alone in a faraway place yet surrounded by others who are also struggling to establish new, sustainable lives. The visible presence of so many like-minded others leads nomads to reach out to connect, share their personal stories, and exchange support. Moreover, Bali's reputation as a leading hub of remote working and a place of personal reinvention means that individuals arrive there with the intention of being open to participating in deep, emotional exchanges with others.

It is our view that digital nomad communities are a unique and contemporary manifestation of larger societal changes, and we take as our task explaining *why* and *how* they are formed. Digital nomads are largely Millennials (born between 1981 and 1996), and therefore digital natives, who are comfortable with intimate online sharing and with blending in-person and online contacts. However, their insistence on the necessity of an in-person community in Bali and elsewhere shows that online community is not enough even for the most enthusiastic remote workers. We have found that digital nomads identify strongly with their shared personal narratives and journeys, and this unites them by priming them for intimacy; as a digital nomad hub, the structure and culture of Bali encourages them to recognize, revere, and create safe spaces for realizing that intimacy. Digital nomads' strong individualist values, and in particular, their emphasis on novelty and the freedom to choose their location, leads them to create communities that embody these same ideals. Nomads embrace the fluidity in their community, celebrating the continual influx and outflow of new members rather than feeling threatened by it or resisting it. Bali, with its culture of *Eat, Pray, Love*[5]–style personal development/adventure tourism, is an ideal location for digital nomadism as visitors of all types have already normalized the celebration of a fluid and intimate community. Almost all digital nomads whom we met indicated that they would move on from Bali at some point. Thus, digital nomads seek both location independence and community, but they also require an individualist, obligation-free, no-strings-attached mindset.

DEFINING DIGITAL NOMADS

Digital nomads are people with mobile work lives. They can live and work anywhere in the world, as long as they have access to the internet. They use this freedom to become what they call *location independent,* meaning that they either sell or store their possessions and divest or rent out their properties to allow them to leave home to travel and live as they please.[6] Although any particular destination might be temporary for a digital nomad, many view this lifestyle as a long-term choice. To demonstrate their commitment to this decision, they cut ties to the material trappings of their old lives and they engage in rituals to demarcate their mobility decision as a meaningful and symbolic step in the larger process of adopting an entirely new way of life. For instance, one way that digital nomads often celebrate their new life choice is by getting tattoos that feature images of maps, globes, and cultural symbols of countries they have visited. In addition to adorning their bodies with elaborate Buddhas, dragons, Hindu gods, lotus flowers, and tribal symbols, they also get minimalist line tattoos displaying quotations ("live each day as if it were your last") or words ("yes," "go," "fearless," "freedom," "wanderlust") that remind them to stay on their new path.

Surprisingly, despite the "nomad" label, these location-independent workers often choose *not* to keep moving regularly. For them, the point is not how often they travel but that they now possess the *freedom* to do it while working. In our research, we observed three phases of nomadism, defined by one's length of residence in a single country. Though we acknowledge that individuals sometimes identify with categories that do not fit their length of residence, we find that one's length of stay is a useful and meaningful way to understand the experience of nomadism and one's role within the ecosystem of a digital nomad hub.

The first phase, which we label the *honeymoon* stage,[7] includes individuals who join Bali's place-based digital nomad community for the first time and who have been there for less than two months (the tourist visa time limit). Thus, all digital nomads start as honeymooners. Although honeymooners are most closely aligned with the stereotypes of digital nomads who are promoted online and in popular media, our research suggests that few digital nomads can sustain the frequent passport-stamping lifestyle for long periods of time. As one nomad put it: "Honestly, you can live out of a backpack for a while and post these pictures of the 'office of the day,'[8] but in my opinion, nobody I've ever met is as productive when they're moving around all the time as when they're not, and I think they're lying if they say they are." Nevertheless, this is the largest subgroup of digital nomads in a hub because it includes a wider range of people who are experimenting with the lifestyle.

Of course, some digital nomads find that they want to stay beyond the two months allowed by Indonesia's tourist visa. Those who wish to extend their time in this digital nomad hub execute *visa runs,* leaving the country just long enough (sometimes, only for a few hours) to restart their visa clock. We label these individuals *visa runners*. We define them as nomads who have left the country at least once to renew their visas, and then they have returned. Although not all honeymooner nomads become visa runners, they are a surprisingly large segment of the digital nomad community. Furthermore, when nomads go on a visa run, they are broadcasting their more serious commitment to the digital nomad lifestyle and community.

Finally, some digital nomads stay in the same place for a year or longer. Although they must continue to make visa runs as needed, these individuals often take additional actions to signal their devotion to nomadism and their specific intent to remain in Bali an extended time period (e.g., signing a long-term lease on a rental villa and getting a pet). We label this group *resident nomads* in recognition that despite their seeming stability, these individuals still identify as location independent. By contesting the idea that they are functionally based in Bali, resident nomads cling to their identities as unencumbered free agents who may choose to leave at any time.

Digital nomads are different from other kinds of expatriates. Much of the previous research on the general category of expatriates has depicted employees of large multinational organizations, many of whom are involuntary pawns who have difficulty adjusting to new cultures.[9] Alternatively, another image of expatriates that consumes the popular imagination is the class of affluent, self-satisfied globe-trotting elites who move from one stimulating cultural experience to the next. Newspapers, glossy magazines, internet sites, and social media outlets depict these kinds of expats as frivolous trust-funders on holiday, attending the circuit of arts festivals (e.g., Art Basel, Cannes, Venice, and Burning Man) and ideas conferences (e.g., TED, Davos, and Aspen), as they cavort with billionaires and celebrities.

In reality, digital nomads are fundamentally different from typical categories of expats. For instance, they are clearly not like the corporate soldiers and privileged jetsetters whom one may imagine. Instead, digital nomads are self-initiated expats who span a broad economic spectrum, and they largely launch their nomadic lives lacking significant wealth that could cushion them in the case of failure. They report that they have been pushed into their new lives by personal crises and work-related burnout, as well as pulled into the nomad lifestyle by the promise of travel, freedom, and time to reconsider their work-life balance and implement a new career plan for the future. Traveling alone and without great wealth or a corporate patron, digital nomads share some traits with a third expatriate category: the travel junkies—hippies, seekers, and other vagabonds who seek adventure. However, digital nomads' commitment to long-term, independent working and their strong work identities also set them apart from this standard expatriate group. Digital nomads do not wish to drift; they have left home to focus on creating sustaining and meaningful careers.

WHY NOW? THE EMERGENCE OF DIGITAL NOMADS

The emergence of digital nomadism is tied to changes in technology, mobility, and work that have converged to create new opportunities for creative professionals. The challenges facing these knowledge workers, including boredom, overwork, and burnout, are hardly new phenomena. What *is* new is that an increasing number and variety of professionals are becoming aware of the benefits and possibilities that location-independent working provides. According to a 2017 Gallup report about the growth and mainstreaming of remote work, 43 percent of Americans spend some time working remotely, and 31 percent of Americans who work remotely do so 80 to 100 percent of the time—a 7 percent increase from 2012 to 2016.[10] This shift toward remote work, together with the mobility offered by inexpensive international air travel, provides a growing segment of professional workers with unprecedented discretion in choosing their work environments. Now more than ever, talented individuals who become disaffected with their work and home lives can leave them behind and seek new environments of their own choosing in which to work. Some, like Carol, a thirty-seven-year-old technical customer service employee whom we profile in chapter 4, continue working for the same company. Others change employers, become freelancers, or enter the world of e-commerce as entrepreneurs.

As creative work becomes more routinized in the knowledge economy, it loses its luster for many talented people. Technology both enables new forms of remote work and spreads information about new work opportunities. In an era of inexpensive global travel, courage and talent easily substitute for wealth in enabling travel. Sam, a twenty-eight-year-old programmer from England, read an advertisement about building digital startups and decided to leave his job to work for half the wage in Bali. Like many nomads we spoke to, Sam was weary of the conveyor belt of routinized knowledge work. As he told us, "My work is my identity," and he was unwilling to remain a well-paid cog in a corporate machine. Joining a support group for new digital nomads fueled his confidence: "When I first went to Bali I went to Project Getaway and met these twenty entrepreneurs, and I'm chatting to these people, and I'm thinking, okay, you're in Bali and working on some cool stuff, but if these guys can do it, shit, I can do it for sure." As individuals like Sam meet like-minded others on similar journeys, they quickly gain access to new sources of knowledge—in-person in locations where nomads congregate, online in private social media forums, and through trial and error in traveling—that provide tools and tips to help to sustain the lifestyle.

CREATING A DIGITAL NOMAD HUB, BALI STYLE

As we shared our curiosity about digital nomads with friends, colleagues, and students, people often asked us why someone would travel 8,000 miles just to work in a coworking space or café. After all, they can plug their computer into a Starbucks at home. Our conversations with digital nomads left no doubt that they believe Bali's digital nomad hub is completely different from remote working in typical Western cities, where the coworking environment encourages introversion and privacy, and where one remains embedded in societal norms and obligations. Digital nomads are not seeking to rent office space at WeWork,[11] and they relish the novelty of working alongside a changing cast of people from many countries and backgrounds. They have a deep desire to escape Western cultures that they view as pathological to the pursuit of their life and work aims. Listening to their explanations about how the role of Bali as a place differs from Vancouver, London, Paris, and New York, we recognized parallels to topics that have long engaged urban sociologists.

Places have constellations of characteristics that support different types of activities. For instance, top-tier cities often possess amenities that attract more highly educated people,[12] but the intensity of big-city life is often theorized to be troubling for citizens.[13] Bali's physical environment, lifestyle, cost, and culture come together in a unique fashion to provide amenities while minimizing stressors for those interested in creative work. There, the sensory stimuli are altogether different from those found back home—wherever that home might be. This novelty, coupled with a traditional arts culture, is immediately recognizable as an amenity to creative people. Yet Bali's novelty is cushioned by its natural beauty, laid-back, island lifestyle, relative freedom from societal rules and obligations, and modest cost of living for Western-style luxury. Indeed, Bali's long-established expat culture of retirees and spiritual seekers has created a foundation for nomads, complete with contemporary conveniences and an English-language hospitality industry. Thus, part of Bali's allure to digital nomads is the place itself.

Still, the dynamics of expatriate life in Bali depend on the people who choose to come there.[14] It is well known that people self-select when they migrate. Accordingly, the expats who make Bali a destination share characteristics and traits (e.g., socioeconomic status, ethnicity, life-cycle stage) that influence their behavior and associations. Clustering together there, they have transformed Bali into a digital nomad hub.

The transience of Bali's digital nomad community differentiates it from prior research on place-based subcultural communities, which tend to assume or find that communities flourish under the conditions of stability and continuity. This is not how digital nomad hubs work. Many nomads have stayed in Bali much longer than other places, but they are not staying for good. It is a place where they feel they can dive deeply into personal development and reinvention, eventually launching new businesses and careers that will take them on to other destinations. With so many people seeking these outcomes but not planning to be rooted, Bali provides what nomads termed an "ideal," "amazing," "perfect," "magic" digital nomad community. In meeting their needs, Bali's digital nomads have created a vibrant community: one characterized by significant connection and intimacy that is nourished by its population fluidity. Individuals come and go, but the character of Bali's digital nomad community exhibits some resilience to these fluctuations.

THE RESEARCH

We began this project in the summer of 2016, when the first author traveled to Bali for two and a half weeks of fieldwork. Beginning during that trip and continuing for the next ten months, we conducted most of the seventy extended, semi-structured interviews that form the core of our data. We then embarked together with our two children on three months of living in Bali (April–July 2017), where we conducted fieldwork in the digital nomad communities in Canggu, Ubud, and Sanur. During this time, we worked and socialized extensively with digital nomads, living alongside them in these communities. Although our fieldwork finished in July 2017, we continued contact with digital nomads online through social media throughout our time writing the book. As a result, we have stayed in touch with many of those in our primary sample into the spring of 2020.

In terms of demographics, thirty-six of our seventy formal interviews were with women. Our interviewees hail from eighteen countries: Austria, Australia, Brunei, Canada, Denmark, England, France, Germany, India, Indonesia, Ireland, New Zealand, Romania, Russia, Sweden, Switzerland, Ukraine, and the United States. Among interviewees, seven are Asian, three are Black (one Canadian, two American), and one is half Latino (i.e., 16 percent were nonwhite). The rest are non-Latino white. The mean age is thirty-three, and thirty-nine (or 55 percent) are in their thirties. In terms of educational attainment, there is a range: high school degree; some college

("I never finished it because I already started my business"); alternative training (e.g., Chinese medicine); college degree (often called a waste of time); some graduate work; master's degree or MBA; doctoral degree. Most have a bachelor's degree, though their majors ranged widely (e.g., accounting to philosophy). One woman served in the US Navy, one man in the Austrian military.

PLAN OF THE BOOK

To better understand Bali's digital nomads, we begin chronologically with a depiction of their pathways to this lifestyle and community. In organizing our description of their journeys, we leverage Everett Lee's (1966) classic theory of migration, which argued that migration is determined in part by *push factors,* things related to the area of origin that push one toward the decision to leave; in part by *pull factors,* aspects of the area of the destination that are attractive; and by personal factors (e.g., age, education, sex, race, and other factors that affect individual decision making) and obstacles (e.g., factors such as cost, distance, and transportation that increase selectivity).

Chapter 1 examines digital nomads' narratives of the push factors that drove them from their home countries into the digital nomad lifestyle abroad. We detail how the failures of the creative class city, in terms of both livability and work, triggered their decisions to flee unfulfilling jobs, unsatisfying communities, and unsustainable lifestyles despite any obstacles they might have perceived.

Bali has long been known as an exotic paradise, full of novel influences that Westerners are eager to experience. In chapter 2, we discuss the history and contours of Bali's expatriate ecosystem, including an outline of the types of expats found in Bali (e.g., digital nomads, new age spirit seekers, retirees, and tourists). We then turn to the pull factors that attract nomads: the island provides a source of inspiration, access to modern conveniences, and a low-cost lifestyle.

Chapter 3 addresses the seeming paradox of self-initiated, location-independent nomads in search of face-to-face community with minimal obligation. We describe digital nomads' place-based communities and consider how they meet the diverse needs of so many nomads. We also articulate the common values that make it possible for their community to meet their needs.

Digital nomads came to Bali to *work*. We begin chapter 4 by unpacking nomads' sources of earned income through entrepreneurship, freelancing, and full-time employment, and we describe their typical occupations, which cluster in marketing, e-commerce, coaching, and technology. We then articulate the digital nomad ecosystem as a social, place-based experience and explain the processes through which digital nomads build and sustain their work-centric communities.

Ethnographies often use extended vignette chapters to enhance existing data and provide a more holistic comparison of how different members of communities interpret the same context.[15] In chapter 5, we present three vignettes that profile the three phases of participation and immersion in digital nomad communities. The first vignette, the honeymooner nomad, features the story of Pauline, a twenty-eight-year-old American who came to Bali after quitting her high-pressure music industry job in New York City. Now an enthusiastic member of one of the most popular coworking spaces, Pauline arrives there first thing in the morning every day, feeling buoyed by those around her. Our second vignette focuses on Lucy, a visa runner and media content creator, who left what she called her "soul-destroying" job in advertising and entertainment after, as she told us, "working pretty much nonstop for nine years." In contrast to her old life of heavy drinking in London, Lucy is now extremely health-conscious, practicing yoga daily and avoiding alcohol. The third vignette features Lorelei and Norman, a western European couple who, since arriving in Bali over three years ago in search of personal and professional reinvention, have become successful entrepreneurs and resident nomads.

The final chapter presents our conclusions. Place matters—so much so that disillusioned knowledge workers move around the world to get away from places they find toxic and so much so that even these *digital nomads*, who value freedom and mobility above nearly all else, seek places where they can build face-to-face community with like-minded others. This final chapter summarizes our findings, discusses their relevance for theories about community and the creative class, and offers insights about the future of work and cities. Digital nomads challenge conventional thinking about what makes work, community, and life "good" in this mobile, digital age. We hope that this peek into their lives will inspire scholars, businesspeople, and creative individuals to consider new options for living in today's complex world.

CHAPTER 1
Goodbye to All That: Escape Stories

Pretty much everyone who makes a big leap in life and moves to a foreign country, or kind of drops everything and moves to another country, they're escaping something, or they're moving away from something, or running away from something. For me, it was thinking I had everything that was supposed to make me happy in the US. I had the corporate job, a nice car, fancy designer clothes. I lived in a big house in the middle of LA. We would get bottle service every weekend, and I still wasn't happy. I realized, "Am I just wasting my life chasing someone else's dream?"

Kenny, *thirty-three-year-old American entrepreneur*

I told my cousin who works on Wall Street that I was leaving New York, and he said, "Why would you want to leave the center of the universe?"

Mark, *forty-three-year-old American software engineer and entrepreneur*

Many people harbor the idle fantasy that they might one day leave their lives behind to travel the world and do what they please. When we began our investigation of digital nomads, we imagined them to be people who simply said "Yes!" to their daydreams of escaping the office. While it turns out that there was an element of truth to our initial stereotyping of digital nomads, their narratives about the factors that pushed them from their home countries into their lifestyles abroad were rarely simple. In these narratives, which we term *escape stories*,[1] nomads revealed that leaving one's old life is often as much a desperate bid to flee unsatisfactory conditions as it is to chase a dream.

Digital nomads' escape stories reflect two overarching themes, both of which are tied to the topic of "creative class cities."[2] The first of these themes questions the viability of living in the very cities that are supposed to provide knowledge workers with fulfilling lives. Creative class cities are expensive, and the cost of living in them has been outpacing wage growth.[3]

Moreover, nomads reported that they were unable to enjoy city amenities because they felt stressed, overworked, and deprived of free time; also, creative class cities have a culture of busy-ness, partying, and materialism that interferes with work-life balance and quality of life. The second theme in nomads' stories concerns the actual work that first drew them to creative class cities, work that often failed to be meaningful, stable, or even creative. Digital nomads report that the dominant cultural response to these negative conditions is passive acquiescence, and that friends, family members, and colleagues would often dismiss their concerns and their search for alternative solutions. As a result, nomads increasingly experienced social distance from their peers, which further contributed to their decisions to free themselves from what they viewed as broken, discredited, and hopeless systems of life and work in the West.

Because the individuals we studied ultimately migrated away from their home countries, we offer some context by discussing patterns of mobility and migration. We then move on to a discussion of creative class cities and their shortcomings.

MOBILITY PUSH FACTORS AND DIGITAL NOMADS

Overview of Mobility Research

Geographers and demographers who study internal (i.e., mobility within a country) and international migration refer to individuals' reasons to leave home as "push factors."[4] Examples of push factors associated with internal migration include sociological, geographic, political, and demographic factors at the individual, household, or neighborhood levels (e.g., age, homeownership status, life-course events, neighborhood turnover rates, and crime rates) that create dissatisfaction and lead one to move.[5] Researchers working in this tradition see individuals as acting within certain constraints, but still voluntarily making calculations about the trade-offs to moving and acting on this decision.[6]

Of course, moving to another country is less common than moving internally within a country, in part because of immigration restrictions, distance, and cultural and legal barriers. Research on international migration tends to focus on two topics. One stream of research examines "forced moves" from locationally disadvantaged places (e.g., places plagued by conflict or natural disasters) and populations who have been forcibly displaced or who are at risk (e.g., refugees, asylum seekers, and victims of human trafficking).[7] A second segment of international migration research examines the location-based variables that lead individuals, especially men, to search for better opportunities in other countries (e.g., socioeconomic, demographic, life course, political, environmental, educational, and transportation-related factors).[8] Social networks can influence these migration decisions, leading individuals to move to places where family or other contacts might help them to adjust and find employment.[9]

However, very little international migration research has considered relatively privileged populations who move from relatively privileged nations. The extant research that does explore this topic focuses on expatriates,[10] but the literature on expatriates tends to concentrate on individuals whose employers have transferred them and their families to another country. This body of research largely views organizations, rather than individuals, as the drivers of international work.[11] Scholars have recognized the need to better understand new and growing forms of self-initiated expatriation,[12] and researchers have begun to consider the wide variety of possibilities for working abroad.[13] In general, one important conclusion of newer scholarship on expatriation is that migration across countries is no longer as unusual or as uniform in character as it once was.[14] Even so, little work to date has attempted to capture the self-directed transience of digital nomads.[15]

The Case of Digital Nomads and Mobility Trends

Digital nomads, like others studied in migration and expatriation research, are people who are moving to improve their life circumstances. Like elite expats, digital nomads have skills that can bring highly compensated work. Yet more similar to less fortunate migrants, nomads migrate toward places where they may find networks for work rather than to a specific job. Given their relatively privileged cities and jobs back home, it is somewhat puzzling to observe digital nomads wanting to leave their successes behind. Understanding why they do requires consideration of the relational processes that link individuals to their structural conditions through time and space.[16] For digital nomads, this means understanding their life-course trajectories in pursuit of careers within changing global economic markets, and within cities where they face rising housing prices, stagnating wages, and insecure and unrewarding work.

Digital nomads' escape stories reveal a wide range of push factors, both contextual and individual, suggesting the need for an integrated, less compartmentalized, and more "biographical approach" to migration research.[17] After all, the traditional reasons for international migration, and especially work-related international migration, are a poor match for nomads. In traditional models, places with superior quality of life, rich opportunities, and high status are not places people seek to flee. However, an overarching theme in our study is that while creative class cities have desirable amenities, draw talented populations, and benefit work organizations, they also burn out the people who work and live there, leaving many of them unfulfilled and unhappy. In this way, nomads' decisions to leave are based on factors that are either ignored by or counter to prominent macrolevel arguments about creative class cities.

Some might find it surprising that nomads describe lives of burnout and dissatisfaction. However, the digital nomads in our sample—most of whom are Millennials—are distinct from the typical members of their generation in at least two significant ways. First, the kinds of people who become digital nomads have a stronger preference for mobility than their generational peers and bristle at the notion of settling down or "planting roots." This is in contrast to the finding from a 2017 Pew Research Center report that in the United States, young adult geographic mobility is at a fifty-year low "even though today's young adults are less likely than previous generations of young adults to be married, to own a home or to be parents, all of which are traditional obstacles to moving."[18] In other words, although technology and transportation infrastructure offer unprecedented opportunities to move while maintaining contact with loved ones, research shows that many younger workers remain close to home. We acknowledge that our sample includes many people from outside the United States and many who traveled while growing up, so it makes sense that they would fail to fit the profile of an average Millennial in the United States. However, it is safe to conclude that reductions in barriers to mobility have not resulted in the general US population of Millennials moving away more frequently, whereas digital nomads have come to develop a preference for more frequent mobility across longer distances.

A second way that digital nomads differ from their generational peers is that their work is less likely to be tethered to physical location compared to peers who are not doing knowledge work. Alternative working arrangements are becoming more common,[19] suggesting that the location independence that digital nomads seek is increasingly available in their home countries through flexible working, remote working, or freelancing. In technology, freelancing is a well-established pathway through which individuals can reclaim a measure of autonomy from corporate cultures and organizational hierarchies.[20] Flexible and remote working are also common for non-technical knowledge workers.[21] Individuals have been working remotely from home for years, and coffee shops like Starbucks increasingly cater to remote workers and freelancers by providing free Wi-Fi, specialized seating, and electrical outlets for laptops.[22] More recently, the rise of dedicated coworking spaces where individuals pay a fee to work alongside other remote workers has provided a way to congregate with others and potentially form a kind of independent work community.[23] Some even believe that coworking can be a progressive political force for organizing individuals to recover more meaningful work lives and counter the dehumanization of transactionalized work.[24]

Yet even as this growth in alternative and remote employment affords workers new levels of flexibility, nomads find it is not enough. This is where digital nomads appear to be part of a vanguard taking greater advantage of the possibilities for locational freedom. What truly separates digital nomads from their generational peers is that they have both the will *and* the capability to move. Nomads are not forced into moving to find a job somewhere or to solve a narrow problem of work location. In fact, most of those whom we interviewed had every reason to stay put: their families and friends preferred that they remain nearby, employers often wanted to retain them, and their careers were moving on a forward trajectory. Digital nomads we interviewed were also not trying to drop out of mainstream life to live in a commune or avoid work. On the contrary, these individuals are highly invested in their work identities—work is central to their self-concept. Yet their dissatisfaction combined with their willingness to move eventually became sufficiently strong to prod them to make radical mobility decisions that took them away from lives that were, outwardly, mostly successful.

When we began our research, we knew we would be exploring an emerging subculture that would reveal much about the future of work, cities, and community. However, when we asked nomads standard questions about their biographical backstories and their reasons for moving, we were amazed at how many told us that they moved to Bali because they felt traumatized by their old lives. We soon learned that nomads' seemingly favorable status within the global work and place hierarchies concealed a darker story about the failures of the creative class urban lifestyle. Whether they were living in New York, London, or Sydney, nomads' moves were not triggered by the pull of well-planned and well-funded futures working abroad. Instead, their moves were fueled by a desperate desire to break from lives that seemed broken. Many reported that they felt starved of work-life balance, creativity, purpose, and a sense of control over their lives—factors known to interfere with health and well-being.[25] To better understand the dynamics of these push factors, we discuss both creative class cities and creative class work in more detail in the following sections.

THE FAILURES OF THE CREATIVE CLASS CITY

Creative people cluster not simply because they like to be around each other, or because they all happen to prefer cosmopolitan centers with lots of amenities, though both of these things happen to be true. Creative people and companies cluster because of the powerful productivity advantages, economies of scale, and knowledge spillovers such density brings. . . . Finding a place that makes us happy has a powerful effect on our "activation." Such places encourage people to do more than we otherwise would, such as engage in more creative activities, invent new things, or start new companies—all things that are both personally fulfilling and economically productive. This kind of innovation . . . stems in large part from the visual and cultural stimulation that places can provide—parks and open space, cultural offerings . . . symbolic amenities. This creates a regenerative cycle: the stimulation creates more energy, which in turn attracts more high-energy people from other places, resulting in higher rates of innovation, greater economic prosperity, higher living standards, and more stimulation.

Excerpt from *Who's Your City?* by Richard Florida[26]

Many factors that pushed digital nomads to abandon their societies are rooted in nomads' negative experiences of their relatively privileged but also stressful lives residing and working in creative class cities. The best and most numerous jobs for creative professionals tend to be concentrated in large cities.[27] Most notably, Richard Florida has become an academic influencer by arguing that cities are often more successful and competitive in the global economy when a larger share of their workforce can be classified as members of the creative class (i.e., conventional knowledge workers and the "super-creative core" in arts, design, media, science, engineering, education, computer programming, and research).[28]

Florida is correct that creative class cities are packed with amenities that cater to creative professionals, and this is by design. Urban policymakers and thought leaders have argued that cities are effectively in an arms race as they compete to draw jobs and talent. Local leaders feel pressure to upgrade urban centers in ways that are likely to be attractive to innovative people and businesses (e.g., bohemians; lesbian, gay, bisexual, transgender, and queer [LGBTQ] people; and others who tend to be drawn to creative professions).[29] This is why city and regional planners, business leaders, and mayors espouse the view that cities must specifically cater to Millennials and knowledge workers by developing a mix of amenities that include cultural institutions, lively entertainment districts, art galleries, and shopping boutiques, all interwoven with carefully positioned green spaces and a variety of desirable housing options.[30] Critics argue that the creative class city strategy is a neoliberal formula that prioritizes business interests over the needs of the average urban family (e.g., living wages, quality public schools, and affordable housing). In essence, the argument against prioritizing the creative class is that efforts to lure creative class employers and employees to boost the economic and cultural stature of cities do nothing to disrupt the forces that cause and perpetuate inequality, and may even worsen these aspects of places.[31] In response, Florida has since acknowledged that creative class cities have failed in many ways: rising inequality, gentrification, and unaffordability and displacement for poor and nonwhite populations.[32]

Whatever the merits of Florida's economic theory of creative class cities as a policy for regional development, digital nomads report that, for them, *as individuals*, creative class cities have been a failure. Here, we unpack this failure in two parts: (1) the cost of creative class cities in terms of money, time, and unhealthy culture; and (2) the false promises of creative class work.

Costs of the Creative Class City

Too Expensive

The cost of living is obscene. The cost of property is rising at an alarming rate. It's being fueled by Chinese and Russian money, like a lot of big cities. The cost of renting for most young people has gone up by like 60 to 70 percent in the last ten years, and meanwhile, the wages? We've had stagnant or no wage inflation to match that. Right? So, graduates who are leaving right now are getting the same offers in terms of money as we had ten years ago, but the costs are much higher.

Ellie, thirty-three-year-old English freelance writer and entrepreneur

Cities that score well on creative class amenities, including New York, Boston, Los Angeles, San Francisco, Seattle, Portland, Vancouver, Toronto, London, Dublin, and Sydney, are notorious for their high cost of living. As speculative real estate investors, tourists, and the global rich flock to creative class cities, the cost of living has skyrocketed, causing residents to flee.[33] Magda told us she felt life there was untenable. A thirty-year-old Romanian, Magda has an MBA and was working in London before coming to Bali. She explained life in London this way:

London is really, really selling off to rich Arabs and Russians, and everybody else is being priced out. If you look at things in the traditional way, everyone else who belongs to London is being priced out, and these people don't even live in those houses. They just want to have a fancy house, and then the whole neighborhood is all polished, and crazy overpriced, and empty. So, I thought that was very sad, but it also happens in New York and other places, too.

For creative class urban residents, the cost of living translates into a constant pressure to secure and maintain highly remunerative employment. In aggregate, economists might wave away this problem because creative class jobs should pay sufficiently to live in the city somehow, whether with roommates or in tiny apartments in less desirable neighborhoods. Further, there is always a large supply of hungry newcomers who are eager for desirable jobs in cities. However, on the individual level, the creative class city's high cost pressures are a constant source of stress for residents.[34] This is especially true when people also experience generalized feelings of insecurity about their jobs and income. Such stressors are demoralizing and can even be damaging to work success.[35]

Grace described her efforts to succeed in Los Angeles (LA). A thirty-year-old African American public relations consultant, Grace had dreamed of breaking into the entertainment industry. She spent her free time reading memoirs and biographies of hip-hop artists and business leaders, desperately networking in the crowded world of LA hopefuls where "you have to audition to be a waitress." After a series of low-paying internships, she was struggling:

> I was then interning full-time, and I just had enough money for one more month of rent, and then my roommate was going home for the summer. So, I was brainstorming on every way that I could make money. They were temping me here and there, so that would bring a little bit of money, and then my boss knew. But I was eating on like, $1.75 a day. I was always so happy when my boss would order lunch for the office.

Finally, she landed a coveted and seemingly glamorous job with a public relations agency where her major client was an award-winning hip-hop celebrity, internationally known as a rapper, television host, and entrepreneur. But over time, Grace became overwhelmed with the work, which required nonstop availability for all kinds of appearances, press situations, crises, publicity issues, and social media promotions. She knew she needed to change her life; she never had the luxury of downtime. In addition to being "on-call twenty-four/seven," she said that her income was barely enough to keep up with her bills and debt: "LA was so expensive to live in, so I'm also like, 'I can't afford to just sit and think while I figure this out.'"

One might think that this tough period is just a phase, part of a process in which younger workers put in extra time, but later find the work to be more balanced, fulfilling, and well-compensated. One might think that being surrounded by interesting people at the job would be worth the sacrifices. Tessa initially thought this way. After graduating from college and working for the Obama campaign in 2012, she obtained a position in marketing with a company in Orlando, Florida. Yet she quickly began to resent her long commute and uninspiring work. Moreover, her colleagues were nothing like the ones she met while working for Obama; the new work environment seemed complacent and provincial. Even the more senior employees were apathetic, often complaining to her about how their wages were not keeping up with the cost of living:

I was surrounded by people who—like this was *it* for them. They'd never even seen snow before. Our creative director was socially clueless. And this other guy, he did the IT. He would talk about how he could barely afford things. The big drive into work, all that stuff. Like, "Oh my god." So, I kind of knew. I started researching. . . . I was starting to get my teaching certificate online. Then, I finally got my tickets to Southeast Asia on my lunch break. One day, I was just like, "Okay, you're just going to do it." I pulled the trigger, but it was not an easy feat. I remember that summer I refused to get the AC fixed in my car as sort of this pushing factor. Like, "I'm going to leave."

Thousands of miles away in Paris, Dennis, a thirty-two-year-old marketer and filmmaker, echoed a popular sentiment among digital nomads in creative class cities. He described the nonstop hamster wheel in which he felt like he "lived to work." "One of the reasons to leave Paris was [that] I felt there was no room for my dreams. Because you put too much energy into actually living there. You live there, you work there, and you work to live there. It's kind of an endless curse."

Alongside the basic expenses, many creative professionals reported that they felt compelled to maintain the materialist lifestyle that dominates large cities. Though many urban professionals are paid better than they would be in smaller cities or towns, the reality is that wages are quickly depleted in creative class cities. Michelle, a thirty-three-year-old business coach from Vancouver, Canada, told us that in order to avoid a long commute to her demanding job, she bought a condo in the city. Michelle explained that despite her high-paying job, money was tight. At first, her home symbolized success and security, but she found that she had difficulty saving money for activities that she actually enjoyed and felt pressure to keep up with people around her:

At $120K salary, 40 percent gets put to taxes. I bought a house, and then I have this car I never drive. I don't know what model it is—with all the fixings, and it was always parked in the garage because you don't want to drive it in traffic, and I was living downtown. I was not giving up the luxury of downtown living. I was eating out every day. I was drinking because I was in corporate, and it was very common to go out to the bar after a workday.

Oscar, a thirty-eight-year-old Canadian who worked in the film industry in Toronto, Canada, also struggled with his city's high cost of living. Today, he is a coach who also runs a podcast focused on self-improvement, goals, and accountability. He has a strong opinion on the ways money interferes with the pursuit of happiness and success, both for himself and his clients. He said that he has noticed that people who chose to become digital nomads seem fed up with and ready to challenge many of deeply held values that dominate large Western cities:

> If money is all that matters to you, leaving New York isn't going to give your life meaning. . . . There's this jostling for position and this scramble in the West that I'm a little afraid of. I can live here [in Bali], and I have one of the cheapest apartments. . . . In Toronto, living in some little apartment, I'd feel like a loser and a failure. So much of the measure of who you are is on what you have. Now, maybe that was just me and where I was at that time, but I think I'm afraid of going back because I don't want to take that back on. . . . A lot of my internal struggle came from not feeling valuable enough in terms of money. I wanted to be a provider. . . . I think that money has been a big thing for me in my life and feeling that until I have lots of it I wouldn't be worth anything as a human, like a multimillionaire. And I run into this a lot with people that I coach. . . . Tim Ferriss talks about this in *4-Hour Work Week*. People's lives cost less than you think. . . . A big part of my journey is to get to a place where I see my own value separate from money. . . . I think that money is symbolic for most Westerners. . . . [T]he American Dream seems to me to be predicated on this idea of, "How much can I have at the expense of other people?," seems really bankrupt. . . . As far as money goes, it's this idea of defining ourselves based on some structure that someone else put in place that very few [people] ever question.

Like Oscar, many nomads have come to realize that simply moving to different Western cities or different companies would make little difference for improving their life satisfaction and work fulfillment. As Brandi, a thirty-two-year-old employee of the US government, put it:

> I was living in Bethesda. If you know anything about Washington, DC, Bethesda's really nice, but it's really expensive. And I just felt like there's got to be more than this. There wasn't one specific moment, no, but I just felt pretty unsatisfied in a variety of areas, and I felt like getting a new job isn't going to make this different. You know, moving to San Diego isn't going to make this different. It's going to be the same thing in a different city.

You Can't Enjoy the Amenities Anyway: No Time for Fun and a Toxic Culture

I did *exactly* what society told me. I looked good. I was nice. I was a team player. I got my education. I became an executive at an advertising agency. I did everything. Besides *getting married*. That's the only thing I did not do that society told me to do. And I got to the top of that ladder, if you will, or that hill, and I was like, "Well, where's my prize? My happiness, my fulfillment, my satisfaction, my love, my connection, my joy? Where is it? Why am I constantly—why am I spending a thousand dollars a week on clothes? Why am I having to drink every night? Why am I acting like a crazy person making sure I'm networked with everybody I could possibly network with? And then, why am I exhausted?" You know?

Dara, forty-three-year-old American executive coach

Urban studies has its origins in bashing cities as places where materialism, superficiality, and consumerism thrive. City people were seen as too rational, lacking in spirituality and social connection, and too distant from nature to appreciate its wonders. Classic scholars romanticized rural life (i.e., analyses of the urban-rural continuum).[36] More recent work has offered Marxist critiques of how urban capitalism prevents collective action,[37] and contemporary studies take aim at the negative consequences of efforts at redevelopment and gentrification.[38]

With the rise of discourse on creative class cities, much has been made of the opportunities, conveniences, and cultural benefits of high-density urban areas. Creative class cities' cultural amenities, together with their high concentrations of professionals, promise a rewarding and enriching lifestyle beyond work. However, digital nomads, similar to early urban theorists, reject the idea that their old lives and communities are fulfilling. They claim that the cost and work pressures in creative class cities foster a form of cultural oppression characterized by materialism, busyness, and workaholism.

As we noted in the previous section, large cities tend to have a materialistic culture that imposes financial costs. This culture also creates norms that leave people feeling unfulfilled, distressed, and ready to move away.[39] Vance, a forty-three-year-old Londoner, described the trappings of London and his job there. Around the time that he was getting divorced, Vance came to terms with the fact that he was burned out from his consulting job. Now he has lived in Bali for almost three years, and at the time of our interview Vance was running several online businesses. He was also a partner in a popular café that is known as digital nomad hangout in Bali. Although Vance was successful back in London, he had come to consider London's culture to be toxic. He explained that the professional culture of creative class cities is characterized by a lifetime of social comparison and a perpetual fixation on wealth accumulation:

Before I came to Bali, I had lunch with my uncle. He'd just retired from a US law firm as managing partner of that firm. He'd spent forty years in corporate law in the oil industry, and he was a pretty wealthy guy. He's made quite a lot of money, and all he could talk to me about was how worried he was about his pension, and he's got nothing to worry about in terms of money. I'm sure he's got a lot of money, and yet all he could talk about was money. And I just thought, "Hang on a second. This is just insane." Like, he's in the top 1%, and yet he's convinced that he's got financial problems. I thought, "Hang on." Chasing money is what *you have to do* in London, really, because that's the culture. It's just madness.

Vance also described London as a place with a "destructive energy" that "sucks you in," and he said that he fell into this trap for period of time:

> Nearly all my friends from college went to work in the City[40] in the financial industry, and they just operate in a different financial reality, and for some reason, their wages are just on a different level. And I think there's something about London which I find quite annoying—a lot of the talent gets sucked into this industry. . . . It's just not a particularly pretty industry, and I think, in essence, quite a destructive industry. I think culturally, the City has a big influence on people's approach, their way of life. I think it has a big impact on people's aspirations. And I think if you're outside that industry, you can say, "Well, hang on. I'm not going to have the same lifestyle as my friends or the same size house, or the private education for my kids that my friends working at the bank are." I think it's quite divisive in that sense.

Of the many costs that creative class urban culture imposes on its inhabitants, nomads complained the most about being starved of time. As urban cores become more congested, residents most resent the lengthy commutes.[41] Time costs also include all of the travel necessary to take advantage of creative class amenities; to meet up with friends, family, and colleagues who are scattered across the city due to low-vacancy real estate markets and high rents; and to accomplish mundane daily tasks. As Vance explained, even if you can afford it, working in London leaves little time or energy to experience what the city has to offer. Furthermore, the culture discourages work-life balance in general, and this includes efforts at healthy living, meaningful relationships, and creative endeavors:

> Even if people come there with good intentions to have a fulfilling life and to take advantage of amenities, culture, and friendships, health, and all that—even if they really want that—you really can't have that there very easily because you're forced to work very long hours in London. So, when you're done, you're very tired, and there is no way to really be like, creative or anything because you're exhausted, or even if you're not totally exhausted, the only thing that people really are interested in doing is drinking.

In describing London's work culture, Drea, a thirty-year-old former advertising professional, said that her peers seem to believe that work should be all-consuming, especially at the early-career life stage through one's twenties and thirties. Though she was successful at work, the rat race left her with scarce time for friends or doing the activities that draw people to the city:

> I had left work *actively* early if I left at 7:00 in the evening. That was a happy, "Yes! Celebrate! I have actually got an evening!" But then, I'd be so tired that I wasn't going

to go out and do anything with friends anyway. [Laughs] It's great living in a city where there's loads of stuff *if* you have time to enjoy it, but there is a very different *expectation* as to what you will put into work in big cities than there is outside of big cities.

Lani, a thirty-two-year-old sportswear designer for a major international activewear brand, reported that she, too, was initially excited to move to the city, but later became disillusioned. As a fashion student, she dreamed of getting a job in Manhattan. After succeeding in an internship, she was excited to start her career, and she quickly moved up the ladder. But a decade later, her life consisted of long hours at work, going home to squeeze in some chores, and then "vegging out" alone with take-out menus as she tried to decompress from her day:

In New York I probably made two friends the entire time I was there. One friend, I knew before, and one person I worked with who sat next to me. I barely met anybody. A lot of times I didn't do anything on weekends. I never felt like doing anything after work. I was exhausted. I didn't date. . . . I'm such a stress eater. I definitely was coming home after work, ordering food, and sitting on the couch.

Darla, an entrepreneur, explained that in Los Angeles and New York, she felt financially squeezed, wasted time on lengthy commutes, and experienced a lack of connection to the people she encountered. She had hoped that switching to freelancing would be the solution and she would gain back some time, but now she rejects the idea that she could create a satisfying balance between life and career in any Western creative class city:

I really do enjoy the city, and I grew up in the city for a while, but I was just in New York for Christmas and New Year's, and I honestly feel like the majority of people in cities are pretty genuinely unhappy. Waiters even seemed pretty pissed. . . . That fast pace, no one is stopping. You're always on the go. Even if I want to go to the grocery store, if I want to do any sort of errands, that will take a whole day. To find a coffee shop in New York that has good Wi-Fi and good seating? . . . I couldn't find anything that was a coffee shop that had good Wi-Fi, had open space, that was a creative space. I could take the subway or Uber, so I was Ubering everywhere, but then it was costing me like $30 a day just to be moving around. I was like, "This is exhausting." So then I just started working from the apartment that I was in, and I literally would just wake up and go to sleep in my PJs, and this is not healthy, other than me walking around the corner to get coffee, and then back into my apartment. It's just not a creative space.

Many nomads told us that the 2008–2009 financial crisis exacerbated negative aspects of creative class culture. Rumors of downsizing loomed during this time, and many nomads reported that they constantly anticipated bad news and were exposed to negative forecasting about the future. As one Londoner said: "It was slow, and everyone was just pessimistic about the future in 2009 and 2010. No one was really optimistic about the economy." Saskia Sassen has argued that transformations in the global economy have resulted in a "savage sorting" process, causing a "toxic" generalized uncertainty.[42] Nomads described this period as a dark time in creative class cities that left an imprint in their consciousness. Many became pessimistic about the social contract that their productivity at work would translate into sustaining compensation and job security.

Even if their own jobs seemed to be stable, many digital nomads mentioned that they encountered vicarious stress when friends and family members lost their jobs. As one tech entrepreneur said: "My wife's father lost his job in the IT world, and I was going to school at the time studying computer programming, and I just realized there's no such thing as job security—especially in this industry." Similarly, Tricia, a forty-year-old entrepreneur, explained her yearning to escape the sense of doom that descended on her home city of Denver, Colorado, during and after the financial crisis:

> We started to do more real estate investments, buying houses, fixing them up, renting them out or whatnot. Until the global financial crisis hit. [Laughs] And then everything [revenue] went back down to zero. . . . We literally were just smashed to zero, but we had some savings still. Okay, not much. We had like $5,000, and were like, "Let's just get out of this negativity. Everything you see in the US at this point is so negative."

Maddie, a thirty-two-year-old Australian digital marketing professional, said that downsizing in the aftermath of the financial crisis translated into unmanageable workloads for the remaining employees in her firm and contributed to a fearful and anxious atmosphere. She said these conditions only aggravated the existing workaholic cultures she experienced in Sydney and then later in New York:

> I was working ridiculous hours in Sydney at this job. In digital media and the media industry after the global financial crisis, they kind of worked you to the bone. They cut a lot of staff, and they had a lot of juniors come in, and the economics is that you save money, and you work your staff to the bone. I would be at work at 8:30, and prior to that I would go to the gym, and then I would work 'til, on average, 8:30, 9:00 at night. Once or twice, I had to work on the weekends. That was in Sydney. In New York it was different. I worked even harder in New York.

Speaking to the normalized workaholism and exhaustion in creative class cities, Magda shared a story about the arrival of "nap stations" in

London, private pods that sleep-deprived urbanites book to powernap or "recharge."[43]

> This one is like a coworking café where people can just go and take a nap. It's not even a capsule. If you're too far from home and on your way somewhere, just come and take a nap. And that, to me, is the perfect symbol. . . . I looked at it, and I was like, "I know exactly why a nap station would be such a popular thing in London."

Travis, the owner of a Bali coworking space, described the creative class city's push factors by posing the questions that many ask about nomads' motives:

> Why would somebody leave a city like this? Why would somebody leave a job like this? It's all personal. It's absolutely personal. Some people just have a higher tolerance for—I don't know—for punishment. There are many paths to happiness, but the truth is, lots of things are not working for lots of people. The people that are coming here often are very successful in their various roles.

Whether because of the financial stressors, the lack of time, or the toxic culture, the costs of creative class cities have left many digital nomads feeling burned out before reaching middle age. Perhaps they might have viewed these burdens as worth it if they had found the fulfillment and security they sought in their jobs. However, as we report next, the specifics of jobs in creative class cities were also a letdown.

Creative Class Jobs as a Cause of Nomad Disillusionment

In creative class cities, individuals' expectations for what work should deliver are higher than ever. Though the scope of creative class work is broad, it generally requires significant levels of education and training.[44] The process of developing one's human capital for knowledge work encourages individuals to build their entire identities around their skills and work.[45] Employers, keen to exploit this human capital to its fullest potential, use various strategies to encourage or demand that employees adopt work-centered identities and lifestyles.[46] Thus, both individuals and employers set expectations that work should be the dominant source of identity. Unfortunately, so-called creative jobs are often disappointing; digital nomads experience them to be too boring, too micromanaged, or too demanding to be creative.

In principle, it makes sense for highly capable, creative, work-focused individuals to be matched with organizations that need such labor. However, organizations seeking to maximize cost effectiveness have increasingly approached human capital management in ways that standardize and transactionalize knowledge work.[47] Fueled by trends in globalization, technological change, the decline of unions, and labor surpluses,[48] employers have sliced work into smaller and smaller chunks that are organized into the digital equivalent of micro-job assembly lines. Such arrangements are now an ongoing and growing part of the landscape of work,[49] and creative work is particularly prone to being divided into short-term "gigs."[50] While there have been calls for knowledge workers to band together to resist this phenomenon,[51] major shifts in the balance of power away from employers have yet to become a reality.

When organizations systematize and transactionalize knowledge work, workers bear the brunt of three negative effects. First, the increasing routinization of large swaths of knowledge work leads to highly trained individuals being hired into jobs that lack the creative, interesting, and meaningful work that they have been socialized to expect. Second, as the transactionalization of knowledge work has reduced job security, individuals have come to resent organizational life's routine indignities. Third, as knowledge work has become transactionalized, organizational cultures devote less effort to providing positive role models, developmental opportunities, and desirable career paths. Below, we further detail each of these work-related push factors that digital nomads encounter in creative class cities.

When Creative Class Work Is Not Creative

Paid work has a psychological significance for one's well-being and self-worth[52] that is critical to workplace creativity.[53] People can become so immersed in creative work that they lose all sense of time and experience enhanced psychological states;[54] but such engagement requires tasks that are appropriately challenging within an environment of autonomy and meaningful work.[55]

Despite all that is known about how to develop environments where employees thrive, many jobs are still designed in demotivating ways.[56] These problems even extend to more cutting-edge creative jobs (e.g., among the super-creative core). For instance, Lani, a thirty-two-year-old American, was thrilled when a competitive internship led her to a job designing women's sportswear for a leading global company. However, after the initial excitement wore off, she was disappointed to find that this so-called creative job left much to be desired in the way of realizing her skills and talents:

> I'd say 4 percent of my job was actually doing creative work and designing, and the rest of it was making updates, getting ready for meetings, going to meetings, going to costing

meetings. . . . A lot of it was me doing a design and then going and sitting in a meeting and having someone from the costing team saying, "This is too expensive. You have to change everything." And so, just a constant negotiation with me going like, "Well then, it's going to look completely different. What if we only change this part, but I keep this part?" And then they do their numbers, and they say, "You need to change one more thing." . . . I definitely felt like I signed up for a creative position, and I'm not allowed to be creative at all.

From an organization's point of view, routinizing knowledge work increases efficiency, but this comes with costs for worker satisfaction. Many digital nomads remarked on how their former employers always pushed them to increase their *quantity* of work, so that even when the work was engaging, the heavy workload was overwhelming and compromised quality output. Kyle, a twenty-nine-year-old Australian, formerly worked at a top advertising agency in his native city of Sydney. He explained the paradox of creating quality work while juggling more and more accounts: "The thing was, if I tried to attend to every account equally, they would all get bad service. . . . At the end of the day, the company is trying to make as much money as possible and pay you as little as possible."

Sam, a twenty-eight-year-old English web developer, described the conditions at the marketing agencies where he was employed where they made hasty decisions and inferior products resulted: "It was all about speed. They wanted execution, and I was like, 'I want to make a good product.' . . . It very much felt like a conveyor belt." Liam, a thirty-two-year-old Englishman and veteran of two well-known blue-chip technology companies, explained his exhaustion from the time crunch he experienced every day, which degraded his work no matter how much time he spent in the office. He said being available to work all of the time is an implicit bargain that creative employees must make when employed at "hot" tech companies that have become household names:

The job was quite grueling. . . . That's very applicable to many jobs in these companies. They hire very smart people, but sometimes they get you to do really *awful* stuff, and they just compensate it through the culture being great. They give you free food and good salary. That does exist. It's a bit of a phenomenon. It's quite common. . . . There wasn't time to be creative. . . . It was all operational.

As another nomad said: "Companies like Google that are trying to please Generation Y and others just think that they can put a Ping-Pong table in the hall, and people will be happy there. No."

Some digital nomads acknowledged that their jobs back home did allow creativity, but they found that these jobs were still a poor match for their values, aspirations, and capabilities. For instance, Lucy, a successful vide-ographer whom we profile in chapter 5, complained that her creativity was wasted to promote products that offended her. Similarly, Noah, a thirty-one-year-old American, had what many would consider to be a dream job producing movies for a major Hollywood film company, but he felt a sense of creative alienation from his organization and its embarrassingly low-brow products:

> I was given the opportunity to be creative, but it felt very *difficult*, especially knowing
> that I was working at a production company that was producing really crappy movies.
> I didn't feel like I could be creative because it wasn't the kinds of things [that] I wanted
> to create. . . . It also seemed a little bit shallow, and a lot of it was just who you know and
> not necessarily how great your quality of work is. So, it felt like an industry I just didn't
> want to try to hustle in. Like, I didn't have a drive to hustle *that*.

Rejecting Organizational Life's Routine Indignities

Much has been made of Millennials' desire for meaningful work, especially early in their careers.[57] In discussing this book, whenever we would talk to older people about Millennials, they seemed mystified, if not outraged, by digital nomads' expectations that their work would be meaningful and that organizations would be well organized. Again and again, people have labeled Millennials as a whole, and digital nomads in particular, as entitled. Critics demand to know: "Why do these young, talented people refuse to pay their dues just like everyone else?" Why not just accept the many perversities of organizational bureaucracies?

The passive acceptance of organizations' unfair, unnecessary, outdated, or overly restrictive policies and actions may have made some sense in the era of long-term employment, but that time has passed.[58] In the new world of instability in both employment and career paths,[59] talented workers may be less tolerant of organizational impositions on their lives. Indeed, changing conceptions of employment stability have fueled digital nomads' thinking about work, and along with that, the routine indignities of contemporary organizations have fed a sense of revulsion toward corporate life. Among the many indignities they reported, the most serious is the perception that organizations are excessively controlling employees through unpredictable workloads, unnecessary face time requirements, and meaningless work. Ultimately, among work-related push factors, these are the issues that most triggered nomads' mobility thoughts.

Drea, the former London advertising agency employee introduced above, is representative of nomads who reported norms of burnout and exhaustion in creative class jobs. On top of her extremely long hours, Drea had no control of her schedule. She said that she never knew in advance when her workday would end, which greatly affected her social relationships and life satisfaction:

> I couldn't make plans with friends in the evening. I had friends who had more normal jobs—like accountants where everything's quite organized in terms of time and stuff like that—and I'd try to make plans to meet them at 7:00 or 7:30. Even *right by my office*, in the same area of the tube stop as my office, and I'd have to cancel. I wouldn't be able to make it, and especially in advertising agencies, you're—it's client service, so you're kind of, to some extent, dependent on the client. You're not entirely in control of your own time, so it's much more easy for things to come in at the last moment. You can think you're going to be fine. "I'm definitely going to be out of here at 6:30," and you're there 'til midnight.

Nicole, a twenty-six-year-old Parisian marketing professional, said that her main complaint was a fluctuating workload with many periods of boredom from underwork. Though she was initially motivated when she secured a job with a top international luxury goods company right out of business school, she quickly realized that the normal flow of work was uneven. She felt frenzied when she was forced to work extremely late during busy times, but then her job became tedious during slow times when she was expected to tolerate being idle and unchallenged. Further exacerbating the monotony of the sluggish periods, she resented that her employer insisted on maintaining the old-fashioned and impractical ritual of face time: "I couldn't really make myself understand why sometimes I was done at 3:00, and I wanted to leave at 3:00, but still I had to wait until 6:30—even if at other times I was not done at 6:30, and I was staying until later."

Like many bored workers, Nicole devised strategies to alleviate the tiresome hours at the office. When asked what she would do during slack times, Nicole gave us what turned out to be a common answer among digital nomads: "I had a blog at some point." Though many members of older cohorts of workers are accustomed to the routine of sitting around the office without work to do, and some we met told us that Millennials should just try to welcome slower work as an "easy gig," the nomads whom we met loathed work norms like this. We met many people who were ambitious but had suffered from underwork and boredom, and like them, Nicole was disappointed that she had ample time at work to sit around and blog when she craved interesting work where she could acquire and execute new skills: "I love to work, but I don't love to *pretend* that I work."

Other nomads, like Lani, the sportswear designer, had an added problem. In addition to overwork and pointless office face time waiting around, the work was of poor quality and felt meaningless in terms of creativity. Though she craved autonomy, Lani told us that her company's design review system involved a large team of people each demanding certain modifications to her original designs. She said that it "felt pointless" to spend so much effort being creative only for the design to be so compromised that she did not even want her name to be associated with it. In this way, Lani was like other digital nomads who moved because their jobs forced them to produce low-quality products, and thus they became cynical and alienated from creative work.

Lani's personal goal of having meaningful, creative work was starting to feel unattainable. She said her workload at peak production times translated into feelings of personal failure and loss of integrity as she was unable to meet her own design quality standards. Adding to these stressors, the workflow had many bottlenecks, and Lani's employer required her to sit around doing nothing but waiting for authorizations. Again, like many nomads, Lani took exception to a stale work culture with rigid policies that prohibit remote work. To Lani, her boss's rule that she had to remain deskbound for no reason represented not just a lack of consideration for her time, but a fundamental distrust of her judgment and work ethic. She felt this treatment was especially unfair and disrespectful, given that she worked late hours and kept a hectic travel schedule, sometimes flying from New York to China on one day's notice:

> That's one of the things that led me to quit in the end. We would be sitting there and just waiting for someone to have a meeting in case they needed something. It would be 7:30 at night, and I would just literally be sitting at my desk, just doing nothing. That, for me, is the worst possible scenario. I think it means they're not treating me like an adult, and they don't respect the fact that I can be accountable for my own work. It just made me feel like a child. I've been here. I've been working for certain people for years. I get my work done. I've never missed a single deadline. I would never leave if there was anything pressing to do. Not to mention, we're always reachable. We've got work phones. If you need me to come in, I can be in the office at my desk within a half an hour, so it was completely pointless, and it just felt a waste of my time.

Echoing the theme that creative class work is not meaningful, Magda, the Romanian mentioned earlier in the chapter, told us that she cares deeply about finding a positive work environment doing something meaningful. To this end, she held a variety of business roles in marketing and finance and moved to different countries before landing a highly desirable job in London. Looking at her colleagues and supervisors across these jobs and places, she concluded that she needs to be in a place and with people who are aligned with her core goal: meaningful work. When she considered her future taking these so-called desirable jobs and moving up the ladder in big cities: "It just looked to me like no soul, no meaning, no purpose."

A common thread in so many nomads' experiences was that creative class cities were filled with jobs that leave people stuck in lives that they do not want. The jobs seem creative, but the policies, people, and work structures left them feeling robbed of autonomy, dignity, and meaning at work. As we detail next, nomads began to recognize that their problems were not merely those of early-career jobs but symptoms of a larger problem in organizational culture.

Pessimistic Views of the Future: The Degradation of Organizational Culture

As organizations have transactionalized knowledge work and workers have come to realize that their jobs may be short-term and promise no security, employees may increasingly scrutinize and criticize their organizational cultures. Many nomads told us that as they imagined their futures in their careers, they looked to their more senior colleagues for reassurance that their organizational cultures would be nurturing, forward-thinking, and positive work environments. Instead, many digital nomads complained that their older colleagues and so-called role models have responded to changes in the economy and organizations by tightly grasping on to what remains of the past, often resisting technology, practices, and policies that could improve morale and productivity. Camelia, a twenty-seven-year-old European human resource manager, liked the content of her work but found that her older colleagues had a limiting mindset and created a stodgy overall environment:

> My job was very interesting, but the people that I was working with, I just did not have good chemistry with them. They were *all*—let's say—I mean, age doesn't matter for me, but when you *do* have stereotypical things attached to the age, that's how it was in my case. I was the youngest person on the team. I was twenty-five at the time, and then people there were extremely conservative, like very narrow-minded. "Things are done like that. They're done like that for years. I don't want to have any innovation. Let's just do it like this." Some stuff like that. This is where I really felt, "No. I don't want to work in such an environment."

Many digital nomads reported that their colleagues and mentors were complacent, provincial, and pessimistic. As young professionals seeking mentorship and camaraderie from more senior people who would inspire and motivate them, many were crushed to find a lack of positive role models, a shortage of progressive mentors, and few desirable career paths.

Ellie, the London writer and entrepreneur, learned early that the jobs to which she could be promoted would not lead to interesting work where she could be empowered and grow: "A lot of people don't have positive role models at work, so then it's sort of like, 'Well, why am I climbing the ladder to try and get this job? This doesn't seem like a good way to spend the next twenty years.'"

Camelia and Ellie both described feeling alienated from their more senior colleagues. Like many nomads, they believed that organizations seemed to instill fear in employees, many of whom had become consumed with worry about job security and were clinging to outmoded ways of working. Oshmi, a thirty-three-year-old from India, worked for a large bank in New York for three years after earning a master's degree in computer science. She decided to become a nomad after she became convinced that her organization was ruining her future career prospects by clinging to obsolete technology. She was perplexed about how such a large, prestigious firm lacked any mechanism for updating employees' skills and became especially disillusioned that her colleagues did not share her outrage. She said that longer-serving employees seemed aimless and hopeless, even as they knew their skills were becoming antiquated as long as they continued to use old technology: "I saw fortysomething people walking around with their coffee mugs, and I thought, 'I don't want to be like them.'"

Noel, a thirty-two-year-old American marketer with a background in engineering, said that staying at his Fortune 500 firm would have entailed a sacrifice in idealism that he was not ready to make:

> I was looking around at people that have been there like twenty, thirty-plus years, and obviously they're old, but they're so cynical. They're so downtrodden about what they had to do to survive at their job. I already knew deep down there's no way I'll be here thirty years. There's no way I can last.

Magda, like many digital nomads, looked to mentors at work for glimpses of her future and recoiled at what awaited her: "I think the most unattractive thing was looking at my older colleagues and seeing what corporate life made them be—this very lonely, extremely competitive, 'I'll walk over dead bodies to get where I need to' kind of mentality."

Laurence, a former technology consultant for a Fortune 100 firm, is now a fashion entrepreneur. He noted that the only colleagues whom he admired were those who had the courage to quit:

> The people I looked up to the most in the company, or learned the most from, were people within three to four years of me experience-wise, and most of them went off and did their own things at some point and made that jump, whether it was starting their

own consulting practice or going on to a different job that was a little more targeted to what they liked. I didn't really see a lot of the partners or VPs that I would interact with as "That is where I'd want to be."

LEAVING "THE CENTER OF THE UNIVERSE"

Personal Crisis: Coping with Stress and Trauma

Crisis[60] is a well-known instigator of personal change. This is why self-help programs often include stories of "hitting bottom" as a precursor to major intrapersonal reinvention and healing. Individuals' experience of stress depends on group memberships, status, roles, and relationships in their lives. Individuals' connections with others can therefore be thought of as contributing to the spread of stress, much like a contagious disease.[61] Unchecked, stressful episodes can escalate into crises. In creative class cities, nomads found that the social structures of life and work generated a great deal of stress. These same conditions also amplified their reactions to other stressful and traumatic life events. Among those we interviewed were individuals whose lives had a cumulative effect that led them into anxiety, depression, suicidal thoughts, and self-harming behaviors. Others experienced more acute events, ranging from the work-related stressors of job losses and business failures, to serious personal traumas including rape, illness, divorce, and the death of loved ones.

For some, feelings of extreme stress or trauma were the impetus to finally take the action to leave home. For instance, Maddie decided to leave her high-powered marketing job in New York City after her boyfriend broke up with her while they were on vacation in Bali. To make matters worse, he did it on the second day of a trip that would stop in Australia for both her thirtieth birthday and her brother's wedding. Faced with continuing the trip alone and explaining to her family and friends the reason her boyfriend was no longer with her and why she hated her glamorous job and life in New York, she cracked:

> I literally had a moment of like, "Fuck this shit. I'm not doing it anymore. I'm not doing what society wants me to be doing—being in a really good job and moving toward this career." I'm good at what I'm doing, but that doesn't mean that I want to do it for the rest of my life.

After her epiphany, Maddie stopped at a library on the way to her brother's wedding and emailed a resignation letter. At the end of the trip, she flew back to New York, cleaned out her apartment, and moved to Bali.

Although several interviewees told us that traumatic experiences had contributed to the push to leave, not all trauma-based escape stories stemmed from a single disruptive event or severe crisis. A second group of nomads experienced some form of what has been called a "quarter-life crisis," a phenomenon in which people in their twenties and thirties feel concerned about the direction of their lives.[62] This part of the life course is often seen as a time of opportunity, career growth, and freedom from the demands of family and school. However, emerging research suggests that some people suffer from a feeling of being "locked in" to adult roles and commitments that they no longer want.[63] Individuals experiencing these feelings may take some time to realize that they can change their life commitments, but when they do, they are likely to separate themselves from these sources of dissatisfaction.[64] Indeed, many individuals had prolonged negative emotions that had not yet become crippling but had interfered with their life and work satisfaction so much that making a clean break seemed to be the only way out of the cycle. Often, nomads realized their experiences of stress were situational, so they began searching for other options, and just happened across information about the digital nomad life-style. Awakened to an urgent need for empowerment over their lives, this segment of nomads believed that staying put was no longer tenable.

For instance, Lani finally left her job after staying far longer than she had wanted. The immediate trigger was when her boss, on just two days' notice, told her she needed to lead a major corporate trip from New York to Texas. For years she had endured her boss's abrupt demands on her time and weekends as a form of work indignity, and this trip was the final straw:

> We were in this meeting and talking about travel for the upcoming season, and they were like, "We want you to go to Austin on Thursday," and it's like, Tuesday, "and be the group leader with other designers, and plan the trip, and come back at the end of the day, and tell others where you're gonna shop, and what you're gonna do." Like, Thursday to Monday, and "Who cares if you had weekend plans, and you're not getting overtime for anything like that ever?" And they always have you travel over the weekends, so you're missing your weekend. And I was just like, "No. I'm not going to go to Austin. I don't want to go. I have plans, and I do not want to be a group leader because I hate this place, and I do not want to put on this front of, 'Be group leader. Organize everything. Be everyone's mom.'" . . . And it was between seasons, so it was a time, professionally, where I could say I had finished my work for this season. So I knew I'm not walking out, dumping shit on them. Because again, I didn't want to burn bridges. I didn't want to go out in an unprofessional manner. So, I noticed that "This is my window. I gotta do it."

Fed up with both her work environment and the cost of living in London, Ellie quit what many would consider a plum job in financial journalism. Not wanting to commit any more time to a life she was uninspired by, she resolved to move to Australia to look for a different job and try something new in life. But she took a freelance gig before her move, and her boss gave her the opportunity to finish it remotely while attending a friend's wedding in India. This led to an epiphany:

> I was on a hammock, sitting in India when I did this work, and I sent it off, and then I invoiced them, and I was like, "Okay. I just worked from Goa." And I was like, "I don't need to do *that* many days' work to live here." I mean, I don't want to stay here forever, but it was just this whole realization of like, "Oh my god. This is possible."

After this realization, Ellie jumped into the nomad lifestyle with both feet and never looked back, telling us: "I just kept going. I just kept working."

Crisis of Self: Reckoning with Authenticity

Whether triggered by a stressful life-course event or a more vague sense that there must be something better elsewhere, many nomads' decisions to leave were acts of desperation. However, we also met individuals whose escape stories, while related to the failures of creative class cities, did not seem tinged with sadness of any kind. This third group of digital nomads left because they had been planning it all along.

Caleb, a thirty-five-year-old Australian digital marketing specialist, was a child of hippie parents from Europe. He had traveled with them from a young age, and he always knew that he wanted the same freedom to travel and that a conventional job would not fit into his goals. Originally trained in alternative medicine and acupuncture, Caleb gravitated toward computers when he realized that he could more easily become location independent if he worked online. Knowing that he needed to build a professional skill base, he spent five years working for digital marketing agencies, but hated the "very high stress" environment where "they overload you with work and expect you to do it no matter what." Like many nomads, he particularly disapproved of the values that his coworkers and peers promoted and the conservative cultural milieu that consumed so much of his time:

> I fucking hated it. I couldn't be myself, basically. I'm alternative. I'm a surfer. I kind of integrated into a corporate culture that wasn't mine. I did well, but I didn't like it, and I didn't have much to relate to. People watching television and sports? Didn't relate. I didn't *want* to go out for drinks. I just wanted to go home and live my life.

However, Caleb entered this work environment with a goal to eventually leave, viewing office-based work as a temporary step toward a loftier plan. Gradually shifting from his status as a corporate employee toward his ultimate goal of successful freelancer, Caleb methodically built his networks and skills until he reached the point where he could sustain a life of working while traveling. Perceiving himself in conflict with the dominant values at home and valuing freedom above almost all else, Caleb was determined to craft a lifestyle around his own beliefs. Here, he explains how his goal to be location independent predated the emerging trendy marketing messages promoting digital nomadism:

> There was no crisis. It was a dream to become free and to do what I want, when I want. The generation now? All these young people are being pushed by Facebook marketing and all this kind of stuff. You know, "Work in the sun and sand." And they're being motivated by that, but that didn't exist when I was around. That's the thing. There's always marketing out there, and it's cool. It's great, but when I was doing it, it was a life decision that I made. It wasn't like, "Wouldn't that be cool to do?" It was like, "Alright. This is what I want to do with my life, and I have to make it happen."

CONCLUSION

A common theme among digital nomads is that the creative class lifestyle, as it is lived in large, Western cities that are the locus of so much of the early twenty-first-century new economy, is inherently destructive to the lives and well-being of creative professionals. Whether burned out or just fatally disillusioned, they ultimately chose to leave.

We probed nomads to explain their choices: Why not just pivot into a different, more meaningful career, but stay in place? However, most digital nomads made few attempts at such changes. Just as they were "all in" for their creative class lives, they preferred radical choices when they decided to leave. Nomads provided several reasons for such choices: (1) their work identities tended to be construed narrowly around their professional skills; (2) many so-called meaningful careers are creatively limiting and bureaucratic; and (3) they would still be tied to the culture of office face time, which would limit their freedom. Lena, a thirty-four-year-old Canadian mechanical engineer–turned–vegan chef and nutrition coach, summed up her extreme reactions (and those of other nomads) like this: "I think when you said why didn't you just choose something a little bit different, I think what happens in life for people is that they go through contrasts, and the deeper the contrast, it's like a trampoline—the harder down you fall the higher up you go." Thus, jumping toward entirely new lives seemed like a more realistic path to happiness than attempting to change their paths within the culture back home.

When we talk to people about our findings from this study, one of the most common questions we receive is, "What are digital nomads' backup plans?" Many people are cynical about the viability of the location-independent lifestyle. Surprisingly, we found that very few nomads had contingency plans, in part, because to them, having a "Plan B" indicates a lack of commitment to creating a fulfilling life. While many nomads made short-term plans to secure freelance work or find less desirable remote work as a starting point, almost nobody told us that they were considering a return to office life at home. Most nomads in our sample were middle class; they benefited from the socioeconomic privilege of years of schooling and experience on the corporate ladder and could be secure in the knowledge that their networks back home could help in the case of an emergency. These safety nets are the foundation that allowed digital nomads to feel confident in their abilities and to take the risk to strike out on their own. Most believed that they could go back if they really wanted or needed to do so. At the same time, they seemed convinced that such a time would never come.

Digital nomads engage in a mobility decision-making process that involves choosing an appropriate destination for a life of remote work. In chapter 2, we look more closely at the other side of digital nomads' mobility decisions: the magnetic pull of Bali as a digital nomad hub. We introduce the concept of work tourism, explain the ways in which work tourists consume the marketing and branding of the digital nomad lifestyle and digital nomad hubs, and outline the reasons that Bali has become a place known for meeting both their preferences for a certain "magical" experience of nature and culture and their practical needs for a low-cost, convenient, coworking community. Chapter 2 also sets the stage for a larger discussion about the importance of place-based community for location-independent workers, which we examine in depth in chapter 3.

CHAPTER 2

Practical Magic: Welcome to Silicon Bali

Silicon Valley, meet Silicon Bali. . . . For years now, experts have been predicting that, with ever-increasing internet speeds and improving video communications technologies, the future of work will involve more telecommuting and working from home. Bali's tech scene participants champion the inspiring scenery. . . . These workers say that they can be location-independent because of the fast internet speeds available in far-flung locales, as well as a growing acceptance from clients that work can and will get done, whether it is from a skyscraper in Manhattan or a bungalow in Bermuda.

BBC.com[1]

Bali is a ninety-five-mile-wide island in the Indian Ocean, located 2,830 miles from Australia and eight degrees from the equator. With the sixth largest population among Indonesia's 17,508 islands,[2] Bali's economy is dominated by tourism, which generates approximately 68 percent of its tax income.[3] Bali also ranks at the top of topics most related to Google searches of the term "digital nomad."[4] Why Bali? Although Bali has long been considered an exotic paradise that is bursting with the kinds of novel influences that many Westerners dream of experiencing firsthand, why has such an out-of-the-way place become a mecca for remote work? In the last chapter we showed why it is important to understand the reasons that digital nomads leave behind their old lives (i.e., push factors). However, a more complete explanation of migration decisions requires us to identify the "pull factors" that have influenced where digital nomads choose to move. Phrases like "nomad" and "location independent" suggest that nomads have a sense of placelessness, or at least an indifference to place, but we found that digital nomads, having given up so much in return for the freedom to choose where to live, are hyper-conscious of and intentional about place.

Nomads' reasons for choosing Bali tend to fall into three major categories: magic (i.e., Bali's array of natural and cultural endowments), practicality (i.e., the expatriate infrastructure and the inexpensive cost), and community (i.e., "no strings attached" relationships with like-minded people). It is the combination of all three of these "pull factors"[5] (i.e., migration decision-making factors associated with the destination area) that makes Bali so alluring to nomads. In this chapter we explore Bali in terms of what nomads characterize as its "magical" and practical sides. We devote the next chapter to the subject of Bali as a place-based community for digital nomads.

REMOTE WORK AS TOURISM: DESTINATION BRANDING IN THE INSTAGRAM AGE

Places are geographically located, but socially and culturally constructed. Social constructionist approaches to place recognize that our understandings of places are not based solely on objective facts; they are realities that people construct and understand subjectively and in conversation with larger social forces.[6] In recent decades, researchers have increasingly acknowledged the process by which places are socially constructed, but their conclusions have been drawn mainly from studies of urban residential neighborhoods and business districts in Western cities.[7] However, technology and social media have increased the accessibility of more remote parts of the world. Today, learning about, traveling to, and even living and working in far-off places have all become forms of cultural and social capital, and travel experiences are often at the center of individuals' expressions of identity in person and on social media. In the past, tropical islands like Bali were places where a very select group would have the privilege of "unplugging" from their lives; now, such far-flung tourism destinations have become places where more and more people go so they can "plug in" and work.

Introducing the Concept of "Work Tourism"

With globalization, places compete more intensely for economic investments, including tourism dollars. In order for a place to attract attention, its unique assets must be branded and rebranded. Around the globe, government administrators and tourism boards at the national, state, city, and community levels use branding consultants and marketing techniques to increase and manage tourism.[8] Indeed, the competition between cities for creative class jobs through the provision of increased amenities might be seen as an extension of their competition for tourist dollars.[9] Historically, the literature suggests that the central strategy for attracting travel consumers is leisure, ranging from vacations that are "free of obligations" to those that are more like pilgrimages where people acquire spiritual meaning.[10] More recently, even mundane commodities such as food and beverages have become attractions for visitors.[11]

In contrast to these "pure" leisure pursuits, the rise in remote work has led many young and middle-aged people to take advantage of travel while working, offering a new lifestyle combining professional, personal, and spatial freedom. Responding to this newfound freedom in the new economy, locations around the globe are attracting individuals who work remotely and who have the potential to inject both tourist and business dollars into the local economy. *Work tourists* use paid vacation time from a job at home, savings, or severance pay from a layoff to explore alternative options for work reinvention, traveling to internationally recognized digital nomad hubs for the primary purpose of working remotely or developing their human capital to engage in remote work within a community of like-minded people.

Many work tourists are either planning to quit an unsatisfying career path, have recently quit, or were laid off by their employer.[12] However, we also met work tourists who had no intention of leaving their jobs back home—they just wanted to try working remotely on a pet project or a passion project (i.e., work that they had always wanted to do but never had time for in their normal lives). In contrast to traditional vacationers, work tourists seek to join place-based communities of like-minded others; they view themselves as part of a revolutionary group pioneering a new way of living. Some work tourists eventually become digital nomads, fully adopting the identity and lifestyle of location independence, but most do not. After all, work tourism is *tourism*, and like most vacationers, work tourists expect to return home to their jobs, families, and societies after this short experimental period.

Work tourism should be understood as distinct from travel as it occurs on the one-year "working holiday" visas that many countries offer (e.g., Australia, New Zealand, Singapore, South Korea, and Ireland) to young people (usually under thirty years old). This kind of visa is mainly for those who are earning extra money to sustain them as they engage in cultural tourism. Likewise, work tourism should not be confused with standard transactional business travel wherein individuals visit a location to meet with place-based suppliers, associates, or customers. Nor does work tourism include the travel experiences of expatriates who have been involuntarily relocated by their companies. Thus, we distinguish between what we call work tourism (including digital nomadism) from the past research on expatriates and work that we discussed in chapter 1.

Place Branding for Work Tourism

Given their growing numbers, their enthusiasm for travel, and their prolonged timelines, work tourists represent an identifiable niche for place branding. The place branding literature usually assumes a top-down strategy wherein government officials coordinate a variety of media outlets to implement marketing.[13] For instance, the state of Florida in the United States has worked with a marketing firm to develop a social media campaign centered around what they call "bragging season." An example of the campaign was presented in the January 14, 2018, issue of the *New York Times* travel section that featured a woman in a bikini lounging by the ocean. The ad featured a photo of her posting to her social media account on an iPad with this tagline: "Be the envy of your social feed." Recognizing this opportunity at a national level, a few countries have begun to implement legal initiatives to encourage work tourism. For instance, Estonia and Thailand have recently developed policies to attract technology entrepreneurs.[14] These legal loopholes are not widespread and are in their infancy, but their existence suggests that work tourism is beginning to appear on the radar screens of officials who craft top-down approaches to place-based branding.

Despite a few pioneering efforts at top-down branding, work tourism has primarily gained attention through more bottom-up, viral campaigns that are separate from officially sanctioned place branding. This approach makes sense in terms of scale—work tourism remains very much a niche market compared to more traditional tourism—and also skirts issues of work tourism's uncertain legality in some countries. In their bottom-up campaigns, remote working enthusiasts and the businesses that serve them actively create and sell remote working communities, mainly by initiating online promotional activities and by modifying conventional tourist infrastructures. The marketing of work tourism is particularly concentrated within the social media ecosystem (e.g., Twitter users, microbloggers, Instagrammers, YouTubers, and administrator-managed Facebook groups),[15] which is well suited to bottom-up initiatives that appeal to international digital workers. Just as cities now use Twitter accounts to send one-way notices of festivals, concerts, and fairs in their jurisdictions,[16] those who promote work tourism share information through blogs, travel sites, and social media groups. Nathan, a thirty-six-year-old Canadian entrepreneur, explained that he learned about Bali through this digital word of mouth: "I heard this was a digital playground, a nomad playground, so I thought, 'Okay, I'm going to check it out.' So I decided to come here in March to focus on the business. I wanted to just focus on work and focus on me at the same time."

Following the popular proposition of the "experience economy" that suggests consumers should prioritize transformative, memorable, and visually impressive experiences over the accumulation of material possessions,[17] the digital nomad lifestyle is a product that nomads are developing, selling, and consuming. Marketing aimed at digital nomads and work tourists captures the experiential element of working in paradise in a personal and visual way, complete with revealing accounts of introspective journeys, posts about achieving personal goals or "bucket list" items, and Instagram-worthy images of travelers working in breathtaking settings. Those who promote work tourism destinations must calm their audience's fears. To do so, they share lists filled with practical insider information about how to navigate life and work in specific locales. For instance, in Facebook groups dedicated to work tourism, it is common to see cryptic messages, crafted to avoid obvious violations of immigration policies, advertising remote jobs that need to be filled, remote services for hire, and digital or place-based courses offered by and for work tourists. It is also typical to see words of advice or warning to naïve beginners who make careless online posts or expose themselves and the community to legal scrutiny. On the site "Baliexpat," someone posted a typical admonition to the rookie digital nomads:

> If you do decide to work as a digital nomad in Bali, make sure to keep a low profile. Never offer your services like web design or photography to anyone locally. Work in a private space. Don't tell anyone what you are actually doing online. If you get questioned by immigration and they ask how you make money, it is probably better just to say you are living from your savings/investments.

Of course, as Bali is a popular international destination for conventional tourism, the Balinese government has its own top-down approaches to place branding, mainly through the commodification of cultural tourism and promotion of the singularity of the Balinese way of life.[18] And Bali *is* unique: though Indonesia is a mainly Muslim country (87.2 percent of Indonesians practice Islam) and is the country with the largest Muslim population in the world, Bali is predominantly Hindu (80.9 percent).[19] The island is celebrated for its retention of ancient Hindu cultural traditions, which include rituals and arts that blend Buddhism, Hinduism, and animism and that are distinct from Indian Hindu practices or Chinese Buddhism, for example. Capitalizing on this uniqueness, the Bali Tourism Board's website mentions that the Balinese civilization is grounded in the Hindu life philosophy of "Tri Hita Karana," which asserts that well-being requires three forms of harmony: harmony with God, surroundings, and humanity. Peace and happiness are central to Bali's official branding strategy, as is the claim that these ideas are authentically rooted in Balinese religious beliefs and rituals. This version of place branding is enticing to Bali's conventional tourists who seek to enjoy warm weather and want to witness and partake in spiritual ceremonies that honor gods, nature, and community.

However, it is far more complicated to commodify remote working in Bali. As a work destination, Bali is marketed in a way that blends the conventional enticements with work conveniences to provide a highly differentiated experience. Once viewed as an island paradise simply offering hedonistic amenities, Bali now promises an experience of immersion in a new work lifestyle that also functions as a path to personal development and identity reinvention. At the end of the experience, the souvenir is not a tan, a family photo, or a T-shirt, but a business idea, an app, a new skill, a community, or a collaboration experience. Bloggers, e-book authors, coworking spaces, coaches, lifestyle entrepreneurs, and companies that cater to "people on the move" spread the word that Bali is a favorite place for world travelers who work remotely. They do this place branding in conjunction with Bali's hotels, restaurants, and other hospitality businesses. Although the Indonesian government is not orchestrating Bali's branding as a work tourism hub, this bottom-up construction of a work-based place identity has drawn thousands of work tourist visitors over the last four years.[20] As a result, Bali's largest coworking organizations are expanding their facilities, and new coworking spaces are opening. Though the importance of social media for branding Bali should not be overlooked, Bali's status as a digital nomad hub also appears in reputable mainstream media outlets (e.g., the BBC, *New York Times*, and *Washington Post*) and online media sources, podcasts, and "listicles" that reach techies (e.g., Forbes, Huffington Post, Medium, and Buzzfeed). The messaging is simple, inclusive, and visual, and it especially targets aspiring entrepreneurs and freelancers in search of freedom (e.g., one *Washington Post* headline proclaimed, "For digital nomads, work is where the laptop is").[21]

A MAGICAL PLACE: BALI'S NATURAL AND CULTURAL DRAWS FOR DIGITAL NOMADS

Bali lets you get away with stuff. Not bad stuff. It's not permissive like Thailand would have a reputation for being, I don't mean [it] that way. Much more in the way that like, "I am just going to go in here and try to be a new me." It's that. Plus, it's got mountains, water, great surfing, nature, beauty, and very inspiring people.

Travis, forty-year-old coworking space owner

It is 6:30 in the evening, and traffic in central Ubud, which is always con-gested, even at off-peak times, grinds to a halt as hundreds of Balinese men, women, and children, clothed in ceremonial dress, march past on the way to the monthly full-moon ceremony at their Hindu temple. The women and girls have their hair pulled back with flowers, and wear kebayas—long, tai-lored lace or cotton blouses, bright sarongs, and sashes tied at their waists. The men and boys also wear sarongs, but in darker colors, with sashes, simple button-down shirts, and finished with the iconic "udeng" headband worn asymmetrically.

Later, they will reverse their route, heading home to their intergen-erational families' traditional compounds that adhere to Hindu and Buddhist architectural rules intended to safeguard against evil spirits, welcome good fortune, and honor ancestors.[22] Tourists, hearing the chiming of the gamelan, a form of traditional Indonesian ensemble music featuring hand drums and bronze percussion instruments played with mallets, leave their tables mid-meal. They join the throngs of bystanders who line the sidewalks and open doorways of restaurants and shops. With a sense of awe, they watch and listen together, sharing in the pageantry, the displays of Hindu gods and spirits, and the sounds of children and men performing as a mobile orchestra as they walk down the main thor-oughfare, Jalan Raya Ubud. Tourists learn that Balinese have many cere-monies: some are annual festivals, some are for family births, weddings, and cremations or for children's rites of passage (e.g., loss of a baby's um-bilical cord or when teenagers' canine teeth are filed down to ward off spirits), but many more happen monthly or several times a month, cen-tering on the phases of the moon, blessings for temples or local people, or seemingly mundane occasions like the opening of a new taxi stand. As suddenly as it began, the spectacle is over, and the families move on into the night, leaving in their wake a multitude of cars and motorbikes that had paused to let them pass.

Within the mindset of the experience economy, the identity and status conferred by travel communicates to the world that one is enlightened, open-minded, adventurous, sophisticated, and prepared for the future world of internationally networked business. The positive character traits attributed to travelers are a main reason that so many digital nomads are proud of the *number* of places they have been, and these traits also moti-vate their goals to actively and methodically collect passport stamps to new places.

Psychologists label people who have a preference for new experiences as having a personality trait called "novelty-seeking."[23] Researchers have noted that this tendency may lead some toward travel,[24] and we interviewed many digital nomads who expressed a general preference for novelty similar to that of Kyle, a twenty-nine-year-old Australian freelance marketer: "I always need new. I love the feeling of it."

Yet digital nomads, similar to the mass tourists who are just visiting Bali briefly, often become enchanted with the island and its lifestyle. They begin to linger as they explore, or else leave, and then decide to return. Dennis, the French marketer and filmmaker, put it this way: "Initially, my presence in Bali was for a month and a half doing a web documentary, and then I was supposed to move on, but then I postponed and canceled my departure to New Zealand and, finally, stayed. I went back to France for a month and a half and came back here." Over and over, we heard stories of individuals who intended to move on, but instead, they restructured or canceled their travel plans once they found what they wanted in Bali. In this section, we explain how Bali's natural and cultural environment contributes to nomads' reasons for finding that Bali is such a "sticky" place.

Nature: A Place in the Sun for Laptop Workers

To the Western eye, Bali is exotic. It has an ocean with offshore coral reefs and a variety of beaches, the beautiful drama of active volcanos, thick jungle vegetation filled with birdlife and macaques, and terraced rice paddies that utilize the traditional irrigation system, producing a patchwork landscape of layered shades of green. Most digital nomads cluster in or around the beach town of Canggu, on Bali's western coast, or in the spiritual center of Ubud, nestled seventeen miles inland (about an hour's drive in Bali's notoriously heavily traffic) on the south-central part of the island. Smaller communities of digital nomads can be found in Sanur, on the southeastern coast, and scattered in other spots on the island. No matter where they are, visitors can easily access a variety of outdoor settings that serve as envy-worthy backdrops to shareable photos and offer a variety of activities tailor-made to check off from their bucket lists.

Nature as a Backdrop to Work and Life

For digital nomads who are "escaping the cubicle," Bali's setting alone is a significant source of inspiration and creates a sense of possibility. Bali's tropical climate is also important as a pull factor for nomads. We found that avoiding cold, cloudy, and snowy weather was a high priority to informants from Canada, the United States, and many European countries. Bali is always hot, and in the dry season, very sunny. Many described the climate as perfect. A favorite nomad pastime is using social media to gloat to friends back home about how warm they are in the winter, sometimes with a hashtag that takes credit for their situation, like "life choices."

Many digital nomads explicitly told us that nature is vital to their work goals. Rebecca, a twenty-nine-year-old marketing consultant from Toronto, explained that Bali has provided her with a climate and setting that easily allows her to feel immersed in nature, removed from distractions, and progressing toward her creative work goals. Here, she explains what Bali offers:

> First off, is nature and environment. The fact that I am looking outside, and I have greenery all around me and bird noises—and in some cases, I'm looking over rice fields—provides you with that mode of isolation and focus that is really important with creativity.

Many nomads are thrilled that nature is no longer reduced to the view from their cubicle or office window. They embrace the idea that easy access to nature and working near natural light make them more productive, help them sleep better, offer meaningful breaks to recharge creatively, and are better for overall well-being. Normalized immersion in nature, even while working, is part of nomads' efficiency mindset. Many nomads are "productivity hackers" – they pride themselves on redesigning systems in their life, finding shortcuts and work arounds, constantly adapting their lives and habits in order to reach their goals. Productivity hacking and habit monitoring have become mainstream and lucrative industries in recent years, but they are especially central within the digital nomad subculture as nomads seek to prove that they can be productive without spending long hours of face time at their desks in an office.

Boris, a twenty-five-year-old technology freelancer and entrepreneur from Ukraine, considers himself an extremely productive person. An obsessive efficiency hacker, Boris is always conducting experiments related to both work (e.g., making money and "cool" products) and his personal life (e.g., getting fit and learning new skills). He is so devoted to and serious about this pastime that it is almost comical. Whether he is focused on a new product, a fresh workout routine, or his capacity to "get likes" on his Facebook page, he methodically develops time-saving habits and goals, carefully measuring his effort and performance. Unlike most nomads who move to Asia to reduce the cost of living, Boris told us it would be easier and cheaper for him to remain in his home country, which is relatively inexpensive. Instead, he relocated to Bali to live in nature, which inspires his work: "If [while] sitting in the basement I could be as productive as [I am] here, I would sit in the basement."

Speaking to the role of nature for both her work and overall well-being, Barb, a thirty-two-year-old American technology entrepreneur, said her former city life left her starved for a connection to nature. She said she had always known that office life was not for her, but as a professional living and working in an industrial city, she suppressed her feelings and just relegated her time with nature to short vacations:

> Environment is quite important to me, like what inspires me, what makes me feel good, all this stuff, and I always kind of envisioned myself living on an island. I was like, maybe Hawaii. . . . Because I somehow, I feel happy, and I just feel good when I'm near the ocean, and kind of, more one with nature.

Many nomads enjoy visiting cities to get a taste of culture but have come to believe that city life, however attractive for career prospects, conflicts with overall happiness and a basic human need to connect with nature. Maddie, an Australian marketing professional introduced in chapter 1, explained how detachment from nature factored in her decision to leave New York:

> I worked in Midtown Manhattan, and I was working for a large digital media agency. . . . I wasn't happy at all, and I was considering moving to the West Coast, where I thought I might be a little bit more suitable, because I'm more of an outdoorsy person. New York's all that being indoors. It's very concrete, and I'm a green person. . . . I had written in my diary, "What do I really, really want? I really want to be around more greenery. I want to be more active outdoors. I want to be conscious about my health." . . . Fast-forward six months later, I'm living in Bali. Yep. Didn't really expect Bali, but here I am. I really manifested that.[25]

As these stories illustrate, nature is essential to nomads' sense of creativity and productivity, especially for those avoiding or leaving cubicle life. Nomads also believe that proximity to nature is necessary for their health, work-life balance, and happiness, which they now define as indispensable to having a productive and positive work life.

Nature as a Source of Activities and Accomplishments

Nomads' "office of the day" photos suggest that they value nature primarily as a backdrop to working. However, their genuine desire for novelty leads nomads to consider nature as important to their travel decisions and how they spend their spare time. Nomads routinely pursue bucket-list items, such as life goals, experiences, and accomplishments, as companions to their work goals. Such lists often feature nature encounters (e.g., solo backpacking, hiking a volcano at sunrise, going on safari). Often, nature experiences are meant to counter their screen-filled lives, and they are part of the life hacking ritual of taking a "tech sabbath"—a day or more away from technology. One business and life coach posted on social media about his intent to visit a famous waterfall in the jungle for the weekend, noting, "I'm going to be fasting from technology and food."

Ned, a twenty-eight-year-old Swiss technology start-up employee, stated that immersion in nature is an essential part of his identity and happiness, so working in an environment where excursions in the wild are convenient and spontaneous helps to offset his long stretches of time in front of computers:

> I'm really a nature guy, so I need to get in the jungle from time to time, and [in northern Bali] it's amazing. There are lakes and jungles and things. I love to just explore the nature of it. Like, just go, for example, across a field to the jungle, down the river, and be with different waterfalls. Go with my tent, sleep on top of the mountain. . . . I really love those moments. . . . In that area, it's like 1,000 meters above sea level. Mosquitos are actually not a problem, and it's not hot. . . . I've done a lot of travels sleeping on beaches, always in a tent everywhere.

Although Ned's "nature goals" tend toward solo explorations of the wild, other nomads focus on more typical tourist nature pursuits. Some enjoy casual access to swimming, while others mentioned hiking, snorkeling, and scuba diving. Bert, a former teacher from Austria, runs several businesses catering to both digital nomads and more conventional tourists, including thrilling mountain bike tours through the jungle. One Chinese American digital nomad we met from California is both a dropshipper (see page 123) and a certified scuba divemaster. He explained his decision to locate in this region versus closer to home or in Europe: "It was always kind of just in my head thinking, 'I have to go to this beautiful, exotic location.'" When we asked if he had always wanted to dive, he said: "Nope. Never thought of the possibility. It was something I thought was reserved for people on *National Geographic*, and when I did my first dive, I just thought, 'Wow. I can't believe nobody told me this is possible. That I can do it.'"

One popular nomad goal is to surf Bali's iconic waves. Bali's tourism industry includes many "surf camps" with accommodations, classes, and island-hopping excursions at every price point. For instance, at Echo Beach in Canggu, just a block from the Dojo coworking space (see page 61), women and men take surf lessons from Balinese locals and ride swelling waves. Some nomads do this between what they call "work sprints" (i.e., task-specific intense productivity bursts of around ninety minutes, which are part of life hacking).

Nomads view surfing as part of a web of behaviors that comprises a new healthy lifestyle in which it is normal to regularly and openly appreciate and take advantage of nature and the warm climate while still being productive and work-oriented. Nigel and Ken, two former tech workers from the United States who are now freelancing and exploring entrepreneurship, reported that their lives back home were far from healthy, with social lives that revolved around bars and overindulging in alcohol. Both said that surfing has become an active and pleasurable outlet for male bonding. They also assert that surfing has greatly benefited their work because they now rise early, surf, and enter the coworking space guilt-free, proud that they have already engaged in habits consistent with their health, life, and work goals. Ken even bragged to us that he had not consumed any alcohol since arriving, attributing this to Bali's health-oriented expat culture and the supportive community in which sobriety is hip and does not interfere with one's social life.[26]

Even those who do not surf often find healthy inspiration from the beaches. Nik, a thirty-three-year-old marketer and entrepreneur from Siberia, told us that the "super-beautiful beach" inspired him both to be more active and to involve his nomad community in this pursuit. "One day I was there, and I was like, if I live in Bali, why wouldn't I just run there every morning because it's beautiful? So, I just started running. I was suggesting my friends to run with me, and so we ended up with a running club." Lani, the sportwear designer who left New York City, agreed that the beach has brought her back in touch with the outdoors. She told us that she specifically moved to Canggu in Bali because "I love the beach. I'll walk on the beach for like, an hour, hour and a half every day."

Whether as a backdrop or source of activity, digital nomads relish Bali's natural wonders. Yet Bali is far more than a scenic, tropical tourist destination. In the remainder of this section, we turn to the role of Bali's distinctive culture in drawing digital nomads.

Culture: Arts and Spirituality

In tandem with its natural beauty, Bali's cultural milieu is rich in arts and spirituality, a draw for both conventional tourists and digital nomads. Most nomads, though acknowledging their outsider status, reported that they felt a special attachment to the Balinese people, often idealizing aspects of their culture.

Fifty years ago, Bali was briefly one of the world's most violent places,[27] but its significant role in the Indonesian genocide of 1965 and 1966 is hard to reconcile with most Westerners' experience of Balinese culture today. Digital nomads commonly described the Balinese as plainspoken but philosophical, patient, calm amid seemingly chaotic events, and able to find beauty all around them. Camelia, a twenty-seven-year-old European human resources professional, explained:

> I think they are the most raw and genuine people I saw so far. They are so straightforward and honest. Simple. Not simplistic, but simple. They don't overcomplicate. They live one day at a time, and this is why I think the happiest people are here. I think that is actually a very valuable lesson.

Dina, a thirty-two-year-old remote worker from Germany, told us how refreshing everyday street life in Bali is: "Here, people react in a very human way. Of course, things don't always go right, but people are genuinely friendly. You smile at them on the street, and they smile back. I really like the people."

The nomads who most appreciated the Balinese were those who had more in-depth interactions with them, either by living in a homestay (i.e., a rented room within a Balinese family compound that is the least costly form of accommodation), hiring them as drivers or for regular work somehow (e.g., personal services or for a business), or by employing them as caregivers to their children. Nadine, a forty-one-year-old Australian entrepreneur who has lived with her husband and children in many types of housing, has employed Balinese caregivers over the three years she has based her family in Bali. She observed that her children have picked up on Balinese ways and creativity:

> My kids can draw really well, and I can't draw and [my husband] can't draw. I really think that part of this is from growing up in Bali, because they are continually exposed to a very high standard of very casually displayed, high-quality art and craft. . . . Every Balinese person can draw a landscape. There's craft and art, and the Balinese do this. We're just constantly getting inputs of this sort of creativity. Everywhere you look there's people carving things, paintings for sale. It's just very casually on display everywhere, and I think the Balinese are very artistic.

Art and spiritual practice routinely merge in Balinese daily life. The Balinese spend an enormous amount of time and resources assembling offerings every day, as well as on their frequent holidays, moon phases, temple ceremonies, and local "banjar"[28] or community events. Elaborate offerings are a status symbol and are thought to protect the banjar and bring prosperity. These rituals cannot be casually learned or imitated. They are steeped in belief and family and community-based traditions that outsiders are unlikely to fully understand.

During our fieldwork, we observed firsthand the Balinese integration of the spiritual and artistic. For instance, we were awakened each morning in our rental house by an elder member of our landlord's family entering the courtyard to place offerings and conduct prayers at an altar. At a "warung" (an inexpensive café owned by locals) on the beach in Sanur, the owner's son taught our seven-year-old son how to make simple daily offerings. Offerings are one example of the routine integration of craft and spirituality, illustrating a way of living that fuels nomads' own aspirations to integrate creativity into their new, balanced approach to life and work. Yet, like most Westerners, nomads also separated artistic and spiritual aspects of their experiences. Given that nomads' artistic and spiritual practices were typically Westernized pursuits, we describe them separately here.

Artistic Immersion Reawakens Creativity

Balinese arts include various forms of painting, dancing, theatre, wood and stone carving, cloth weaving, and silver making. Opportunities abound to intimately experience enchanting aspects of non-Western culture and interact with local people (e.g., cooking lessons, art villages, local markets, coffee and spice plantations, family compound tours, and Hindu temple visits). Travis, the coworking space owner, pointed out Bali's longtime reputation for hosting expats who are interested in the arts. He explained the "magic" that drew him to Bali and the inspirational atmosphere that draws so many creative people:

> I did choose Bali. Why Bali? Because Bali is magic. That's probably the most honest answer I can give. Bali has been attracting writers, artists, and other creatives for hundreds of years as a place to go and be inspired. It has a very long artistic culture, so when people come, they're like, "Oh, my God, the wood carving. Oh, my God, the brick work. Oh, my God, the artisanship." . . . There isn't actually a word for art in the Balinese language because it's just something that is. It's not something like, "Now, I'm gonna do art." It's just something that's like, "Art is there." It's kind of how I have to explain it. I think that for people who are looking to be inspired, this is where *Eat, Pray, Love*[29] comes in, and all of that. It's all related to the same thing.

The normalized and integrated practice of art has emboldened many nomads to close their laptops and revisit the creative passions of their youth. Magda, the Romanian event planner, explained how traditional Balinese painting has reawakened her inner artist:

> I had an exhibition of painting when I was twelve, thirteen, but I decided I wasn't creative enough, and so I just stopped. Now, since I've come to Bali, I've started to explore a bit of that again. The Balinese have a different painting technique, and it was interesting to me to explore a bit of that, and it was interesting to go to this painter's house, and hang out, and learn how that is being done.

Similarly, Maddie has found success in Bali running her own digital media agency, but she has also embraced her artistic side. She now has a following on Instagram and a website selling ceramics she has made. Maddie explained that the ubiquity of ceramics art, studios, and classes inspired her to take some classes, rent studio space, and even commit to working on ceramics as a serious pursuit. What started as a two-week intensive course became a seven-month unpaid internship. She has made and sold many pieces and is now crafting a collection of dishes and pottery. Maddie insists that none of this would have been possible with her hectic schedule back in New York: "Being here in Bali and not having the pressure of a full-time job where you only have x number of days per year [for vacation] gave me the freedom to pursue this two-week workshop."

Maddie's story is far from unique. Many nomads told us that Bali has provided a setting to reconnect with the creative identities that their corporate jobs had forced them to suppress. Drea, the former ad agency employee, explained how her London job had distanced her from her artistic talents and identity:

> I worked in advertising agencies in London. We work with corporate clients. . . . I worked for big and small agencies. Like, I worked for the biggest one in the UK. . . . I worked in advertising for about seven years, and then I went client-side to work in-house in marketing. . . . I wasn't a creative in those jobs. I managed client relationships when I was in ad agencies, so I didn't think up the ad ideas or anything like that. I used to do a lot of art when I was younger, and I'd been paid to do paintings in restaurants before and stuff, and I used to paint a lot, but once I started working in London I kind of mostly stopped that until the last year before I went away.

Kevin, a forty-four-year-old Londoner who studied art in college, was lured away from a creative path by the promise of a more lucrative business career. After moving up the corporate ladder, he became disillusioned and moved to Bali to become a health coach. He said that Bali makes him feel more creative, in part, because he is surrounded by others who seek a creative lifestyle rather than "city life," which he believes prioritizes the Western values of work, materialism, and consumption:

> I went to art school, and then I basically decided that I wanted to earn some money, and then I went to the City to earn some money. . . . I didn't finish the art degree. In those days I got an interview for a job that was local with an insurance company and did very well with it. I was managing twenty-odd people by the time I was twenty-one, and I had kind of reached a ceiling in that particular company, so the next logical place to go was the City. So I started low down, and then worked my way up to different positions over twenty years. . . . When I left the City [for Bali] I was an executive director of a multinational reinsurance broker. . . . I always liked art, [but] I'm more creative when I'm in a good place for creativity to come through. . . . Nowadays, I make a conscious choice to be around like-minded people. . . . I didn't used to do that. I just partied quite a lot in my twenties and worked hard and earned money and spent it. Yeah. I mean, it was a city life.

Digital nomads often view the decision to move to Bali as a continuation of and a commitment to their authentic, creative selves. They view the choice to live there as a pledge to themselves that they will avoid the conventional paths taken by their peers, parents, and bosses. For instance, many nomads participate in the ritual of tattooing an image on their bodies to visibly convey their commitment to nomadism and all that it encapsulates: nonconformity, travel, freedom, and creativity. One nomad described her new tattoos as a rite to mark her renewed creative journey and as a promise to herself to stay the path:

> [The artist who inked her] is a roving tattoo artist, incredibly talented. He worked out of his little villa—super-professional setup and books everywhere, overflowing with previous designs. He used to be a muralist and then transitioned over to tattooing. I got the tattoo on the interior of my right arm, which is my writing hand, partly to encourage me to let the ideas flow through my brain down my arm and into my hand—to get it out. Partly because I was having an internal dilemma around whether the topic/idea was something I could "hang my hat on" long-term . . . By getting the tattoo, I made that a reality immediately. I'd forever be associated with it; it became the cornerstone of what I believe my mission or purpose is.

When asked if the tattoo also serves to help her "stick it out" on a more creative path and to prevent her from reverting back to a more secure life trajectory, whether a corporate job or just moving back home, she said:

> Yes. Absolutely. I'm at a crossroads right now, actually. Does this [life] work sustainably? Why hasn't it so far, as much as I would have liked? . . . So this month I changed all my plans, parked most of my projects, started a book-writing [group], and began a

1,000-word-a-day challenge—the Stephen King method.[30] For the first time, I think [the tattoo] acted as that anchor, alongside a few other nudges the universe has given me that I'm meant to share this message. "This," as in "digital nomadism." It's a daily reminder. Just like my [other tattoo] on my wrist.

Given how much Bali's tourism industry promotes the arts to visitors, some digital nomads have become jaded about "touristy" activities, seeing themselves as too savvy to get overcharged and pulled into events designed for the other kind of tourist—the mass tourist—easily identified by clothing styles, gullibility, and ignorance about the norms of the island. Tracy, a thirty-eight-year-old Australian health coach, has great disdain for Bali's aggressive tourist industry, which interferes with digital nomads' participation in the local arts culture and sometimes causes them to detach or become blasé about it:

> I sometimes go to the dance. I love the gamelan. Whenever the local temple is playing the gamelan I'm just in ecstasy. It's so beautiful to hear the gamelan—just from your home and outside the temple. I go to the dance sometimes. Not enough. I should go more because it's awesome, but it's just—you have to sit around with all these tourists to watch it. I don't like it so much. That's what holds me back from it.

Despite mass tourists' contamination of Bali's local arts culture, Tracy still reveres the local attitudes and customs that nurture and celebrate creativity and aesthetics. Summing up many nomads' feelings, she described the ubiquity of Bali's creative cultural milieu:

> It's more that the art is all around. I feel like my house is a work of art. The attention to detail that they have. It's so beautiful. I feel like you *live in the art. You live in the art.* It's like the whole thing is artistically beautiful and energetically harmonious. They actually create a space to live in which is art. It's creative. You don't have to necessarily *go to do something* to be a part of that, is what I'm trying to say.

Spiritual Magnet

One cannot overstate how much spirituality permeates every aspect of Balinese people's lives, and as a result the island has a reputation as a mecca for spiritual travelers. In addition to the local Hindu practices, Bali now offers a brand of new age capitalism in which locals and expats have commodified a wide array of spiritual and alternative health practices.[31] Entrepreneurs exploit Bali's identity as an *authentic* spiritual place, and they cater to the many travelers who want to sample or even fully immerse themselves in some combination of new age and Balinese healing experiences. For digital nomads, many of whom are still recovering from their separation from their home societies, Bali's spiritual climate provides a gateway to reflection and healing.

Tourists seeking out ancient Balinese cultural practices might engage in mystical readings, Hindu traditions with music, healing treatments using massage and herbs, and ceremonies that allegedly improve "energy imbalances." For instance, many tourists and digital nomads visit Balinese "holy water springs" or water temples, the most famous of which is *Tirta Empul*. There, in a complex of koi ponds, tropical plants, statues, and pools, they bathe alongside Balinese families in sacred spring water believed to provide ritual purification and curing powers. As Travis alluded to above, mass tourism to Bali was boosted by the memoir *Eat, Pray, Love*. In the film, Julia Roberts reaches self-actualization with the help of a Balinese healer (played by an actual healer rather than an actor). This pop cultural touchstone certainly popularized Bali's spiritual healers, who are estimated to outnumber doctors four to one in Bali[32] and are easy for spirit-seeking tourists to find.

As outsiders, tourists often only superficially dip their toes into locals' intricate rituals. Indeed, aside from interactions related to the services they provide (e.g., hospitality, transport, childcare, and healing), many tourists spend little meaningful time with the Balinese. Still, Westerners often are captivated by Bali's brand of spirituality. Keith, an Irish expat retiree in his mid-sixties, moved to Bali after fleeing corporate life in Australia. He explained his transformation in Bali, where locals believe that the dead are reincarnated and that healers can make contact with them:

> It is a vacation area, but there is an aura or an atmosphere of connectivity to nature and to the super-being, if there is one. The supernatural. I think there's a strong connection here, which you can actually feel in yourself when you're here, because I feel more connected to Mom here than I ever did in Australia, and she's dead more than twenty years.

Whether or not they mainly chose to come to Bali for this purpose, most digital nomads recounted some aspect of their spiritual journeys to us. Carol, a thirty-seven-year-old Australian remote employee of a tech start-up, observed: "Bali just has something about it. The way that religion and culture's just so integrated. There's something very special about Bali. . . . It's a mysterious island that lures you in. . . . I love Bali because it's such a spiritual place."

Why would business-minded digital nomads concern themselves with spirituality? Part of the answer is found in popular media, where business moguls such as Ariana Huffington, Mark Zuckerberg, Jack Dorsey, and Richard Branson espouse the necessity for successful people to set goals, adhere to enhancing daily routines, and practice mindfulness in all areas of their life, including the spiritual realm. Digital nomads, like many businesspeople, tend to subscribe to a self-help ideology that echoes commodified versions of Eastern religious beliefs. Digital nomads often link their worldviews and personal aspirations to ideas that they believe are found in sacred Eastern texts. Examples of such concepts are mindfulness, karma and balance, manifesting and the law of attraction, and the abundance mindset. In chapter 1, we noted that many digital nomads left their old lives because of burnout and stress. In Bali, they are free from the office, but many are still detaching from stress and the culture of busy and find that spiritual practices help them to do so. One nomad argued that overlap between tourists who are spirit seekers and digital nomads is increasing:

> It used to be completely separate communities, and now, when I go to like a yoga studio? Like, two years ago, it would be completely separate. Everyone at the yoga studio, they were just *Eat, Pray, Love*. They would almost feel like making money is a bad thing. Now, when I go and do yoga, I will always meet someone who either reads my blog or follows my podcast or is a digital nomad themselves, so it's very integrated now.

As Oshmi, the former Wall Street computer scientist, said, "I feel like Bali attracts people solo traveling. . . . There are digital nomads who are here only because of costs, but also people who are trying to find something spiritual here."

We mentioned that many expats and tourists do take part in, or at least appreciate, some spiritual practices unique to Bali, but that a large portion of Bali's expat spiritual industry consists of other traditions and new age practices separate from Balinese life. Perhaps the most prominent example of this kind is Bali's thriving yoga industry, which is digital nomads' most common spiritual practice. Yoga is not a common practice among the Balinese. Yet almost everyone we spoke to, both men and women, had practiced yoga at least occasionally in Bali, and many said they have a regular practice either individually or at a studio.

In the West, yoga is a mainstream, multibillion-dollar industry popularized by celebrities. Athleisure clothing brands, such as lululemon, market the yoga "lifestyle." However, Western yoga largely ignores or minimizes the original traditions, focusing more on a series of physical poses or asanas, and offering only the minimum amount of mind/body rhetoric needed to satisfy consumers' cravings.[33] Highly commercialized, today's yoga takes place at trendy studios, mainstream big-box gyms, and franchised yoga centers with branded training, certificates, and instructors.

In gentrifying neighborhoods, yoga storefronts are even seen as markers of the middle-class invasion, a prerequisite for creative class cities, as well as the surrounding suburbs filled with moms in yoga pants in search of a flexible, lithe yoga-body. Many serious practitioners, including those who fly to Bali, long for a return to authenticity, complaining that its cost, high-end retreats and classes, and expensive clothing, mats, and accessories have corrupted and diluted it.

Yoga enthusiasts consider Bali a place for more authentic versions of spiritual experiences. Yoga is not merely a workout with a fitness instructor; it is a personal practice learned under the guidance of gurus or teachers. Classes are in natural and peaceful settings, often open-air bamboo structures with a view, filled with Hindu statues, burning incense, flowers, and men and women seeking a transformative experience. Bali expats view yoga as a profound spiritual experience tied to Hinduism and with a *serious* yogi community. Many come to Bali for the sheer variety of yoga options—classes of every type, in a range of locations, of all sizes and styles, and at various price points. According to Maddie: "I did some investigation into the best places to do yoga teacher training. India and Bali came up as the most authentic and most affordable."

Tourists and trendy eco-hipsters consider Bali an opportunity to experiment with yoga in a beautiful setting, something they would never or only sporadically do at home, but Bali expats take their yoga very seriously. Digital nomads often explained the community's hierarchies of dedication to it. For instance, some told us about their fondness for yoga classes, but then prefaced their stories with the disclaimer that they do not consider themselves "real yogis." Barb, the American technology entrepreneur, articulated a sentiment we heard from many others, distancing herself from "woo-woo" spirit seekers:

> I think, by default, after you've been in Bali for so long you can't escape, *but* I'm like, the biggest skeptic. I question everything, and like, I wouldn't say I go as far as like, "Oh, I'm doing crystal healing now." You know, but I will go experiment, and just see what the hell it's all about, and make my own judgment for myself. I've never fallen for any of these like, very spiritual [activities]. There's all kinds of weird shit in Ubud, especially. . . . But I definitely started picking up yoga. I like it just because of the benefits of being able to stretch out your body.

Many people view The Yoga Barn in Ubud as a new age spiritual institution. In addition to hosting the Bali Spirit Festival every April (i.e., a week of music, wellness, and yoga where one can buy a special "abundance pass" for $850), it boasts retreats, a café, and even housing, and offers many esoteric specialty classes that would be hard to find at home: sacred women's circles, master classes focused on yoga's "ancient wisdom," handstand classes, movie nights featuring mind-body healing documentaries, women's wealth "abundance" classes, vision quest classes with "craniosacral therapy and shamanic awareness," and "Bollywood" workshops with music, singing, and sound healing.

Digital nomads mentioned dabbling in several other kinds of alternative spiritual modalities. Often led by a Western "shaman" or guru, these lessons are marketed as "sacred retreats" consistent with Balinese practices. Examples include sound healing, where people gather by candlelight, repeating mantras, accompanied by crystal sound bowls. Also common was breathwork, a term used to describe conscious breath control meditation. Many people mentioned that a "must-do" at The Yoga Barn is "ecstatic dance" (described in more detail in chapter 5). Classes and events like these are supposed to get people out of their comfort zones so they can let go of shame, fear, and judgment.

Bali is also a place where some digital nomads combine spiritual practices with mind-altering drugs. The use of psychedelics to improve mental health was popular in past decades and has had a resurgence in popularity, in part, because of mainstream science writers like Michael Pollan.[34] For instance, several nomads told us about using ayahuasca, a hallucinogenic tea that users drink as part of sacred Latin American religious practices. In the ceremony, a coach or "shaman" will administer the drug and users will undergo a trance as a way to discover spirituality and a life purpose. Because illegal drug possession is severely punished in Bali, nomads are understandably reluctant to openly advertise this kind of service. As one nomad semi-transparently said, "I've been exploring consciousness expansion while I've been here a bit, but not just through meditation, through other instruments. But I'll say what Bali has is definitely a strong spiritual energy that I've sort of let myself fall into, let it come to me, or whatever you want to say."

Bali's brand of new age capitalism is also known for its holistic approach to health through specific foods and diets. Most Balinese believe in the use of natural and supernatural remedies for problems when possible (e.g., rubbing tea tree oil on our son's belly for indigestion). They eat a simple and repetitive diet consisting of noodles or rice mixed with vegetables, chicken, or fish, and seem disinclined to fetishize culinary pursuits. However, as in Western gentrified communities, Bali's new age tourists and digital nomads are obsessed with food, which many see as part of their spiritual practice, or at least part of their healthy self-improvement aspirations. Organic and vegan restaurants are numerous, and nomads are passionate about adhering to restrictive nutrition that is thought to produce better energy, such as raw "high-vibration" foods (i.e., organic nuts, vegetables, fruits, and herbs). Nomads tend to eat most or all of their meals in such restaurants with their like-minded peers. Many nomads shop at local markets, enroll in cooking classes and certification programs to learn more about organic living and horticulture, and share raw food recipes. Similarly, many have experimented in or subscribe to Ayurveda therapy, including consultations about "detoxing," and participating in various routines, treatments, medicines, and healing activities that remove disease-causing "toxins."

Bali's people and the island's artistic and spiritual cultural endowments inspire nomads and are often as important to them as the environment's natural splendor. Yet Bali's so-called magic is most appreciated by digital nomads because they can experience it in a cheap and convenient way that allows them to work. For nomads to set up an effective home base and embark on a new life of remote work, they need more than just magic and inspiration.

BALI AS A PRACTICAL COMMUNITY FOR NOMADS: COWORKING, CONVENIENCE, AND COST

Mention Bali to people from nearby Australia and what usually comes to their minds is their popular holiday destination, Kuta,[35] where many Australians visit. For decades foreign tourists have come to this beach resort to party and let loose. One clichéd image of a Kuta beach is a blonde, sunburned family, parents drinking beer and getting massages, while Indonesian women administer pedicures to little girls and braid their hair into cornrows, perhaps after a day at the water park or a meal at the Hard Rock Café. Those who prefer an upscale but still thoroughly Western experience can head to the neighboring area of Seminyak, home of the beachfront W hotel and other stylish resorts and restaurants.

Digital nomads are *not* usually found living in these kinds of places. They are too thrifty to stay in upscale Seminyak, so this area is reserved for special meetups and excursions. Kuta is out of the question. Nomads pride themselves on being knowledgeable and worldly tastemakers. They have a strong aversion to the mainstream, including throngs of families, retirees, and Australian "buck and hen" nights (i.e., bachelor and bachelorette parties). They are simply too cool for Kuta, which they consider to be the worst of Bali, offering only debaucherous mass tourism, low-brow food, and generic activities and nightlife similar to the US Las Vegas strip.

Instead, nomads flock to Canggu for a hipster beach environment or else to Ubud for a more artistic and spiritual experience (see the Bali map). In both towns, the vibe is relaxed, Wi-Fi is widely available, and restaurants offer healthy alternatives to typical Western tourist cuisine (e.g., pizza, burgers, pasta) without limiting one to the narrow Balinese diet of staple dishes like *nasi goreng* (fried rice with vegetables, egg, and chicken).

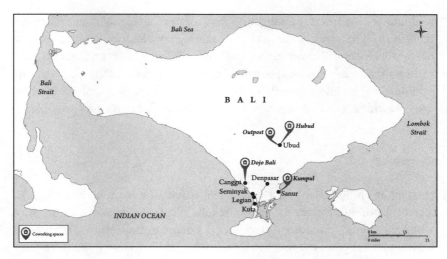

Map 1 Bali

Canggu, about a six-mile drive northwest of Seminyak, is the last in a string of tourist beach towns that spool out from the capital city of Denpasar along Bali's western coast. The vibe in Canggu is reminiscent of Southern California Southeast Asian–style. Just a few minutes' walk from the surfers' beloved Echo Beach is Dojo, a large coworking space where nomads work in bare feet with an ocean breeze and a dog snoring under a nearby desk. At nearly any time of day, the waters off Canggu's beaches are dotted with surfers waiting for the next wave. After an early morning surf lesson, many digital nomads recharge at one of the Western-style restaurants serving avocado toast breakfasts and gourmet coffee—a luxury on an island where the standard "Bali coffee" consists of low-grade, instant coffee powder that is partially dissolved in hot water. While nomads on a budget might grab a Balinese meal at a local warung, those who are more indulgent or finicky can head to places such as the Shady Shack, a nomad favorite for raw and vegan food. Here, for $4 US, one can sit outside gazing at a rice field and indulge in a smoothie bowl filled with frozen fruit and almond or coconut milk, and topped with bee pollen, maca (a Peruvian herb), cacao, or granola.

In landlocked Ubud, twenty-eight kilometers northeast of Canggu, the spiritual and artistic sides of Bali are on full display in many galleries and workshops. Its jungle ravines seem worlds away from coastal Canggu, yet if one were to replace surfboards with yoga mats, similar rituals would be observable among the nomads as early morning yoga classes segue into breakfast at one of many cafés catering to expats. In Ubud, Bali's expat spiritual community and its digital nomad community are in much closer proximity, and even business subjects are more likely to be discussed with reference to spiritual or wellness-related ideas. For instance, a business meeting at Alchemy, a well-known restaurant specializing in raw, vegan cuisine, might take place at a table in front of a rack of enema bags, sparking conversation about the value of so-called personal cleanses to achieve greater focus in life and work.

In Bali, nomads can be seen relishing their new freedom to choose their schedule, pace, and surroundings as they see fit. In this section, we describe the coworking, convenience, and cost structures that make this possible.

Coworking

It is *hot* at Hubud, Bali's first coworking space. The main work area lacks air conditioning, but every seat is taken. While no one knows for sure when the first digital nomad stepped off a plane in Bali, Hubud ("Hub-in-Ubud") launched in the town of Ubud in March 2013 and quickly became a center of the digital nomad community there. The brainchild of three Canadian expat friends, Hubud offers[36] a space with a Balinese bamboo architectural style, a lively, buzzing community, and a range of membership options.[37] Hubud is located across the street from Bali's celebrated Sacred Monkey Forest Sanctuary, a wildlife preserve home to some 700 macaque monkeys[38] who mingle with tourists and occasionally encroach into town to wreak minor havoc on neighboring businesses and passersby. Hubudians, as members call themselves, sit elbow-to-elbow with few comforts beyond excellent internet connectivity and a view of a rice field out the back. Hubud's appearance as a kind of hacker clubhouse in the jungle might intimidate new arrivals, but its reputation is just the opposite: the staff and members exude warmth and friendliness. Hubud is internationally known in the nomad world for fostering positive community among its sweaty but enthusiastic coworkers.

In the lobby area, Tim, a very fit and energetic man in his forties, is mixing salad in plastic bags at a high-top table. Tim is a leadership coach from the United States who has been in Bali for seven months. In search of professional and personal renewal, Tim says that being with so many like-minded people at Hubud has strengthened his sense of purpose. He is not alone. Many informants reported that they intentionally selected Bali so they could participate in community at the coworking spaces. Vance, the business consultant and entrepreneur whom we mentioned in chapter 1, told us: "I was sitting in a coworking space in London called Impact Hub, and I saw an advert. It said, 'Why don't you work at Hubud in Bali?' And I was like, 'Hang on. Yeah. Why *don't* I work in Hubud?'" Although coworking space owners throughout the world profess that they have unique cultures, Bali's coworking spaces have achieved rare acclaim among digital nomads. Michelle, the Canadian coach who specializes in helping cubicle-dwellers transition from their traditional Western corporate jobs, explained how coworking spaces form a practical support network for people who largely arrive alone and who are looking to make significant changes in their lives:

> When I started to go to Hubud, I met a lot of people who were in my phase of my life where I was starting things and doing things and also still in self-exploration. Then, I gained these more intimate relationships with people there, and friendships can bond, can form *very quickly* in a place like Hubud because everyone's in the same way of change, so it's very supportive. No one thinks your ideas are stupid. Everyone's willing to help you out because they're going through the same thing, needing support, so you build family very quickly here because no one has family when they move here.

Hubud is essential to the story of how Bali became a nomad hub. Its success proved that there was significant demand for coworking in Bali, leading to the establishment of many other coworking spaces across the island. Each one offers physical space for working, technical accoutrements, and access to a network of highly skilled labor and entrepreneurs. Although the basics of coworking are straightforward—open, "hot desk"–style office spaces (i.e., open seating on a first-come, first-served basis) with some private rooms for meetings or calls, fast internet, and community programming—each of Bali's major coworking spaces is distinct. For instance, people who prefer Outpost, also located in Ubud, appreciate that it is fully air-conditioned, has a quiet policy in the main working area, and that it projects a Western standard for its coworking atmosphere, albeit with a hotel-style pool and views of rice fields and the jungle.

Kumpul, in the sleepy resort town of Sanur on Bali's southeastern coast, focuses on attracting Indonesian coworkers and has a grant from the Indonesian government to help support the development of local technology freelancers and entrepreneurs. Back on the west coast in Canggu, Dojo Bali attracts surfers and others who want to be near the beach with a laid-back vibe that belies the fact that many serious professionals use the space. At the time of our fieldwork, all of Bali's major coworking spaces were expanding their operations in one way or another, and coworking spaces sometimes collaborated with one another on programming. As promoters of work tourism, coworking businesses regarded the market as too large for them to serve individually, and therefore, they tended to focus on increasing the health of the overall digital nomad ecosystem as a means to ensure their own prosperity. In 2019, Dojo and Hubud coworking spaces merged, and Outpost opened a second Bali location in Canggu. Whatever these changes may reflect in terms of future competition between spaces, the fact that memberships now give individuals the option to move between Canggu and Ubud for coworking fits nomads' preferences to be able to shift their work location at will.

Although not all digital nomads use coworking spaces, most acknowledge their importance to Bali's reputation as a practical destination for remote working. Tracy, the Australian health coach who works mainly at home or from cafés, told us: "I don't really [go to coworking spaces]. I have thought sometimes I should because there's a lot of people doing cool stuff, and it's good to be around that kind of energy." We return to the role of coworking in digital nomad community and work in chapters 3 and 4.

Convenience

Digital nomad hubs must offer modern and familiar conveniences in order to draw people to work and live in them. Though access to technology allows Westerners to maintain connections to home, nomads prefer places with creature comforts and conveniences if they are to stay for long periods. The tastes and standards of prior waves of expatriates are reflected in the housing, restaurants, shopping, and nightlife designed to satisfy both short-term and longer-term visitors. One can find personal services as well as schools designed for expat children, allowing longer-term visitors and those with families to arrange their lives to more closely meet Western expectations and standards.

English is the common expatriate language, and many Balinese in expat areas have basic English language proficiency.[39] The shared language allows more interaction and promotes social support, easing adjustment to a new environment.[40] Many Balinese speak English with an Australian accent, in part, because for decades the island has hosted Australian expats who participate in so-called amenity or lifestyle migration as long-term tourists. Australian retirees have invested in income-generating properties in Bali, developed extensive social networks, and participated in local community life.[41] Many consider Bali an established Australian retirement enclave, where those with long-term visas (i.e., one-year retiree visas can be extended annually for up to five years) can find villas and services that cater to their tastes. Indeed, Australia continues to provide the largest number of tourists to Bali.[42] Although experts urge corporate expat workers to adjust to their new country and build trust with locals by signaling to the host country "a strong desire to adapt," including making efforts to eat "strange foods," have a "willingness to make sacrifices," and give "up our own norms to conform to theirs,"[43] digital nomad hubs form when a Western base of services and amenities is already in place, and the ability to communicate in English is one part of this foundation.

In Bali, digital nomads are able to step into a functioning ecosystem of expat life where they can get right to work. For instance, Western food that suits their tastes is easily obtained even though it is extremely different from local cuisine. Tessa, a marketing manager for a start-up, explained how this translates into a comfortable transition for working nomads: "There's lots of expats here, and it's not just teaching. If I want tacos or gluten-free pasta, I can get it. I'm not roughing it."

Piggybacking on the coworking establishment and on the concurrent boom in rental villas, expat entrepreneurs have launched a variety of coaching services to entice would-be digital nomads to come to Bali. For instance, many newcomers with means indulge in so-called soft-landing packages that ease the transition. Whether run by a coworking space or an independent organization, these packages offer housing and support services (e.g., cell phone cards, scooter rentals) to get newcomers off to a fast start. Oshmi, the Indian writer and consultant, described what she valued about her soft-landing experience:

> It's supposed to be a community for digital nomads, so that it gives you a community feeling because everyone is working on their own. So I *do* feel like if I just go to Hubud, then everyone is like, kind of working on their own thing. There are sometimes events, or speaking, or sessions, or workshops that you can go and attend. But beyond that, if you want to go and talk to someone, you go, and talk to them on your own. There's no facilitation. There are parties and all, but you have to create your own network on your own. What [this experience] did for me was it was already a group of people who wanted to have some structure. So what we used to do was like, on Monday, Tuesday, and Wednesday at 10 AM we used to have some meetings, and it could be something simple, like having an accountability meeting, in which we would commit that this is what we are going to work on this week. And next Monday, we would just, everyone would check, "Okay, this week, did you get that done?" It gives a sense of having a tribe even when everyone was working on their own stuff, and that, to me, was very, very helpful the first month. So I'm glad I did that.

Although soft-landing services continue to meet demand, arriving in Bali has reached a level of ease such that the more adventurous and well-traveled digital nomads rarely require this kind of hand-holding. Facebook forums, Airbnb, and even more conventional travel sites, such as TripAdvisor, offer a broad range of accommodations, and the success of coworking spaces means that finding community on arrival gets easier by the day. Liam, the English tech employee, came to Bali through a soft-landing package but thinks it has become obsolete:

> [This service] has existed for so many years, but this year was a complete flop. . . . I think people now know that they can come to Bali. There are so many people out here already, so there is less need for group-organized activities. . . . It can just happen naturally.

Cost Incentive

As we noted in chapter 1, when companies make decisions about where to locate, they tend to choose cities with high-skilled labor, minimal bureaucracy, and favorable tax treatment, sparking competition among cities to provide the most favorable incentive packages.[44] Similarly, digital nomads openly admit that the economic conditions in Southeast Asia are a driving factor in their migration decisions.

One of the most important considerations for digital nomads, whether starting a new business, self-funding a start-up, or downscaling a professional life to begin a new path as a freelancer, is to secure a Western standard of living at a drastically reduced cost. This idea of earning money in a Western currency while spending it in a lower-cost society was popularized under the name "geoarbitrage" by Tim Ferriss, author of perhaps the greatest touchstone of digital nomadism, *The 4-Hour Work Week*.[45] It is no coincidence that digital nomads, backpackers, spirit-seekers, and vacationers all go to Bali. Southeast Asian countries vary in their total travel costs, but in general, Thailand, Laos, Cambodia, Vietnam, Malaysia, the Philippines, and Myanmar are inexpensive by Western standards. Although not the cheapest of these destinations, the cost of living in Bali still compares very favorably to that of the Western world, especially when one resides farther from tourist centers. In the major categories of lodging, transportation, food, personal services, and availability of basic internet connectivity, Bali's options begin at a very low price point.

Hundreds of blog posts, websites, and Facebook groups offer digital nomads advice about how to save and budget as they prepare to leave their cubicles to start over in Bali. The first consideration is the flight, the price of which depends on the time of year, the number of connections, whether it is roundtrip or one-way, the airline carrier, and the departure city, but it can run from $600 to $1,600 in economy class from New York City. Travel insurance is another cost on which experienced nomads tend to splurge. However, the type and cost of insurance depend on one's country of origin. Upon arrival, digital nomads pay for a thirty-day visa ($35), which is extendable for another thirty days. In addition to hotel options, accommodations in Bali range from low-end shared hostel dorms that offer a bed (usually for backpackers in their twenties), to private budget rooms that rely on fans for cooling, to homestays with local families, and finally to independent villas with air conditioning and pools. At the nexus of the hotel, hostel, and villa categories are a few live-work spaces that specifically target digital nomads.[46] Prices are more expensive in central areas, so digital nomads seeking more space, luxury, or fewer tourists tend to live farther from or the beach areas of Canggu. Visitors to Bali can secure housing by the day, week, month, year, or even longer periods through word of mouth in the community, local Facebook groups and lodging services, Airbnb, and international travel agencies such as TripAdvisor. Bargaining is the norm in Bali, and such haggling allows visitors to receive discounts for longer-term stays. Informants told us it was possible to find a shared place to live in 2019 for as little $200 to $300 US per month.

With few intact sidewalks and heavy traffic, Bali is not pedestrian-friendly and public transportation is not readily available. Nomads rent scooters to get around, as is evidenced by their many scraped and scarred legs and arms, bandages, and slings. For nomads, riding a scooter is a sign that you are not a mass tourist but are part of digital nomads' freedom-loving subculture. One can rent a scooter for around $75 US per month, plus the cost of gas (around $10 a month), which Balinese sell from their roadside stands, often in vodka bottles marked "petrol" and filled with yellow liquid. For rides to the airport, nights out on the town, or shared rides on long trips, nomads will sometimes obtain transportation through private car and scooter taxi services. Private cars and taxis may be metered or unmetered, and local cab driver monopolies or co-ops often control them.[47] Whenever possible, nomads prefer to use online apps like Grab and Gojek, which are far less expensive, but these services are controversial and are stigmatized because they conflict with local taxi cooperatives.

As reasonable as lodging and transportation costs are compared to the West, Bali's real bargains lie in the realms of food and personal services. Although restaurants in major tourist sections are priced in line with Western standards, many nomads see themselves as longer-term residents who know where to eat locally, finding cafés where they get the food they want at prices that they believe to be fair. Full meals can sometimes be as low as a few dollars per person, making it entirely possible to live on a food budget of $10 per day while eating out most meals. Although digital nomads tend to bore of the Balinese diet, local warungs are inexpensive.

In general, digital nomads do very little cooking, as the climate is hot, water is not potable, and accommodations tend to have only bare-bones kitchens. Also, nomads are trying to eliminate chores that take up their time, and they may use meals as an occasion to socialize. Many nomads have specific food preferences that require eating out, such as splurging on green juice, smoothies, quality coffee, raw restaurants, and Western-style baked goods, so food budgets are variable. Some nomads reside in places where breakfast is included, while others make smoothies and coffee at home, but eat their other meals out, aiming to spend $10 to $15 US a day on food. Accommodations often come with a bottled water tank for drinking, brushing teeth, and washing fruit, but people also buy water and coconut water while on the go to stay hydrated in the tropical heat. Many nomads avoid alcohol and cigarettes for both budgetary and health reasons, but others indulge their habits, usually smoking Marlboros ($1.50 US) and drinking the local beer, Bintang ($2.75 US a bottle). Liquor and wine are heavily taxed in Bali, so nomads who still drink alcohol tend to reserve these as luxuries for special occasions.

Digital nomads' productivity is greatly facilitated by bargain personal services. For instance, housekeeping costs are often included in monthly rent, and sending out laundry costs pennies a day. A basic massage, a treat back at home, can be had for $7 US. Coworking membership is probably considered the main blow to the budget at around $190 US per month (as of July 2019) for unlimited access, with more limited packages costing somewhat less. Still, this price is at the lower end of pricing in the West (for comparison, similar coworking memberships in Boston in July 2019 were available between $150 and $435).[48]

In sum, Bali has become a premier hub for digital nomads from around the world because it offers so much for the money. Although it is certainly possible to spend large sums living in Bali, many of the island prices remain scaled more closely to the developing world than to international tourist hotspots, especially for people in the know. This allows for a comfortable lifestyle at a relatively low cost, an appealing combination to all nomads, but especially to those who are trying to start companies with very limited capital. Most people we interviewed live on a total of $800 to $1,500 US per month, though we met some spending above and some spending below this range. As nomads repeatedly explained, $1,500 is below the low end of rent expenses alone in many Western cities.

THE DARK SIDE OF PARADISE: INCONVENIENCE, EXPLOITATION, AND CONFLICT

Inconveniences

Smoothies and coworking spaces aside, Bali is part of the developing world. Like many such locations, Bali's push into modernity has been accompanied by significant inconveniences. For instance, the tap water is not treated and contains viruses and bacteria that cause "Bali belly," a combination of bloating and traveler's diarrhea. Some visitors refuse raw food, tea and coffee, and beverages with ice. We learned that mass tourists can be especially distrustful of the water, so much so that they exclusively drink water from single-serving plastic bottles to ensure that locals are not cutting corners by serving them tap water.[49]

Another inconvenience involves Bali's increased prevalence of many tropical and developing world diseases. For instance, many nomads suffer debilitating months-long spells of fever, headaches, vomiting, muscle pain, and fatigue caused by the dengue virus, which is carried by mosquitos. One way to appreciate how concerned nomads are about dengue is to note how they feel about mosquito repellent. Digital nomads tend to prefer healthy and organic food, so we were surprised when they mocked our use of mosquito-repellent bracelets and patches that use natural ingredients like lemon eucalyptus oil. They warned us to only use repellent sprays with "the real stuff" (i.e., high-concentration DEET that is hard to find in Bali).

Animals are also a concern. The Balinese mainly view dogs as a source of security for their homes and communities, although some seem to show a more emotional attachment to them. Tourists find it troubling to encounter Bali's numerous stray dogs, many starving and sick, living in squalor, often eating leftover rice from Hindu offerings. Some of these dogs may harbor rabies, so visitors are warned that vaccines, though expensive and inconvenient, are highly advised for anyone who is bitten. Furthermore, many nomads are animal lovers and deeply distressed by the way dogs live there. A large number of Bali's digital nomad social media posts feature concerns about animals, as well as news stories about their perceived mistreatment by the Balinese (e.g., dogs being stolen and used for food).

As more tourists arrive in Bali each year, crowding becomes a major issue.[50] Traffic and accidents are major topics of conversation when people complain about Bali. With tourism such a large part of the economy, many Westerners can now be seen zipping through Bali on motorbikes, often scantily clad and without helmets amid traffic congestion, stressed and overused infrastructure, and poor-quality roads sprinkled with dogs, chickens, and cows. The Balinese have developed their own system of navigating the winding, narrow, hilly roads, as well as their particular methods and etiquette for avoiding traffic and dealing with clogged roads or streets blocked off for religious processions. The Balinese are generally patient and lightly double-honk their horns as a friendly signal that they are coming around a bend or even down a straightaway with space for only one car at a time. Indeed, the only people we saw become visibly angry while driving during our fieldwork were Westerners. Socialization into driving norms is a lifelong process, with Balinese children as young as eight years old steering motorbikes or sitting on them with multiple family members, babies, pets, and cargo. The internet abounds with images of Balinese people driving scooters overloaded with large unwieldy items such as bamboo, bricks, and appliances. It is normal to see whole families of Balinese—and now nomads—driving a scooter with a toddler as well as a dog by the handlebars.

Despite the fact that nomads are new to the driving culture, they are thrilled to finally ride motorbikes in Bali, a true symbol of expat acculturation. Even after showing us their injuries from accidents (one informant was confined to a wheelchair for several months, others showed off casts and burn marks), they ridiculed our decision to use a private driver and car, insisting that it is safe for us to drive a motorbike with a three-year-old and a seven-year-old in tow.

Another drawback to Bali is that many Westerners perceive Indonesia's laws as compromising their civil rights. Though Bali has a relatively liberal atmosphere (e.g., drinking alcohol is permitted in Bali, though this is a source of conflict with some sectors of the Indonesian government), Indonesia adheres to conservative Muslim standards. Indonesia also has strict laws against drugs of all kinds, including marijuana. Informants told us that even the possession of sex toys is prohibited, and that airport workers often confiscate these from tourists upon their arrival. In addition, the government selectively and sporadically censors media and internet sites, much to the frustration of digital nomads who miss their full array of Netflix choices, pornography, and other media that the government views as "negative" (including LGBT content and extremist ideology).[51]

Further, many Westerners consider Indonesia's political avenues to be ineffective and corrupt. Nomads often mention "bribe points"—Bali's roadside police have checkpoints where they target Westerners on scooters to see if they have the required Bali driver's license, and sometimes they threaten to take the bike until a few dollars are exchanged. Many expats are frustrated with the red tape and obstacles involved in extending their visas and securing longer-term visas. That said, the long tradition of Bali's expatriate communities has resulted in the development of an infrastructure to manage some of these problems. For instance, visa agents are available at reasonable rates to assist in navigating Indonesia's complex and potentially frustrating system for visa renewal. Ultimately, most of these "inconveniences" occur simply because Bali is not part of a Western nation, and it has norms and systems that differ from those to which visitors have become accustomed.

Exploitation

Bali's many benefits for digital nomads and other Westerners are very real. All of this tourism also helps to create jobs in Bali. Yet any discussion of advantages invites questions about how and why such benefits are possible. A thorough analysis must therefore acknowledge that Bali's work tourism industry is not exclusively beneficial to the Balinese.

Tourism can be seen as an extractive industry, starting with the greenhouse gas emissions of all the flights.[52] Throngs of work tourists add to already growing problems with traffic, overcrowding, and water and air pollution on the island. Waste generation is a serious problem, as Bali does not have widespread trash collection or recycling, so plastic and trash litter the land and sea. This growth paradox—fast and unsustainable development—has taken place in many tourist destinations around the world.[53] When relatively wealthier outsiders descend on an entire society, unintended consequences often result (e.g., effects on the environment, ad hoc development, burdens on local capacity, and leakage—tourist money leaving the host community rather than being distributed among the locals).[54]

Another overarching criticism of any idyllic view of Bali concerns the imposition of Western economic incentives on traditional society and how this has negatively impacted many long-standing structures and cultural norms. The productization of the digital nomad lifestyle for work tourism leads to uncomfortable associations with Western privilege, exploitation, gentrification, and neocolonialism. Even businesses that cater to nomads could be seen as a form of Western gentrification and cultural displacement. Most nomads are aware of the neocolonialism narrative, but they usually accept and neutralize their role in the ecosystem, comforting themselves with the knowledge that they are at least contributing to a poor region's tourism-dependent economy. As Ellie explained:

> I don't really see it as neocolonialism. It troubles me with any tourist spot. I was in Barcelona the other week, and there's wide plazas and the Spanish outside drinking wine, and that's not the Balinese culture. Balinese people don't sit outside drinking wine and beer. They eat privately in Balinese compounds, and just like in any tourist place, it's set up for tourists. You give them what they want, and then it's like Western people demanding Western-style service from Balinese waiters who don't understand. They don't understand the restaurant culture that we have in London or New York. They don't get why you have to have things delivered in a certain order, or why things have to come within a certain amount of time, and you just see people giving them shit about that, and that's not nice but that happens in so many tourist centers.

Our own experience supports Ellie's observations. When friends visited us as tourists in Bali during our fieldwork, we noticed that they were mystified and annoyed by the lack of Western-style service norms in restaurants.

Visitors to Bali often exploit the non-confrontational norms of Balinese society by using their freedom to behave in ways that offend locals. One digital nomad noted that when Balinese people witness expats violating local norms, such as sunbathing in a swimsuit in front of a temple regardless of signs that prohibit this, they remain silent:

> They will not say anything because [they think] it multiplies the shame. So, as it stands, [the Balinese] feel shame on behalf of the inconsiderate tourist, but if they say anything the tourist may also feel shame themselves, and then the accuser feels shame for delivering the judgment. Instead, the offender is simply a recipient of the friendly Balinese smile.

We sometimes heard digital nomads complain about Hindu rituals interfering with their lives. We once witnessed a hotel advertising that management was seeking non-Hindu employees who can work on Hindu holidays. The ad mentioned Nyepi, Bali's Hindu New Year, which is also a day of silence when everyone must remain at home and quiet with lights off and no Wi-Fi. Nomad Facebook groups feature many grievances about Balinese ways and Hindu rituals, though other nomads and the Balinese frequently respond by telling nomads to "go back home" if they feel this way.

Tourism has long been known to increase the potential for conflict between locals and travelers.[55] Western entitlement may be particularly likely to cause conflict when tourists are bargaining for goods and services. Bargaining is normal for economic transactions in Bali, yet it creates the potential for conflict as seasoned digital nomads are incensed about perceived Balinese schemes to overcharge Westerners. Repeatedly, nomads would ask us what we paid for something, warn us about Balinese "ripping us off," and tell us we paid too much for a service. Given the relative affluence of expats and Bali's low prices, wariness about exploitation *of tourists* is off-putting. However, nomads are on a budget and have a free market ideology. Bryan, an engineer and entrepreneur from New Zealand, mentioned that many necessary services, such as rides to and from the airport, require a long search for a reasonable price—research that is worth it because rates for those in the know are often half what tourists are charged. Lucy, a videographer profiled in more detail in chapter 5, explained the nomads' mindset, even as she characterized it as "a trap":

I think you fall into the trap here. . . . If you say, "I'm paying seven million [rupiah or about $500 US]," people are like, "I'm paying six." . . . But that's a difference of sixty pounds. . . . I'm earning $400 a day; that's my daily rate. . . . So why am I quibbling? Why am I like, "I don't want to pay this extra fifty pounds"? . . . But you kind of feel—it's the same with anything. You go out to eat here, but you wouldn't pay $10 for a salad because that's not what it costs here, so you wouldn't pay it. At home, that would be cheap. But here, you're like, "That's twice as much as it is everywhere else, so I don't pay it."

For their part, the Balinese are not naïve; they also evaluate Westerners. In our fieldwork, we observed Balinese behaving similarly to people everywhere in business transactions. Some attempted to take advantage of us, but most were fair in their negotiations with us,[56] and those whom we established longer relationships with reciprocated by doing nice things for us without compensation or else trusting us to pay them back in accordance with Balinese ideas about karma.

Though the Balinese generally frown on open expressions of disapproval and rarely complain to Westerners, online forums capture some of their negative sentiment toward expats. A prime example of conflict between locals and Balinese that has overtones of neocolonialism is the issue of taxi service. Westerners, including tourist resources,[57] construe Balinese taxi cooperatives as "cartels" or mafias—a representation that seems to imply something sinister and illegitimate. Yet from the Balinese perspective, taxi cooperatives are simply an efficient means for local drivers to band together to regulate business so that they get a fair share of rides and receive a consistent wage based on the distance traveled. However, nomads' extreme individualism seems to make them particularly resistant to accepting the legitimacy of Balinese collective efforts to protect their interests so that they are not pitted against each other and exploited for the lowest possible wage. An example of the Balinese perspective is apparent in a post in which a Balinese driver complained about the rise of the online car and delivery service Go-Jek, which local drivers believe interferes with their ability to get fares: "I am sure all of us like cheap price for transportation. But if the price indicates human exploitation inside, will you still [be] comfortable to use this service? Say no to over low price of online transportation. We are not on slavery time." A typical expat response resembles this one:

> It may seem like "slavery" or cruelty to the human race. . . . Well let's face it. . . . For the customer: (A) Who doesn't like a good service at a low cost??—we all do!! (B) It allows one to get more things done in a day by creating another job for someone else that is happy to do it, or he wouldn't have accepted the job.

Exchanges like this one show that there are at least some conflicts lurking beneath the many smiles exchanged between digital nomads and the Balinese. And, as the taxi issue suggests, digital nomads' perceptions of having been exploited back home in their prior lives do not necessarily lead them to a generalized view of fairness toward labor.

CONCLUSION

Without a doubt, Bali is a place that holds great symbolic meaning for many people who visit. However, it is undeniable that the tourist industry and those who take part in it have exoticized the island, a process that is part of a larger Western tendency to "other" islands while simultaneously conceiving of them as paradise.[58] Indeed, marketing scholar Janeen Costa wrote that an island is "a place essentially unlike . . . daily life"; it is "exotic, unusual and different" a "metaphor for the negation of everyday existence" where "rules and obligations are largely suspended, resources are abundant, and hardships associated with quotidian earthly existence are lacking."[59] These features conjure the magical and dark sides of Bali. Ultimately, though, Bali has become a digital nomad hub because it combines these features with a practical environment that diverges from the stereotypes of island life in which one is there to simply relax. Bali is a place where digital nomads can have their magic and their connected work lives side by side. In the next chapter we turn to the third, and according to digital nomads, most important factor pulling work tourists to Bali: the local digital nomad community. Map 1 Bali

CHAPTER 3

Paradise Paradox: Constructing a Digital Nomad Community

We are social creatures. Full stop.

Coworking space owner

The community. I actually travel to places where I feel very good and where I think there are good people because when you travel it can be quite lonely sometimes and having the right people around you—who maybe also stay long-term—it's just very nice to have. I feel like in Bali I have this.

Belinda, twenty-two-year-old digital assistant and entrepreneur

When we asked people why they chose Bali as their location to be digital nomads, these were some of their most common answers: "It was definitely the community of nomads. People come here because of the people." "There's so much synergy here, and everybody's wanting to see other people succeed—that community of like-minded individuals." "Bali is simple: community. So many like-minded people in one place, and of course, under the umbrella of tropical beauty." "I remember in the working world—like anything—there's people you get on with, and those you don't. In this world, I can honestly say, perhaps it's attracting like-minded people, the number of nomads I've come across who I've disliked, I can count on one hand."

In chapter 2 we discussed several pull factors that draw nomads to Bali. We now devote an entire chapter to what our informants said was the most important reason they chose Bali: *community*. On this island, digital nomads have finally found a place-based community with like-minded others, an environment that eluded them back home. But what does a place-based community of digital nomads look like? Why do "location-independent" workers desire face-to-face contact with others who are working remotely? How can nomads form social bonds and a sense of community in a place with so much population turnover? These are the subjects of this chapter.

REVISITING THE COMMUNITY QUESTION

Barry Wellman, an expert on cities, community, and social networks, has long investigated the changing role of territory for community. He asserted that the "community question"—"the question of how large-scale social systemic divisions of labor affect the organization and content of primary ties"—has "set the agenda for much of sociology."[1] Indeed, existing theories offer several insights into which aspects of community digital nomads desire and which they seek to avoid.

Early theorists considered community to be an organically evolving phenomenon—sometimes called "natural"—based on population flows and competition among groups.[2] Soon, a community "lost" theory emerged. Here, scholars argued that close social ties were declining because urban life is packed with pressures that have a disorganizing effect,[3] a view that many digital nomads expressed to us when reflecting on their former lives in creative class cities. In a contemporary version of this argument, Robert Putnam[4] documented how frantic schedules, pressures, and conveniences have led to a "bowling alone" phenomenon wherein individuals opt out of collective identity and participation in structured, local forms of social engagement (e.g., joining bowling leagues, political campaigns, labor unions, neighborhood associations, and churches). As we reported in chapter 1, many digital nomads told us that even when their lives were packed with social participation (e.g., family obligations, socializing with colleagues, and going to bars with friends), they found that their aspirational community remained beyond their reach, and they were not spending meaningful time with the "right" kinds of people.

As a response to these arguments, scholars forwarded the concept of communities of "limited liability," wherein social ties are viewed as voluntary, and individuals choose where to live and the degree to which they socialize according to their own particular needs.[5] Another well-known argument, termed the community "saved" argument, suggests that people may respond to the pressures of contemporary life or their dissatisfaction with traditional social bonds (e.g., family and neighbors) by seeking out people who share their interests and values. They often do this within the geographic boundaries of their local communities,[6] but sometimes they migrate to places that already have concentrations of people who are like them or they join non-spatial communities.[7] Digital nomads subscribe to aspects of both the limited liability and community saved arguments but do not perfectly fit either perspective. Nomads tend to aspire to social lives that are less dominated by traditional and obligatory activities that they view to be largely determined by where one was born or where one happened to have secured a job. They also seek a more volitional social world, pursuing in-person community away from their home countries with people who share their values, engage in social interaction, and provide support.[8] However, most digital nomads would reject the contention that Western cities can offer these environments--places where meaningful communities are thriving, especially for people who hold their values.

Richard Florida focused on shared values in developing his "creative class" perspective on how people find community within new economy cities.[9] Florida argued that by traditional measures, community may seem lost, because individuals' preferences for social bonding have changed--they "prefer weak ties to strong."[10] To the extent that people desire weak ties, it is logical to imagine that social ties might lose their geographical dependency altogether, especially in a technologically enabled world.[11] This argument, the community "liberated" argument, posits that traditional, primary, place-based social ties that link community, work, and family are not lost, but neither do they tend to thrive within small geographical places.[12] Rather, technology has *liberated* people from the constraints of limiting, circumstantial, and provincial aspects of place, enabling them to manage both kin and non-kin social relationships, sustain weak ties, and create and maintain both *non-local* and *online communities* that satisfy needs no longer met by many geographic localities. With the rise of the so-called triple revolution (e.g., social network, internet, and mobile revolutions),[13] many urbanists have now turned to the community liberated framework to understand the changing, and increasingly nonspatial role of community—even those scholars who admit that they idealize neighbor relationships as the solution to urban problems. For instance, criminologist Robert Sampson—whose best-known body of work advocates community informal social control as a solution to crime and other neighborhood problems—wrote in his essay "What Community Supplies": "The evidence is now clear that urban dwellers rely less than they have in the past on local neighborhoods for psychological support, cultural and religious nourishment, and economic needs and transactions."[14]

Digital nomads would seem to be the very prototype of individuals to endorse the liberated, nonspatial perspective on community life. However, our informants clearly and firmly rejected any claims that technology substitutes for face-to-face community. In fact, they reported that they intentionally moved to Bali to create more meaningful, transformative, face-to-face social networks. For digital nomads, technology and mobility create the freedom to work away from the office and to connect with like-minded others online, but it is only after arriving at a nomad hub that they find the most meaningful community. Rebecca, a business consultant and entrepreneur introduced in chapter 2, explained her need for in-person community like this:

> I went off on my own a number of times to start my own creative businesses, but I never got anywhere because I was sitting alone in my office working for myself with no community around me and no one to hold me accountable and no inspiration, and I stalled out. I made enough to get by, but I was so unhappy with it. . . . I'm involved with a lot of Facebook communities and entrepreneurial circles, but no one's really invested in your success. It's just like, "What resource can you give me?" or "What event can you invite me to?" It's very ingenuine. You have to have your guard up a lot.

When asked if she thought the relationships online were more transactional than those that she formed in Bali, she responded:

> Yes, very much so. When I came to Bali, there's a couple of things in terms of creative conditions that are so different. . . . The community aspect is enormous. You're around like-minded people who are trying to have these massive, aspirational, independently driven goals. And being around that? Not only having these accountability buddies, but you're attending these skill shares and think tanks and being inspired by other people's progress, and it's fueling you up while you're fueling them up. It's a beautiful cycle of creativity.

As Rebecca's comments indicate, by far the most vital aspect of community to digital nomads is the opportunity to live and work with peers who share their values. Sociologists refer to this desire to be with a selective, socially compatible community as *homophily*. Personal preference and structural constraints produce homogeneity in social ties.[15] Furthermore, those who share less in common find that their social ties tend to dissolve faster.[16] Given that most nomads have a shared homophily narrative and use it to make sense of their decision to move to Bali, any effort to understand the culture and structure of the digital nomad community requires a consideration of the values that make up their "like minds." If individuals need place-based communities to satisfy their social needs, it makes sense that more successful communities will have members with shared values. Accordingly, to better understand what attracts digital nomads to digital nomad communities abroad, we continue this chapter with an examination of nomads' core values. These are values that nomads view as distinct from the dominant or mainstream values in their home societies.

Back in 1997, an eon ago in the tech universe, a Sony technology executive named Tsugio Makimoto, along with his coauthor David Manners, wrote a book that launched the term "digital nomad." In it, they predicted that a coming wave of technology-enabled mobility would soon allow creative professionals to meaningfully revisit an ancient human choice: whether to become a nomad or a settler. As dramatic as this sounds, to date, most people, and most creative professionals, have remained settled relatively close to home. After all, many came of age before location independence seemed like a viable lifestyle, and they have now become established in their lives and ways. Furthermore, many creative class workers, remote or not, are still attached to conventional ideals, values, and aspirations, such as proximity to one's family, homeownership, acquisition of material goods, and loyalty, sentimental attachment, or affinity to one's country, state, or locality. Perhaps this will change, but for the present, digital nomadism, though growing rapidly, remains confined to a relatively small number of people—probably fewer than 100,000 worldwide as of this writing.[17]

Given that many people share nomads' frustrations with their lives in creative class cities, as described in chapter 1, what differentiates those who selectively migrate to become digital nomads? Our research has led us to conclude that digital nomads share a set of core values that are dissimilar from those that dominate their home cultures. Although these values are not exclusive to digital nomads and may be found among small subcultures at home, nomads are extreme in the degree to which they prioritize their lives according to these values. Nomads are so committed to their core beliefs that they have left home to find a place where they can live and work within a community of like-minded peers, a dedicated community who will support them and reinforce their values.

Below, we outline the five core values found in digital nomad hubs. We begin with the most important one: *freedom*. We also describe four other shared values that, though secondary to freedom, were pervasive and central to the digital nomad community in Bali and elsewhere. We label these *personal development, sharing, positivity,* and *minimalism.* These synergistic values form the basis of communities that digital nomads build, seek, and join.

Value #1: Freedom

No detailed discussion of the digital nomad community is possible without addressing the centrality of the value of *freedom.* As digital nomads describe it, freedom means defining oneself as an individual in explicit contrast to social structures and institutions, especially those that appear to offer security and stability in return for conformity to rules or other collective social obligations to families, communities, organizations, and societies.[18] Freedom is strongly related to individualism, defined as "a worldview that centralizes the personal—personal goals, personal uniqueness, and personal control—and peripheralizes the social."[19] Given that entrepreneurs across societies tend to score higher on individualism[20] and that individuals' autonomous interests drive creativity,[21] it is no surprise that digital nomads, as entrepreneurial, professionally creative people, advocate each component of individualistic values (i.e., a focus on personal goals, uniqueness, and control).[22] However, freedom is a more specific value than individualism; it also emphasizes the individual rebelling against collective social structures.

In describing to us their value for freedom, digital nomads emphasized their self-determination, their opposition to cultural programming, and their unusual view of social life. In their narratives, nomads used the word "freedom" to describe their desire for independence in everything from the work that they do, to where they do it, and with whom they do it. For instance, one digital nomad influencer posted: "The best part of being a digital nomad is the freedom of location independence, to be able to work from anywhere." Another nomad in our sample posted this update on his travels: "Freedom is the courage to do what you want with your life. It's the ability to be in alignment with your dreams and values." Paul, a thirty-nine-year-old English marketer, expanded on this:

> The driver is that you're doing it for yourself. It's a wonderful feeling. I love it. It harks back to that travel that I talked about at the start [when I was younger]. It's a sense of freedom. Back to value systems, what gives me inspiration, zest for life is this idea of freedom. Being able to do whatever I want to do, whenever I want to do it, from wherever I want to do it, is so empowering for me. It's palpable. I can taste it. It's a wonderful feeling, and it far exceeds my expectations of what I thought it would ever be like in those daydreams that I must have had many times.

Nomads also reference the word "freedom" when they describe their visceral and ideological desire to rebel against what they perceive to be the captivity of their former lives. Nicholas, a thirty-seven-year-old Australian entrepreneur, explained:

> In Western culture, there's a paradox of freedom. People think they're free, but they're not. I did a list on my phone about all the rules. I got *sick* of the rules in Australia. Like, *so many* rules . . . it's just ridiculous. It's a nanny state. That's not freedom. . . . I think the first

time I really enjoyed Bali was when I got a motorbike and just went riding around. It was just like—it was just freedom. . . . I was just like, "Fuck. I feel free." I didn't have to wear a helmet. There were no cops around. There's no one controlling me now. It just felt good.

This rebellious dimension of nomads' affinity for freedom, particularly rebellion against forces that require them to *stay* in a location, a job, or situation, is inextricably tied to travel. Terms like "digital nomad" and "location independent" signify freedom from restrictions and obligations that tie a person to a specific geographic place, but they have an even broader meaning that extends to escaping societal role restrictions. One nomad who left New York City listed the domains of his new freedom:

"Physical" is being able to live and work where you want. "Mental" is to think for yourself and explore your consciousness. "Financial" is to spend money on what you want and when. But the version of freedom I've been working on has to do with self-expression, since modern society has conditioned men with a false narrative that prevents this.

Many digital nomads attached their view of freedom to a wide array of unconventional choices that reject societal scripts about work as well as those dictating norms about gender, monogamy, marriage, children, suburbs, cities, materialism, schedules, education, adulthood, and aging. Thus, nomads' internal state of attachment to freedom rather than security dictates their beliefs, attitudes, and orientation to the future. For example, one nomad explained that he felt trapped by the lifestyle encroaching on him back home: "I was thirty-seven at the time. All my friends had started moving out to the suburbs of London, so my social life had started to dry up a lot at that point because people were off having babies and that sort of stuff." Another associated freedom with his desire to escape the West's overprotective government rules for a place like Bali where rules are more informal, enforcement is sporadic, infrastructure is weaker, and people are forced to take personal responsibility for their actions: "If you walk down the street and fall in a hole, tough shit. Watch where you're going." Paul, the London marketing executive, described feeling confined by his prestigious career-track job: "I remember feeling like I'm in a zoo, like I'm caged, like I've got no freedom anymore." Like others whom we met, he described feelings of elation when his company eventually fired him from an even better position: "It was in the top five or top three days of my life. Ever . . . It was like being released from prison. It was a fantastic feeling."

Nomads also use the word "freedom" when referencing their unusual view of social life. Individualists tend to "peripheralize the social,"[23] but what is so striking about digital nomads is that they view community as critical to their well-being while also firmly rejecting the idea that their social lives should entail even the most minor obligations, which they often view as coercive.[24] For example, Lani, the clothing designer, described her provocation when a fellow digital nomad confronted her about skipping a local event in Bali: "Everybody just needs to get out of here with that, because I did not come here to feel obligated." Kyle, a twenty-nine-year-old marketing analytics freelancer, explained that he wanted to get away from the sense of obligation that he felt back home in Australia:

> I just found that in Sydney, my family and my friends are there, but there were too many distractions. There was always social obligations and all this stuff going on. . . . I loved hanging out with friends, and obviously, I love spending time with the family, but I kind of needed to sacrifice that part of my life so that I could seclude myself away from all of that, so I could just put my head down and just kind of go for what I wanted to achieve.

Although freedom is the sin qua non of digital nomad values, achieving and maintaining it has also led nomads to embrace other shared values. We now turn to these other values that support their cherished value for freedom.

Value #2: Personal Development

Personal development among digital nomads refers to their value for striving to increase their self-awareness and capabilities through structured activities. These may include psychological and spiritual practices such as meditation, yoga, and other mindful reflection and rituals; physical fitness and dietary practices, such as exercise routines and restricted diets; knowledge and skill building through reading, practical training, and coaching (though not usually through formal education); and social practices, such as networking with like-minded others.

Although personal development pursuits are consistent with freedom, freedom does not require people to distinguish themselves through the pursuit of learning or other self-improvement efforts. Hence, we identify personal development as a separate digital nomad value. Nomads frequently operationalize their value for personal development by incorporating these activities into their daily routines, but they also aim for loftier goals by periodically engaging in self-imposed challenges—a sort of gamification of personal development that they term "leveling up." For most, the decisions to become a digital nomad and then to travel to Bali are examples of grand efforts at expressing free will and committing to personal growth.

The core value of personal development is also tied to our findings about digital nomads' "push factors" in chapter 1. In that chapter many informants explained that they left their old jobs because the work was too boring, routine, or easy, failing to challenge them on the aspects of work that had the most potential to be interesting and meaningful.[25] This aspect of digital nomads is perplexing to many people who wonder why nomads refuse to simply tolerate their unsatisfying lives and jobs back home. After all, those jobs provided steady pay, health care, benefits packages, stability—and all without the hassle of hustling for work and living away from the comforts of home. But the trade-off is not worth it for nomads. Nicole, who worked in marketing for a well-known international luxury brand in Paris, told us:

> At first it was cool, but eventually I got really, really bored. . . . The job didn't have any creative things. . . . I was really bored. I liked the tasks that I had because I was planning stuff for the agencies, and I'm friends with them now, but it was not enough workload, and it was missing creativity and freedom. The periods where I had too much work were pretty short, and it was exciting. Eventually, something that would take me half a day would take me half an hour. . . . but when I was challenged I was pretty happy.

This desire for self-driven personal growth is clearly evident in nomads' extremely positive attitudes about learning. Though many are highly critical of the institution of higher education, especially its methods and the degree to which it is useful in the real world, nomads view themselves as lifelong learners who are curious, intellectual, and critical thinkers. When they describe their aspirations, and even their current identities, they use labels like expert, genius, futurist, change-maker, innovator, founder, author, polymath, thought leader, motivator, and inspirational speaker. They even refer to themselves using this lofty language in interviews and in their online profiles and biographical summaries.

Digital nomads' professed and proud orientation toward learning is very proximally focused on the self. Their online and in-person community of peers, life coaches, customers, and clients provides them with external validation of positive changes in their knowledge base and levels of insightfulness, as does their ability to meet self-imposed goals (e.g., making a certain amount of money from a business per month).

Nomads' personal development value is especially interesting when they contrast their customized search for knowledge to what universities have failed to provide, a favorite topic of conversation. As mentioned, nomads are not necessarily open to all forms of learning and education, especially schooling that subtracts from one's income-earning, traveling, and self-determined personal and professional development time. Although a few nomads reported positive experiences in traditional educational environments, a more typical attitude is represented in Caiden's story. An

American software entrepreneur, Caiden told us, "I got a bachelor's degree. I honestly feel that it was kind of a waste of time. I learned a whole lot more just programming on my own. In college, maybe two or three classes were useful, but other than that?"

Caiden's life choices illustrate the way in which nomads' value for personal development extends beyond the boundaries of work opportunities to everyday life. Raised as a Mormon, Caiden's eyes were opened to the concept of cultural relativism after a life-changing mission to Asia that resulted in his eventual decision to leave the church. Now he and his family have built a home and are based in Bali. Like all of the other nomads we met who travel with their children, Caiden and his wife are evangelists for unconventional approaches to education. Having "worldschooled" three children across thirty-six countries in nine years, Caiden's identity is more closely aligned with being a coach to others who want to travel with families than it is with the software company he founded, where he derives his income. Like most nomads, Caiden is an aficionado of self-help books and business gurus beloved by self-help influencers like Oprah Winfrey. Similar to many we spoke to, Caiden became especially captivated by Tim Ferriss's book *The 4-Hour Work Week*:[26] "I read that book before we started traveling, and it was really helpful for me. I've since been featured on his blog. . . . I enjoy all of that: [laughs] Liz Gilbert,[27] Tony Robbins,[28] Tim Ferriss. . . . I enjoy that kind of stuff. Eckhart Tolle, *The Power of Now*."[29] When asked if these books have helped with his business, he replied that self-help books he likes have a broader and deeper reach than offering professional advice. He said the lessons are more about "just enjoying life, and being more present, and learning what's going on underneath the surface."

Caiden, like many nomads, left his life back home, in part, because it felt limiting in terms of personal growth and he wanted to "get unstuck."[30] He believed this was unlikely in his home community where people were closed-minded and disinclined to interrogate their own way of life or to pursue knowledge:

We were quite traditional. I was extremely devout in Mormonism, but I wanted to travel. . . . It's just a feeling, too, of knowing like, there is a lot more out there. . . . We lived very much in a bubble. There was a lot I wasn't getting. I wasn't feeling stimulated in my personal growth. . . . Spiritually, I kind of felt like I reached the peak of what I could get from it. . . . We realized, "Well, wait a minute. I have an online business. We don't have to stay here." And we really want to give our kids a more international experience. We want to learn about what's out there in the world. You experience different cultures, different people, have our minds expanded and grow, and have travel be a catalyst for personal growth.

Many nomads told us that they seek to surround themselves with people who will further their need for personal development, people who can teach them things. Sometimes, digital nomads want to learn about subjects related directly to their businesses, work, or projects, but their personal growth paradigm is based on the principle that any interaction is an opportunity to expand the boundaries of their knowledge and interests and has the potential to stoke their creativity, especially to ignite parts of themselves that have been dormant or neglected. Tricia, a forty-year-old entrepreneur who travels with her husband and two young children, summed up nomads' value for personal development: "Maybe one thing you find with digital nomads is that we just like to go to those new horizons and learn. I am such an avid learner [that] if I don't do something new or learn something new every day, it's a wasted day."

Value #3: Sharing

Despite their love of freedom, digital nomads are quick to express that they simultaneously value sharing their knowledge, skills, and time with other nomads. Sharing is the most relationally oriented of the five nomad values; it is their starting point for building social bonds, networks, and community.

Social capital, a widely used and highly elastic term found in many social science disciplines, refers to the idea that others' goodwill toward us can be a useful resource.[31] Relevant to Bali's digital nomad community, sociologist Alexandro Portes once described social capital and social support this way: "By being thrown together in a common situation, workers learn to identify with each other and support each other's initiatives. This solidarity is not the result of norm introjection during childhood but is an emergent product of a common fate."[32] Although lacking one common employer, digital nomads share a sense of commonality and community with one another. Vance, a freelancer and entrepreneur introduced in chapter 1, believes that the shared digital nomad experience of relocating to a new place with few in-person networks leads nomads to embrace a value system that exalts sharing behaviors: "The support from the community kind of comes from the place that everyone is on their own, and that creates empathy because it's their experience, too. Everyone gets off the plane, and they don't know anyone."

Examples of sharing values among nomads are wide ranging and include instrumental or tangible behaviors (e.g., teaching a skill without compensation), informational forms of support (e.g., advising on housing and visas), and emotional support (e.g., attending someone's talk to encourage them). Sharing also leads to a level of intimacy that is more characteristic of a private or personal order of social bonds;[33] this is, in part, because nomads have a tendency to reveal to each other testimonies of their "journeys" or biographical pathways to Bali, including personal, once-guarded stories and earnest teachings about life lessons they have gathered.

When we asked one newly arrived digital nomad about who comprises her community now that she is away from home, she talked about nomad hubs as places with empathic and supportive people who understand her acculturation needs as a digital nomad, have the desire to form close bonds with strangers, and are generous with their highly prized time:

> It's actually other digital nomads. It's mostly people who work remotely and people who are coming and going, and everyone is hyper-connected because people stay in places [for] so short an amount of time, because people are all in that same boat where they need the same things. Like, I need to know where to rent a scooter. I need to know what's the right neighborhood to live in. I need to know where to go to the doctor. So everybody is in that same boat where they needed that help when they got here, so people are really helpful to other new people coming in, and additionally, everyone knows that no one really knows anybody, so people connect to each other really quickly, and they're like, "I know someone you should meet. You two will really get along." You're probably not going to do that wherever, but here everyone is so much more tight-knit, and you're gonna need that friend, actually. And additionally, we're kind of all working from the same space and stuff, so it's easier to do that, too. And no one has set schedules, so everyone has time to meet you for lunch, and take two hours, and then work different hours that day.

In line with the concept of social capital, the sharing values of digital nomads are not necessarily completely altruistic. Vance explained that since arriving in Bali, he has become far more invested in his social life, in part, because it pays off: "I found I care much more about my social relations. [What gives you social status here] is being a kind person, and there's a lot of ways to do it, and it's really public here. Somehow, here, you get more recognition for what you do to help others [than back home]."

In sum, in a place where many people arrive with no social ties, digital nomads embrace a value for sharing as a way to establish social capital. Though many digital nomads are also altruistically motivated to help others, we view their value for sharing primarily through the lens of its utility in supporting their value for freedom and the goal of building bonds in a place-based community.

Value #4: Positivity

Although pessimism, especially about economic well-being, is a growing force in the most advanced economies,[34] digital nomads reject it as a self-defeating mindset and seek to fight back by actively cultivating a value for positivity. We define *positivity* as nomads' values for optimism and pro-activity in themselves and others, where optimism is the degree to which individuals generally expect to have a favorable future[35] and proactivity is defined in terms of a willingness to take initiative and to challenge, rather than to accept, the status quo.[36]

Many digital nomads complained that they experienced their home countries as "toxic" places where people are unhappy, pessimistic, and charged with negative emotions, especially when it comes to the subject of work. Making matters worse, digital nomads experienced their home societies as passive and accepting of this negativity and as disapproving of their desire to actively cultivate optimism and proactivity and attempt to shield themselves from pessimism and passivity. Their constant contact with cynical agents of socialization—whether school, work, family, or friends—propelled their desire to detach from home. When we would suggest jobs outside of the for-profit sector, nomads reported that the culture of pessimism proliferated even among colleagues working at nonprofits and non-governmental organizations (NGOs), and in education. Lorelei, a former graduate student whom we profile in chapter 5, described the unhealthy emotional culture back home: "I tried a lot. . . . It's a toxic environment because we all become competitors." Time and again, nomads' friends, family, and colleagues offered some variant of the following counsel: you are lucky to have a job; you need to be patient and pay your dues; you should lower your standards; you should just try to make the most of your little time away from the office. Digital nomads cherish their value for positivity because it symbolizes their rejection of such hopeless pronouncements.

In their search and preparation for a way out of life back home, digital nomads almost always devoted time to reading business magazines, en-trepreneurship how-to manuals, and self-help books, and listened to or watched motivational speakers who advised them to become more aware of ways in which their social environment has been negatively affecting their lives. For instance, the advice warns audiences that they are "the average of the five people you spend the most time with"[37] or they should actively avoid "toxic" people as part of their improving their "emotional intelli-gence." When digital nomads absorb these messages, they start to follow the call to take action and seek out peers and mentors who will support their decision to make a life change. This is the path to moving to a digital nomad hub—the search for a geographic place where one can be immersed in a positive "circle of influence."[38]

Nomads' positivity value also relates to their sharing values and behaviors. For instance, at first, it may seem counterintuitive that entrepre-neurial nomads would share ideas, as their knowledge may be proprietary, or at least provide a competitive advantage with clients. However, as much as nomads want to achieve individual personal goals, they know that they need help to do so. Their belief in positivity translates into distrust of the inherent need for competition against others, describing competitiveness as part of a "scarcity mindset."[39] Instead, they advocate what they call an "abundance mindset," meaning they do not believe that they are in competition for a limited amount of business or even creative ideas; there is plenty to go around. Noel, a thirty-two-year-old engineer turned freelance digital marketer introduced in chapter 1, described an idealistic view of capitalism common among nomads, one based on a perceived synergy between having both sharing and positivity mindsets:

> It's definitely having a life more [about] giving rather than taking. So shifting from the "taking" motives to the "giving" motives. Abundance mindset. Something I picked up from Bridgewater[40] that we talked about—radical transparency. Meaningful work and meaningful relationships with radical transparency. Trying to build that. That's a foundation of my life for work and business culture, but also everything else that surrounds it. I'm quite passionate about the anti-corruption movement that's going on and bringing transparency to like, power structures around the world, and seeing success more as societal success. Changing society's definitions of progress in terms of like, progress to me now isn't always more efficient. Instead of like, one teacher for forty kids, what if it was one teacher for one kid? Sort of like, that's progress, right? That's not efficient, but that's progress. Sort of like, everybody having health care, or everybody having access to education, or the fact that kids could be raised without curriculums, and they could just pursue whatever they're interested in because we can distribute resources in such a way that labor and jobs are no longer needed anymore. So success, to me, is building and helping that sort of Star Trek future along. Oh, and I will say one of my goals is to be the richest poor person ever. So being financially successful in like, business, but then I can take the capital I build and put it into building the Star Trek future. Not just straight up philanthropy, I would say more like Elon Musk.[41]

Digital nomads acknowledge that some view their desire for positivity as irrational, delusional, or unrealistic, but they see it as necessary for success. In this respect, their values are similar to those found in the start-up culture in the United States, where public criticism is viewed as counterproductive.[42] When nomads' bank accounts are low and they remain convinced that they should stay the course, they are inspired by others who have succeeded against all odds, especially people known as trailblazers, innovators, inventors, and business leaders. They point out that the value of optimism paired with proactivity is what unites geniuses across various disciplines. Though it may be off-putting to listen to nomads talk about celebrities, whether in science, technology, art, or business, nomads identify with visionaries and view them as a source of inspiration during hard times. In sum, digital nomads view their positivity as a value that is essential to their success and well-being, and a historically proven driver of innovation.

Shared Value #5: Minimalism

I travel with a carry-on only, so 45L [linear inches], and I have a little backpack with my laptop. The mental clarity I've had from having less stuff is absolutely amazing.

-Estelle, Canadian freelance user experience/interface (UX/UI) product designer

Most digital nomads subscribe to some version of a "lifestyle minimalism" philosophy in which modern consumption patterns (e.g., desire, buy, dispose) are viewed as oppressive.[43] We define minimalism as having aesthetic (e.g., Japanese or Scandinavian design; Apple, Inc. during the Steve Jobs / Jony Ive era), and ethical (i.e., accumulating things is wasteful, unethical, and harmful to the environment on a global level)[44] dimensions that imply that one should simplify one's life in order to increase well-being (i.e., spend money on experiences and not things). The ultimate goal of minimalism is to calm one's environment, become more mindful of consumption choices, and use one's extra resources on experiences that bring forth meaningful memories, happiness, and satisfaction.

Minimalism has emerged as a social movement of sorts, as evidenced by the mainstream popularity of books like Marie Kondo's *The Life-Changing Magic of Tidying Up: The Japanese Art of Decluttering and Organizing,*[45] which Netflix later turned into a video series, triggering overwhelming donations to thrift stores after its release. In pop culture, one can find podcasts about minimalism, TV shows about "tiny houses," and business gurus incorporating minimalism into their advice about bootstrapping and limiting debt problems. Taken to the extreme, some minimalists pride themselves on owning only a certain number of possessions (e.g., some proudly post lists of the twenty-five or so items they own, complete with brand names such as "two pairs of Eastern Mountain Sports boxer shorts," etc.).

Digital nomads' basic value for minimalism is one of limiting possessions to those things that are truly necessary or personally meaningful and do not interfere excessively with their mobile lifestyle. Limiting possessions is practical for anyone whose life is defined by frequent travel, but digital nomads are extreme in their preferences about this, as they are about so many things. Many have long felt alienated by common materialism and consumption patterns and have noticed that they prefer experiences over "stuff." Ellie, the business journalist and entrepreneur whom we heard from in the introduction and previous chapters, articulated a view shared by many:

> I've never been materialistic. I remember going backpacking when I was twenty-one around Asia with just a tiny backpack, and I'm like, "I don't need stuff." I always knew I don't need stuff, but now I really know I don't need stuff, and a lot of people in London spend their weekend buying more clothes or filling up their house with more crap, and that didn't ever really interest me.

Minimalism is a value that also broadcasts digital nomads' creativity, ingenuity, and alternative value systems. Indeed, nomads jettison their possessions, in part, as a way to symbolize their commitment to this lifestyle. As Michelle, a coach introduced in chapter 1, told us about her decision to sell all of her possessions before leaving Canada, "I had this thought like, 'If I want to really start over and live differently, I want to live minimally.'"

Like digital nomadism as a whole, minimalism is a countercultural value and aesthetic that separates individuals from the mainstream. However, we noticed that minimalism includes consumption and materialism as well, a fact that many nomads seem reluctant to acknowledge. As Pierre Bourdieu asserted, one's tastes and consumption styles are influenced by familial and individual educational experiences, as well as formative experiences over the life course.[46] This includes an affinity for specific types of travel, favoring certain kinds of art, and aspiring to one aesthetic over another.

For instance, we observed that nomads' consumer impulses tend to manifest in the form of fetishizing and purchasing high-quality goods and impressive experiences. Indeed, the predilection and ability to consume relatively extravagant experiences and to buy a small number of expensive possessions is a marker of privilege and a subtler form of conspicuous consumption.[47] Kenny, an American entrepreneur whose quote opens chapter 1, exemplified the focus on owning only a small number of quality brand items:

> By being a minimalist you're automatically less materialistic. I still own and buy a lot less stuff, but when I buy things, I buy the best, most expensive. These headphones are $350 headphones, but instead of owning five pairs of headphones and three monitors and Apple TV and all this crap, I just have the things that I actually need, but that are, maybe, the best quality.

In chapter 2, we discussed the rise of the experience economy and the role it plays in digital nomads' lives. In the stratification of the experience economy, travel to exotic places, including in the developing world, communicates something that trips to Disney World or even Paris do not.[48]

Ellie explained her view of how this creates status for nomads, even when they are not particularly financially successful:

> In the old days, if you wanted to display your status to your peers you'd buy a new car, and you'd put it in your drive[way], and you'd drive around in it, and you'd be able to impress the people on your street and in your local area with your new car, but now [with] social media specifically, how do you impress people? Well, you impress them by taking pics of you doing cool things in cool places, and it's almost like that has become a new defining currency of our era. Me having taken photos of me in exotic places is now almost like the equivalent of the car in the driveway. It's like the new status symbol. And I think that is a driver for people, as well. You impress people with your travels, you're basically living like an international jet-setter in these exotic places. Like, you've got your laptop out by the swimming pool, but [are] making probably less than the average teacher, like maybe half.

Although minimalism may reflect practical concerns and consumption preferences as much as any philosophical rejection of traditional materialism, it remains a value that is central to digital nomads' lives. In an ongoing sense, minimalism both facilitates their lifestyles and symbolizes their freedom from the accumulative tendencies of their home cultures.

DIGITAL NOMAD COMMUNITY: FLUID AND INTIMATE

As digital nomads put their individual values into practice, they create a community that is, paradoxically, both fluid and intimate. A community that embraces transience while simultaneously fostering intensive interactions within dense social networks violates typical understandings of how successful place-based communities function. Yet we observed that fluidity and intimacy do not just coexist in digital nomad communities but are the key to their success.

Fluidity

In the introduction to this book, we noted that digital nomad communities are fluid in the sense that individuals are constantly coming and going, regularly making and breaking social ties.[49] We also observed that digital nomad communities are characterized by a *norm* for fluidity such that community members do not merely tolerate the high levels of transience, but rather expect and actively embrace the fact that people come and go. In this way, the nomad experience creates further social distance from people back home. Grace, who left her job in the Los Angeles music industry to come to Bali and has since returned to the United States, explained that nomads' acceptance of transience stands in stark contrast to people at home who "don't get it":

> You're on the same path, and where you've been someone has been already, so it's nice. We all say how we get to have conversations that we can't have with people back home because you call your friends at home, and they're asking you all these questions that you don't have the answers [to] quite yet. But your friends in this community, they know what it's like to say, "I don't know." They know what it is to say, "I'm not sure when I'm going back home." And they also understand if you have to all of a sudden go back home. There's no shame. There's no guilt. There's just a real sense of compassion within this kind of community because you are all going through something that's very unique to your situation. Like, very unique. So it's really nice. It's only when I talk to people from back home that I have to explain myself.

Grace's comment draws social boundaries between the nomad norm to embrace transient communities and the mainstream norms of certainty, expectations, and stability. Her words illustrate how nomads' values for freedom, positivity, and personal development have led to a community that embraces fluidity. Nomads want to be around others who are like them—pursuing freedom. They view their personal development as partially about being around like-minded others, and this encourages them to accept others' freedom to flow in and out of the community.

When we asked coworking space owners about nomads' perceptions of community transience, they confirmed that up to half of their monthly members are only there for a month and do not renew membership for a second consecutive month. In fact, nomads love to joke that the first thing they ask a new person is: "How long are you staying?" At first, we took this to mean that they wanted to gauge whether it was worth it to invest in a relationship with a newcomer, but when we asked about this, most people said that the question was not intended to screen out nomads who were just passing through town. Rather, nomads' value for freedom translates into an acceptance that one can never be certain how long they or anyone else will be around, and their ethos normalizes and celebrates community fluidity.

In fact, embracing fluidity is ritualized for nomads. Digital nomads enjoy the practical and symbolic value of rituals and routines, especially morning, work, productivity, and personal development rituals, as well as routines for eating, drinking, and exercise. They also engage in rituals that both manage their travel transitions[50] and validate their identities as digital nomads.[51] Two key rituals we observed were those around departure and arrival.

Everyone is jovial even though their friend, Tessa, is leaving. Sitting in a hanging wicker chair at her going-away party in a popular café owned by digital nomads, we listened as Tessa's friends caught up with one another. Some talked excitedly about the thrill of their recent return to Bali, while others discussed their future travel plans. Although Tessa was leaving for the United States after more than a year in Bali, the mood was festive, a celebration of the continuation of a journey. Friendly, smart, and witty, Tessa, an American digital marketer first introduced in chapter 1, made many nomad friends while living and working in Bali and Thailand. We spent lots of time with her on our trips to Bali, going to events, sharing meals and drinks, and sometimes even riding on the back of her motorbike. Earlier on her last day in Bali, we drank from coconuts as she explained her last-minute preparations for leaving: returning her rented scooter, picking up mementos such as a Balinese-crafted silver ring, and squeezing in one last ten-dollar spa appointment. Like a typical nomad, Tessa could not stomach the cost of tourist taxis, so she was trying to find a cheaper ride to the airport. Now, as a rainstorm poured down outside of the café, we did our best to adopt the digital nomad norm of celebrating departures. Even though Tessa's departure was unusual because she was planning, at least for the time being, to leave the nomadic lifestyle and return to her home country, the ritual was the same: expressing happiness for friends who actively pursue their goals and discussing the possibilities of meeting up again in the future, perhaps in another location. With such a large and strong in-person community of travelers, leaving is a common nomad hub ritual.

Rites of departure, such as Tessa's party, mark outflows from the community. Individual nomads *do* experience such outflows as losses, sometimes because they feel a strong bond to the person who is going away, but often for the simple reason that they came to Bali for in-person community and found it and the people they meet there are symbolically important for their own understandings of themselves at these points of reference. Moreover, outflows sometimes feature prominent members of the community, which can upset the equilibrium. For instance, as we were drafting this chapter, Hubud's co-owners announced on their website that they were leaving Bali for an unspecified length of time,[52] demonstrating that even the most rooted and influential nomads sometimes feel the urge to move on.

Yet departures also balance continuity with change. They offer opportunities for new people to gain influence, ensuring that the community does not stagnate or become tightly controlled by a small or elite group. Indeed, departures open slots for new arrivals to make an impact relatively quickly. Due to nomads' values for personal development and sharing, and the general proactivity signaled by their pursuit of freedom, departures actually *add* to the community by freeing up channels for new arrivals' excitement and energy to be expressed. For individual nomads, journeys begin with departure, and the act of leaving therefore provides essential validation of their nomad identities.

Rites of Arrival

Arriving in a new place, whether for the first time or the tenth, provides both a rush of novelty and a validation that one is truly a nomad. In nomad hubs, expats who are new to a location are easily spotted, as they consult maps and phones and ask questions about laws, customs, and logistics. This is a time for nomads' imaginations to be ignited as they picture themselves working and living their dream, so an essential part of creating a welcoming digital nomad space is making sure that the new arrivals have a positive sensory and social experience.[53]

For instance, one morning we watched as a young man excitedly approached Dojo's front desk, explaining that he had just arrived from Sweden. He wanted to join the coworking space, but first, he needed to find lodging. The Indonesian staff, having answered such questions countless times before, patiently offered suggestions for inexpensive housing in locations that nomads tend to prefer. The Swede rushed off, returning an hour later to purchase a coworking membership and start his workday. Thus, newcomers use arrival migration rituals to create their nomad identities, to contest associations with mainstream tourists, and to construct a sense of belonging to Bali as a place.[54]

An important signifier of the benefits of inbound fluidity is the various rites of arrival that take place in Bali's digital nomad community. For instance, coworking spaces frequently sponsor new member meals, receptions, orientations, and other events that serve to quickly introduce newcomers to one another and to those who have been active in the community for a longer period of time. We also observed that Bali's online digital nomad forums often feature newcomers broadcasting their arrival to Bali and announcing their interests and skills and desire to make friends and get together:

> Hey guys! I've just arrived in Bali for the next 3–4 months and would love to meet some of you. About me: 18 months ago I co-founded a business in Australia and am running it remotely while here. My time is usually spent in digital advertising, strategy, and general marketing, and my next project will be utilising facebook messenger ads and chatbots.[55] Personally, I'll be training and learning to surf while I'm here, am interested in all things

tech (especially AI[56]—hence the chatbots) and love talking ideas (big ones and complete nonsense).

Even for nomads who have been in Bali for a long time, newcomers serve as a constant reminder of their initial vision of nomad life and their intentions for their time in Bali. Mindful of the evolving nature of their own travels, nomads try to stay open to befriending people who may be in the community for only a short spell. Rites of arrival therefore stoke the energy of all digital nomads, regardless of how long they have been settled in Bali.

Intimacy

Scholars who study individuals' networks define the strength of a connection between two people as a "combination of the amount of time, the emotional intensity, the intimacy (mutual confiding), and the reciprocal services that characterize the tie."[57] The traditional sociological perspective is that tightly bounded communities with high levels of solidarity are those in which individuals have long lengths of residence and strong ties, especially densely knit ones rather than sparse clusters of networks.[58] It is in these types of communities, usually where kin also live, that people are to find optimal social and emotional support. However, over time, many scholars have pointed out that wide-ranging networks offer more options in life, especially as the traditional structures and roles of family have declined.[59] Non-kin and broader networks offer other kinds of resources and assistance, such as material and personal help and information. Such broader networks, with many weaker ties, may also facilitate creativity.[60] Further, Richard Florida's research concludes that creative class professionals *prefer* weak ties to strong ones and do not aspire to close-knit communities glorified in past research: "They have close friends. They call Mom. But life in modern communities revolves around a larger set of looser ties and . . . most people seem to prefer it that way."[61] In contrast, digital nomads seek to have strong ties and believe that such connections make them more creative, but they believe the place to find them is not in large creative class cities or homogenous strong-tie towns,[62] but in digital nomad hubs.

The fluidity we have described in the digital nomad community shortens relational time horizons, limiting the typical path in which strong ties develop over long periods of time. Moreover, though nomads' values for sharing create a community where individuals can give and receive help, their rejection of any sense of obligation limits person-to-person reciprocity norms.[63] These forces would seem to work against the development of strong communities. To compensate, nomads escalate tie development through enacting norms of self-disclosure, as sharing personal information increases the odds of forming bonds.[64] Indeed, much research shows that developing and maintaining relationships depends on self-disclosure, and that people tend to like individuals who are open in this way more than they like people who are closed off to sharing.[65] In their home societies, self-disclosure involves risking rejection from family and close friends.[66] As we noted in chapter 1, many nomads felt that people at home rejected their dreams. Michelle, the coach we introduced in chapter 1 who works with individuals transitioning to new work lives, told us that it is common for her clients to experience situations where "all your friends and family disagree with your choices." Such experiences, whether real or imagined, discourage self-disclosure at home. In Bali, the punitive consequences of self-disclosure are more distant, and there are proximal consequences to self-disclosure that may be highly beneficial for digital nomads.

Traveling alone is lonely. Steve Munroe, a founder of the Hubud coworking space, told us that loneliness was a major factor that propelled Hubud's early success:

> Within the first month we started getting digital nomads—I'd never heard the term— showing up, and the story [that the nomads told] was that "Look, I read the *4-Hour Workweek*. I got all inspired, I did what he [author Tim Ferriss] said, and I was successful doing it. I found myself on the beach in Thailand, I sent the Instagram photo on my laptop, and I was totally lonely. It was working, but I was totally lonely. Here I was all by myself, a free man, independent, post-community guy, and I was totally lonely." And Hubud kind of became that clubhouse for the digital nomad community.

To combat loneliness effectively during long-term travel abroad, what digital nomads need is not momentary, superficial contact; rather, they crave deep exchanges. Their value for sharing encourages them toward such interactions. Similarly, nomads' value for personal development rituals encourages them to push themselves away from superficiality and toward more meaningful and authentic relations with others. As mentioned earlier in this chapter, a strong current of individualism runs through the literature of personal development (formerly known as "self-help"), but much of the messaging endorsed, promoted, and even led by celebrity gurus (e.g., Tony Robbins) and business leaders (e.g., Richard Branson) also espouses an explicit intermingling of entrepreneurship, health-consciousness, spirituality, and sociality.[67] This self-improvement ethos, imbibed through books, podcasts, TED talks, and many other forums in Bali and beyond, encourages vulnerability and overcoming shame through intimate interactions with others. Such intimate interactions are viewed as a source of inspiration, fulfillment, creativity, and learning among nomads. Bali flips the script of risky self-disclosure through the imposition of new norms in a new environment. In Bali, the people one meets are strangers, they are likely to be transient contacts, and they are like-minded on key values, including positivity. This pushes nomads to share important aspects of their lives and work with relative strangers in ways that signal a willingness to appear vulnerable and encourage others to do the same, creating *intimacy*.[68]

Nomads create intimacy through both formal and informal mechanisms. On the formal side, entrepreneurs catering to digital nomads understand that they must actively facilitate intimacy in the community, and they offer a range of programs to do so. Informally, nomads create intimacy as they revel in the kinds of exchanges that are only possible because they have more control of their daily schedules and fewer externally imposed obligations. Since most digital nomads are single and traveling alone, they are not preoccupied by family concerns and are therefore available and motivated to socialize with one another, often at a moment's notice. Many digital nomads echoed the sentiment expressed by Laurence, a fashion designer and entrepreneur first introduced in chapter 1: "No matter how busy you are, there's always time to have lunch with a friend." Similar to their approach to fluidity, digital nomads have developed a ritual to build intimacy, which we have labeled *telling your story*.

In line with their values for personal development, sharing, and positivity, an important ritual in nomad social life is telling one's story, usually a personal narrative that nomads convey in the format of a "personal journey," capitalizing on the travel metaphor. Nomads spend significant time informally engaged in telling their stories. For instance, we found that virtually everyone we interviewed or even casually conversed with was ready, if not eager, to take the time to tell their story to us. At first, we questioned whether this had something to do with us and perhaps their desire to promote their brands in our book. However, we observed that nomads engage in deep conversations, often taking emotional risks, everywhere and with all kinds of people—in cafés and coworking spaces, on the street, on the beach, and at parties. For digital nomads, telling one's story enacts norms for sharing intense emotional depth with others, even in initial meetings, as a means to build bonds.[69]

In addition to informal storytelling, many, if not most, formal events in nomad culture include opportunities for telling one's story. For instance, Pecha Kucha is a global phenomenon where speakers present twenty slides for twenty seconds each. Although these talks can cover any subject, when we attended a large Pecha Kucha in Bali the themes were all concerned with individuals' personal journeys in one way or another (e.g., overcoming a health problem or quitting a corporate job in order to find one's true calling).

Other formalized venues for storytelling include "Fuck-Up Nights," where audiences applaud and cheer as nomads tell witty and celebratory stories about their "epic" entrepreneurship and career failures, often with slides that feature humorous images, such as the sinking *Titanic* (e.g., working for unethical bosses, losing jobs and homes, and repeatedly talking oneself into staying in hated jobs rather than following instincts and passions). Another example is a series of events called "Startup Grind," which feature a single person telling a story about how they built, launched, and funded a company, and the obstacles and challenges they faced. Although such events are common in entrepreneurial ecosystems around the world, in Bali they may also feature people who are *not* engaged in entrepreneurship. Among digital nomads, telling one's story is more than just an exercise in personal branding or validating an identity. In an environment where nearly everyone is alone and in need of support, telling a personal story builds the kind of intimacy that is a prerequisite for many other types of significant helping exchanges.

THE CONTINUING SIGNIFICANCE OF PLACE, EVEN FOR "DIGITAL" NOMADS

Digital nomads have migrated around the world to join a community of like-minded others. Having left their old lives, in part, because they felt alienated by their jobs and urban lifestyles, dreaded the possibility of a future within systems they no longer believe in, and sensed the prospect of personal change through their exposure to media touting a different way of life available to people with their skill sets, nomads have dedicated themselves to searching for a new way to live and work in the company of others who are similarly committed.

In Bali, these unconventional people—who reject fundamental societal values such as materialism, conventional employment, marriage, living in proximity to kin, and even the idea of a semi-permanent geographic home—come together as a highly self-selected group of extreme people, consistent with Fischer's urban subcultural theory.[70] Yet digital nomadism is not just about rejecting the dominant values of home. Rather, nomads' highly similar values undergird their pursuit of their unconventional community. Digital nomads' thirst for freedom drove them to break from home, but their values for personal development, sharing, positivity, and minimalism play important supporting roles as they seek ways to sustain themselves in the lifestyle.

As this chapter shows, digital nomads bond quickly. Nik, a thirty-three-year-old entrepreneur and marketing consultant from Siberia, explained it this way: "We make friends at the speed of two friends per hour." For those of us leading more traditional lives, it may seem contradictory that digital nomads are building a community that is explicitly fluid and intimate. But nomads' values, and especially the primacy of their value for freedom, lead them to be comfortable with structures that allow, or even require, short time horizons.

Despite their transience, Bali's digital nomads are not blasé urbanites[71] who ignore each other's presence as they work and live. They came to Bali to experience strong social ties to one another. In the digital nomad world, strong social ties do not require that people share the same nationality, religion, or work organization. Indeed, digital nomads relish their international networks, which convert even the most mundane interactions into novel experiences of deep and memorable social connection. Unlike many people back home, nomads' strong social ties are not rooted in the accidental, geographically constrained circumstances of their youth over which they had little control: they have not been best friends with each other since childhood, are not related, and are not bonded by a shared formative history. Moreover, once nomad relationships form, it does not follow that nomads settle down in the same geographic place consistently and for years on end. Instead, strong social ties in the digital nomad universe emerge through work and personal needs that arise in an environment where nearly everyone arrives alone, in search of reinvention, and with little to support them beyond their determination and the contents of their backpacks. As a result, digital nomads accept that people in their networks come and go.

Along with embracing the fact of their friends' departures and arrivals, digital nomads must tolerate the accompanying modulations in the strength of these bonds. This is a sacrifice they are willing to make, but it does not mean that they will then seek to have their social needs met online. As earlier comments from Grace, Vance, and Rebecca indicate, nomads feel most connected when having face-to-face contact with like-minded people. They know that their weaker, virtual social ties are not a replacement for what they get from in-person community in nomad hubs.

Digital nomads seek out individuals to fill various roles in their networks, but given the fluidity in their environment, they are open to a reshuffling of the specific individuals who occupy those roles. Rather than a community "liberated" from place-based ties,[72] the digital nomad community is liberated from the need for individuals to be strongly tied to the same individuals in a circumstantial geographic place for long periods of time. In this way, it is *person-based ties* that seem to be weakened by the digital nomad lifestyle. This does not mean that digital nomads are inauthentic or that they do not genuinely connect to others. Rather, they have concluded that strong ties based primarily on interacting over long periods of time do not lead to the kinds of communities they want. In nomad hubs, the shorter durations of their relationships with specific individuals are offset by their greater intensity. Hence, while digital nomads break long-standing ideas about place-based communities, their lives demonstrate the continuing significance of place even among transient, digital workers.

In this chapter we discussed nomads' distinct value systems and how these contribute to a selective migration to nomad hubs, creating a fluid yet intimate place-based community. In chapter 4 we turn our full attention to the work-specific aspects of the digital nomad community. There, we examine the types of employment that digital nomads undertake and the work-focused community processes that support them in pursuit of sustainable, location-independent lifestyles.

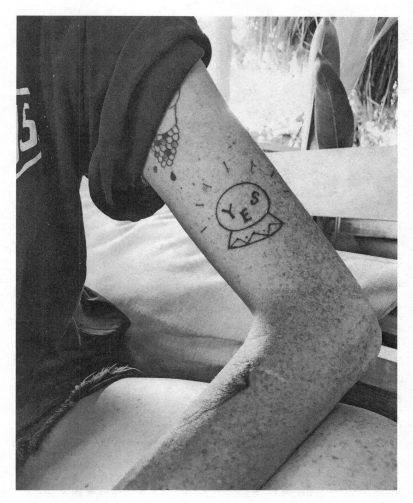

Picture 1:
Digital nomads often get tattoos to signify their new lifestyle.
Credit: Kirsty McKie.

Picture 2:
Digital nomads working at Dojo Bali coworking space during Startup Weekend in 2017.
Credit: Authors.

Picture 3:
Poster advertising a public skill share session at Dojo Bali coworking space in 2016.
Credit: Authors.

Picture 4:
Graffiti in Canggu showing community resistance to the pace of development.
Credit: Authors.

Picture 5:
Digital nomads often post pictures of themselves working. This photo, created by a nomad, is a parody of how digital nomad life is idealized. It lampoons the "office of the day" while simultaneously promoting nomadism.
Credit: Charles Louis Allizard.

Picture 6:
The entrance to Hubud, known as Bali's first coworking space, located in Ubud, Bali. Many spaces in Bali are decorated with marigolds in this manner, borrowing from the symbolism of Balinese offerings found on statues, shrines, and temples.
Credit: Authors.

Picture 7:
The Balinese merge craft and religion in their preparation of daily offerings. These simple palm leaf basket offerings are filled with flowers and are found in temples, shrines, beaches, and on the ground, as well as on taxi dashboards and in Starbucks.

Credit: Authors.

Picture 8:
The Balinese perform ceremonies not just for moon phases, weddings, and funerals, but also to cleanse spaces, ward off evil, and bring luck when opening new businesses. Nomad events and openings often incorporate these Balinese traditions as a way to honor locals, bring good fortune, and include local flavor. Here, at a nomad event, nomads and Balinese sat cross-legged on the ground as a Balinese Hindu priest performed a blessing ceremony with live gamelan music. Balinese women displayed traditional fruit tower offerings, which they construct, parade around, and present on a regular basis for their own ceremonies.

Picture 9 :
Bali's free-roaming livestock can often be found on the roadside, amid crumbling roads and open sewers filled with plastic waste. This one was scavenging for greens among the refuse. Tourist encounters with chickens, monkeys, and cows on the streets add to Bali's novel, exotic, and authentic feel, but also are a reminder of the problems associated with tourism development.

Picture 10:
Pura Tirta Empul, a Balinese water temple, is a sacred place known for healing springs, ornate statues, and purification pools. For those who seek an immersive experience, the tourism industry offers excursions where one can visit the temple, get physical and emotional healing, and acquire a sense of magic. One company offers a "Be Balinese" excursion in which tourists can be guided and instructed on complicated Balinese rituals as they enter the waist-deep pools and rinse their heads under the spouts and present offerings.

Picture 11:
Hubud sits near Ubud's Monkey Forest preserve, which is a sanctuary and temple space set amid a lush forest with walking paths. There, and in many places close to tall trees, long tailed macaque monkeys roam, looking for food and stealing items from tourists. Unexpected encounters with local wildlife add to Bali's unique atmosphere.

CHAPTER 4

Not on Holiday: Making Money and Building Dreams

What I love about Bali is I can obviously work on my own stuff, but everyone around me is doing really inspiring things, too. . . . And there's obviously ways that I can help them, but also they can help me.

Laurence, *twenty-six-year-old American fashion entrepreneur*

It is morning in Bali. The sounds of roosters crowing and birds singing are accompanied by the smell of incense from offerings to Bali's Hindu gods. Among the expat population, yoga enthusiasts, mats in hand, head off to their classes, and afterward, lounge in cafés enjoying green juice. The more conventional tourists leave their hotels to head for the markets, take their excursions, or visit the beaches. However, amid the rising buzz of activity one can glimpse another group of expats. They can be seen on foot or riding their scooters, laptops in backpacks, ready to clock in at their coworking spaces. For digital nomads, it is time to go to work.

Work is the foundation of the digital nomad community. Although not all community theories place work in such an exalted position, neither is this view unprecedented. Writing at the dawn of the industrial age, Durkheim[1] proposed that an increased division of work labor might ultimately bind individuals *more* tightly to community as they become more interdependent and develop organic solidarity. Similar to the industrial work that was the focus of Durkheim's comment, specialized work of the kind performed by digital nomads is only valuable in conjunction with the work of others who perform complementary specializations.

Having abandoned most of the connections and safety nets of their former lives, digital nomads seek new contacts that are more attuned to their current needs. Digital nomads must find markets for their skills, and these new connections to like-minded others are essential for developing a pipeline of paid work to sustain their lifestyles. Yet almost inevitably, these new networks—and the various community functions within which they form—also help digital nomads to imagine and begin to shift their work lives other ways.

We were struck by how often we met people who, now that they had arrived in "paradise," were working as hard, or even harder, than they had in their old lives. Brandi, a thirty-two-year-old whom we first introduced in chapter 1, was working as a freelance writer and podcaster when we met her. She first caught the travel bug while serving overseas in the US military, and she then worked for several years in a "boring" civilian job within an intelligence agency in Washington, DC, before becoming a digital nomad. In chapter 1, we heard from some digital nomads who reported that they were overworked in their old lives, while others told us that they were often bored on the job. Brandi represents this latter category of unfulfilled worker. She complained that she was not busy enough, but rigid employer policies required her to stay at work even with little to do. Like others, Brandi told us that she had started writing a blog as a coping strategy for filling time during slow periods at work. This blog would eventually become part of her new freelancing business when she finally gathered the courage to quit her job. When we asked if there was a pivotal or decisive event that instigated her resignation, she told us that she had reached a threshold in what she could tolerate at work. She said she was overcome with feelings of indignity one day when she was staffing the office all alone and needed to use the restroom:

I wasn't supposed to leave my desk, and no one's there, right? 'Cause it's lunchtime. It's just me, and I'm like, "This cannot be my life. I can't believe I'm scared to go to the bathroom. I'm thirty years old or whatever, and we're a professional office, and I should be able to go to the bathroom." So I get up, and go to the bathroom, and shocker: nothing happens. . . . And then I went online and bought a plane ticket. That was it. This is not my life. I'm buying a plane ticket right now.

When we caught up with Brandi in Bali, she had already traveled to thirty-six countries, with the goal of reaching a hundred. Despite, or maybe because of, her travel ambitions, she was resisting the temptation to be a regular tourist and was maintaining a rigorous, but self-imposed work schedule:

I get up at about 7:30, take a shower, eat breakfast, start working, eat lunch, work 'til about five or six, then do whatever I want in the evening, do more work sometimes. . . .

I just happen to be in Bali, so it seems magical to all these people, but at the end of the day, I want to work eight to twelve hours a day because I want my business to succeed, and it's just me. I can't call in [sick], or I can, but then the work doesn't get done.

As we noted in chapter 2, Bali's low cost of living relative to creative class cities means that most nomads can cover their expenses while working fewer hours than they had in their old lives. To understand why so many nomads choose to work so much more than what is required to maintain their lifestyle, it is necessary to consider how these work-oriented individuals derive meaning in their lives. In *The 4-Hour Workweek*, a book that many referred to as the digital nomad bible, Tim Ferriss explains (and admits) that "four hours" is not actually the total number of hours that he spends on work but rather the number of hours he focuses on work that he would prefer not to do.[2] Digital nomads try to live by Ferriss's philosophy by minimizing the time that they spend doing what they deem to be undesirable work or work that can be outsourced, freeing them to spend more hours pursuing the work about which they are most passionate. As Brandi so eloquently put it: "I don't want to work four hours. I like what I do, and I want to do it. I'm happy to work. I'm not trying to get away from work. I just want to like what I do and be good at it."

In this chapter, we unpack the central role of work in the digital nomad community. We look first at how digital nomads earn money. To achieve their goal of location independence, nomads must have work that can be performed anywhere with sufficient internet connectivity. This limits their choices about how they earn their income. Sometimes nomads' work is driven by passionate interests, but just as often it is simply propelled by their need to earn money to sustain their lifestyles. We show that these dueling impulses to earn money and pursue interests lead nomads to increasingly view their work as a portfolio of projects. We then turn to the features of the digital nomad work environment and to the key work processes that illuminate the central role of work within the digital nomad community.

BUT HOW DO THEY MAKE MONEY? DIGITAL NOMADS' WORK

Three Main Forms of Digital Nomad Income

When skeptics hear about digital nomadism, one of the first things they want to know is how they make their money. Bali's digital nomad enthusiasts tend to emphasize the variety of work that nomads do, and their lists of nomad employment sound like a census of creative class occupations: filmmakers, scientists, writers, architects and engineers, accountants and financial professionals, lawyers, computer programmers, human resource professionals, artists, designers, entrepreneurs, and marketers.

Though we met people in each of these professions, the reality is that the work diversity within the digital nomad community is highly concentrated within four domains: technology (including both conventional software and mobile applications), marketing (including creative design, content, and analytics), e-commerce (selling products and services on the internet), and coaching (including business, health, artistic, romantic, and spiritual providers). The concentration of work into these four domains is beneficial to nomads because it allows them to communicate easily, leverage specific skills for projects, and form businesses together. Notably, the technology and marketing domains also mirror those frequently described in other accounts of digital labor and freelance knowledge work.[3] E-commerce and online coaching are relatively newer domains that, to our knowledge, have yet to be subjected to thorough academic study from a sociological perspective.

Bali's digital nomads vary in their configurations of income sources, but arrangements generally fall into some combination of three categories: full-time or part-time dedicated remote employment with a single organization, freelancing through either longer-term contracts or short-term "gigs," and entrepreneurship. We examine each of these, and then consider how nomads combine them to create sustaining income portfolios.

Dedicated Remote Employment

Some nomads whom we met in Bali were there as full-time, remote-working employees with dedicated employment contracts. For instance, Carol, a thirty-seven-year-old technical customer service employee whom we first heard from in chapter 2, told us that she had been working remotely for four years (mainly, but not exclusively, from Bali). She characterized her company, supervisors, and colleagues as "incredible," so we were surprised when she told the typical gloomy story about her former life in Sydney, Australia:

> My life was spent getting up at 5:00 in the morning, sitting in two hours' traffic, going to the office, and feeling completely stressed out before I even got to the office. I sat on my chair at the same spot as I did every day, having a lunch break, no connections with anyone outside of the office.... Get home 8:00, just eat something on the run, and just do it again. I felt like I was existing. I felt like I was spending so much money. There was all this wasted time and energy that was just not being used or channeled in a way that was serving. I felt very trapped. Stuck.

Carol finally informed her boss that she was going to quit her job and take some time to travel. What happened next seemed almost like a utopian fantasy compared to the stereotype of contemporary organizations as uncaring and transactional in their approach to employment:

> They said, "We don't want you to leave. Once you've finished traveling, just log on, and work wherever you are." I nearly fell off my seat. What corporate company offers that to you when you go to resign because you still have more traveling to do? My boss is amazing. I love him. He's someone I very dearly look up to, and I knew when I joined the company I was going into something special. My boss cares about people. He cares about who he employs, and he's very picky about who he employs. He said in our last meeting, "You can upskill, and go in courses, but you can't learn to be a good person. Being a good person counts before how good you are at your job." And that's just beautiful to hear coming from a CEO of a company. You know you're a part of something special.

Feeling shock, gratitude, and relief, and with strengthened loyalty to her employer, Carol stayed on as a remote worker. She now believes that she can take some credit for creating this outcome just by her commitment to being a valuable worker, and also by being intentional, true to herself, and taking action to move toward the life that she desired: "My life is how I always dreamed it to be. It's what I manifested."[4] When we expressed surprise at her employer's flexibility, she acknowledged her good fortune, but also told us that she has been increasingly encountering others with similar stories and believes this is part of the changing landscape of work: "Now, there's so many companies out there. The likes of Buffer,[5] Google. There're big companies. Their structure, their model now is absolutely that components of these businesses are remote."

Several nomads told us that when they decided to resign, their employers offered them remote-working privileges, clearly an indication of their competence and value. Yet most declined, explaining that working remotely at the same job would not solve their problems (see chapter 1). Instead, these nomads chose to start over, striking out on their own as freelancers.

Freelancing

Although some digital nomads work as remote employees for a company, and some informants told us that the number of nomads with this type of income source is growing, we found that freelance contract work was the most common form of income in Bali's digital nomad community. We define *freelancing* simply: selling a professional skill on an hourly or contract basis but without the obligations or continuing benefits available to full-time employees.[6] Freelance work ranges from short-term gigs such as updating a website or conducting internet research to larger projects such as developing a firm's digital media campaign, to ongoing client retainers.

Sociologists have been highly critical of freelancing due to the many ways in which it divests workers of stability and benefits compared to traditional jobs,[7] but digital nomads reject this negative view as missing the point that the so-called stability of traditional work is often illusory and generally not worth the sacrifice in personal freedom. Freelance income is central to digital nomadism because it allows individuals to enter and sustain the digital nomad lifestyle without a traditional job, significant savings, or a successful business.

Contrary to what outsiders might imagine, most nomads we met began their travels with limited financial resources and without full-time employment or entrepreneurship revenue. Instead, they depended on their professional skills to secure freelance employment in order to meet their expenses. Some nomads' skills were readily transferrable to remote freelance work, and these individuals seem to have the easiest adjustment to digital nomadism. Often, they were able to arrange freelancing contracts with their former employers or bring freelance work with them on the road that they had obtained before leaving. These nomads could bill their services at the typical Western rates while also working with employers who were accustomed to remote freelancers. These individuals strive to retain their freelance contracts, making sure they deliver quality work on time and carefully cultivating ongoing work relationships that originated back home. Typically, this required some effort, with our informants reporting that they often had to work odd hours in Bali to match up to their clients' work hours in time zones elsewhere in the world. Those with multiple freelance contracts in different parts of the world also had to take care to limit the disruption to their own lives that juggling client meetings across multiple time zones might cause.

Not all nomads were so readily able to transfer their skills online. Those who lacked easy access to gainful freelance work faced the challenge of how to pivot their skills to fit remote opportunities. These nomads were more likely to use web-based marketplaces for gig work such as Upwork.com, Fiverr.com, and Freelancer.com to patch together employment and scrape by. To get started as nomads, some worked as virtual assistants (VAs). Virtual assistants perform a range of tasks. Some are relatively simple, such as conducting online research, making slide presentations, and arranging travel schedules, but others are more sophisticated, such as project management for online businesses. Though VA work is an entry to nomadism for people with few technical skills and those without in-hand contracts, it tends to pay poorly because the competition is global and low-wage markets where workers have high English-language proficiency (e.g., India, the Philippines) drive down the pay rates. As nomads build their social networks and skills, they tend to obtain a larger portion of their work through informal and private channels, which usually result in better pay, thus helping to sustain their lifestyles over time.

Though it might seem confusing or disappointing that many nomads continue doing the same work that they did back home rather than venturing into new frontiers, nomads who freelance in Southeast Asia tend to spend far less money on living expenses. Living at such a reduced cost allows them some freedom to adjust their workload while they explore their future career options. For instance, Lani, a clothing designer mentioned in chapters 1, 2, and 3, took a pay cut when she chose to continue working with a freelance client back in the West, but she is making it work for now:

> I'm already doing it remotely, so what's the difference if I do it in Bali? They didn't even bat an eye. They were like, "No problem." I'm freelancing just for them, and so I'm not making that much money, especially compared to what I was making before, but my expenses are also a lot lower. In an ideal world, and if I were smart with my finances, I would try to pick up another job or two and be working more hours a day because I certainly could, but I'm okay with it right now. I'm enjoying the break, and I'm making enough to live off of.

Entrepreneurship

We distinguish between entrepreneurship and freelancing by defining entrepreneurship as active engagement in launching or running a business that consists of *something other than* selling one's own professional skill on an hourly or other contract basis.[8] Digital nomads' entrepreneurial endeavors include physical products, such as health and wellness merchandise, consumer goods, and apparel; virtual products, such as software, apps, e-books, educational materials, and web-based courses; and experiential products, such as retreats and tours.

The popular view of entrepreneurship today, as exemplified in mainstream media success stories of Silicon Valley firms like Facebook, Airbnb, Google, and Uber, is one of venture funding and high-growth aspirations. However, entrepreneurship among digital nomads takes many forms. Barb, a thirty-two-year-old American whom we first introduced in chapter 2, is the CEO of a location-independent start-up that, while not on the level of Silicon Valley unicorns,[9] does have venture funding and substantial growth aspirations. When asked if, like most nomads, her income declined once she began her start-up life in Bali, she exclaimed: "Yes, yes, yes!" But then she immediately explained why the trade-off was worth it:

> I would take having a better life over having a higher salary any day, and that's something you learn when you actually experience the better life. I wasn't so stressed. I felt like I had time for myself, and I felt like I was building something. *That* motivated me. When you finally put this product out there, and you have customers who are like, "Wow! This is awesome. Thank you so much for it," that's like, the most rewarding thing ever.

Barb's business has continued to grow, and we met other nomads whose businesses were gaining traction. However, the vast majority of digital nomad entrepreneurship does not resemble the start-up lore of Silicon Valley. Rather, most digital nomad entrepreneurs aimed toward the "better life" that Barb described by starting businesses that are not designed to grow large and complex. Commonly described as "lifestyle entrepreneurship," these individuals launch businesses to support themselves and actively avoid growth that would require bringing on substantial staff and associated management responsibilities. Lifestyle entrepreneurs typically fund their businesses through "bootstrapping" (i.e., self-funding their businesses through revenue, savings, investment income, or paid employment of some sort).[10]

Most aspiring digital nomad entrepreneurs must combine income sources in order to meet their living expenses. For instance, many use freelancing income to start their new businesses and to sustain them as they nurse these businesses toward profitability. Lani explained that digital nomad hubs have a contagious entrepreneurial spirit and reported that since coming to Bali, she has caught the bug. She now limits her freelancing hours, protecting her time for her own business goals. Bali's inspiring digital nomad community, combined with her new liberated schedule, has meant that she finally has the social support and breathing room to launch a business of her own. Although Lani was traumatized by her mother's early death from cancer, a small inheritance she received has also helped her toward her entrepreneurial goals:

> I'm using some money from when my mom passed away. I hadn't touched that, and I was waiting to use it for something really good, so I've been working on that for three to four months now. I've been working with some local factories, getting some prototypes made, and there's zero way I would have ever been able to do this with my old life. My entrepreneurial spirit is at an all-time high because I'm surrounded by so many people that have their own company. I actually did not have any intention of starting anything on my own, but it kind of just evolved into that slowly as I started to think about why I wanted to leave somewhere else—because the conditions weren't ideal for me, and if I created my own company I could dictate what those conditions are.

As Lani's case shows, nomads who become entrepreneurial tend to blend freelancing with entrepreneurship. Combining multiple sources of income is a practical response to nomads' desires to maintain their freedom, is a statement about their reluctance to be tied to one path, and is a consequence of their immersion in Bali's entrepreneurial digital nomad community.

Work as a Portfolio of Gigs and Projects

We observed that digital nomads commonly conceive of work as something that goes beyond any one employer or single business idea. While we did meet funded entrepreneurs and remote employees who dedicated all of their work time to a single enterprise, most nomads whom we interviewed were either actively involved in, or else scouting for, additional work and business opportunities. Even full-time employees regarded their jobs as projects rather than considering them through a more traditional, occupational mindset.

For instance, we were surprised when we learned that Nik, a nomad we first introduced in chapter 2 and someone we regard as one of the most entrepreneurial people in our primary sample, had later taken a job with a large, multinational corporation in Malaysia. When he updated us on this development in his life, he said he loved his new job. He was especially enthusiastic about the knowledge he was gathering. He told us that he was trying to learn how big companies standardize operations so that he could later apply this information to his next start-up venture. In essence, Nik intentionally took the job as a kind of short-term, skill-building professional development project, all while continuing to make plans to return to his true passion: entrepreneurship. We met several other nomads who similarly regarded stints at career-track jobs, jobs that many knowledge workers would envy as ends in themselves and that others would view as a pathway to management, as simply another self-imposed challenge for improving or adding to a portfolio of skills.

Although some digital nomads pursued work projects sequentially, it was more common for us to meet nomads juggling several projects at once. Though many are critical of the rise of the gig economy as a commodification of work that spreads non-standard employment and risk to the workforce,[11] digital nomads tend to have a different perspective. Accepting the idea that work *is* transactionalized, nomads view the gig economy as a way to manage the risk inherent in any single job. As nomads see it, by diversifying their work into multiple sources of income, they are preparing for work shifts in the future. Furthermore, by controlling the *mix* of gigs that they take—in effect viewing work as a portfolio of differently motivated income sources—they also benefit because they balance their need for work that is financially sustaining with work that is meaningful to them. For instance, Boris, a twenty-five-year-old Ukrainian programmer first introduced in chapter 2, described to us his conception of allocating "fun" versus "money" across his three gigs. In his typical unemotional, detached, and very logical manner, Boris explained how he organizes his portfolio of gigs and his "metrics" for judging them:

> The first company: there's a lot of smart people, and I learn how to build products because they have much more experience than me. And [the] second job, I just earn money because it was my first project I created from zero. And third, it's like, my passion, what I care [about] most. So these three projects all have metrics, two metrics. First is like, "fun," and second is "money." First is fifty/fifty. Second is maybe 10 percent fun and 90 percent money. What I'm doing on [the] third project is zero percent money/ 100 percent fun.

Although not all digital nomads were as explicit as Boris in elaborating the role of each of their projects, we found that many did talk about their portfolios of work as involving conscious choices. We observed three common and sometimes overlapping practices among nomads who pursued portfolios of simultaneous work projects. We term these *funding a creative passion*, *pursuing passive income*, and *coaching*. We comment briefly on each.

Funding a Creative Passion

Several nomads used income from either dedicated remote employment or steady freelancing gigs to bankroll creative work that might not produce income in the short run. One example is Lyle, a thirty-three-year-old Canadian remote employee. He works in e-commerce and information technology and is also a published writer. He told us that back home before becoming a nomad, the only way he had time to write was on his commute. We were stunned when he revealed that he wrote his first novel on a cell phone, composing "two, three, four paragraphs a day on my phone, on the bus." He elaborated:

> It took me a year and a half, and I had a first draft, and I was like, "Wow. This is okay—about 90,000 words." It was garbage, but predictably, right? . . . But I got it done, and that was the most important thing. . . . And then it took another probably, two years, I'd say, of editing, off and on, and really kind of getting into the details of it, and blowing up the plot, and starting over again. And then I have what I have now.

Now Lyle lives in Bali as a remotely employed digital nomad. He told us that the time zone difference between Bali and the location of his company's operating office allows him to control both his work portfolio and the allocation of his energy and motivation levels for each task. Like many other nomads, Lyle strategically uses his freedom to protect his creative energy. Here, he explained how he reserves his most productive time for writing novels rather than squandering his best waking hours on his "real job":

> I really started to work on [the novel] when I went to Bali, and the *reason* was because the time difference between [my company's location] and Bali was four hours, and it allowed me to work on *my* stuff during the morning when I'm at my most creative, and then do my "work-work" in the afternoon when I have less energy. I'm able just to answer emails. So Bali was actually *great* because I could wake up in the morning and be productive on my own projects, as opposed to my work projects.

Lyle's practice of leveraging one source of income to preserve his time and energy for creativity on a very different project was one we heard repeatedly as nomads would reference a wide variety of activities encompassing the arts, entrepreneurship, and more desirable freelance work.

Pursuing Passive Income

Many digital nomads' ultimate goal is to create a stream of "passive income," a popular term among entrepreneurs and investment gurus. Those with passive income receive ongoing earnings from sources that do not require their full-time engagement (e.g., renting out real estate property; investing in or owning part of a business that requires limited management attention; creating apps, e-books, and courses that generate income without continual updating; or benefiting from other financial investment income).

Digital nomads' most common path to passive income is through e-commerce, typically by running online businesses to sell products sourced in Asia to markets in North America or Europe. Most of these entrepreneurs engage in a popular e-commerce strategy called *dropshipping*, a name that refers to a practice in which sellers do not physically handle the products themselves, but instead use a manufacturer or an intermediary (such as Fulfillment by Amazon, often abbreviated as simply "FBA") to ship the products to the customer directly. Dropshippers use market trends or data to identify a product niche, contract with manufacturers to provide the product, and then sell the product through outlets like eBay, Amazon, or Alibaba. Many websites, podcasts, and social media forums provide advice, courses, and information on how to start a dropshipping business.

Although we did met a few nomads for whom dropshipping was their main business, Bali's digital nomads more commonly used dropshipping as part of a portfolio of several sources of income.[12] For instance, Paul, a London marketing executive we introduced in chapter 3, earned most of his income from freelancing, but he also earned money from a dropshipping business related to crafting products, though he admitted that he does not use these products or do crafts.

Coaching

A third typical component of digital nomads' employment portfolios is *coaching,* a personal development career in which one helps clients to set goals, solve problems, and engage in personal growth.[13] Coaching links individuals' business interests to their personal stories and those of others, and it epitomizes nomads' desires to direct their energies toward their passions. As we met more and more digital nomads over the years, it sometimes seemed as if almost everyone is a coach or else aspires to be one. All nomads—even coaches—joke about this. Coaching is a popular job and aspiration, in part, because it corresponds so well with nomads' values for freedom, personal development, sharing, positivity, and minimalism. In our observations, coaches—whether focused on health and wellness, careers, entrepreneurship, spirituality, or some other domain—report that they (1) encourage clients to prioritize themselves as individuals (freedom); (2) help clients to increase their self-awareness through structured activities (personal development); (3) view communicating their knowledge as a gift to the world (sharing); (4) adopt a non-competitive mindset of resource and success abundance rather than scarcity (positivity); and (5) disengage with systems and values of consumption and adopt values that transcend material possessions (minimalism).

Almost all of the coaches we met combined coaching with another income source. Some began coaching after succeeding in their own business or profession and then transitioned into coaching within that profession, such as a few successful dropshippers we met who transitioned into coaching others on how to become dropshippers. We also met successful digital marketers who now coach others on how to get started in digital marketing. However, it was just as common to meet coaches who entered the profession with little to no specific expertise relevant to their professed coaching subject. These coaches were especially likely to supplement their coaching income with *unrelated* work related to dropshipping (e.g., a career coach selling bathtub enclosures online) or freelancing (e.g., a leadership coach who also has web design contracts). Many coaches also engaged in e-commerce related to their coaching practices by selling products such as health and wellness accessories (e.g., aromatherapy and personal care products) or prepackaged training materials, including courses and e-books.

What is most remarkable in summing up the range and combinations of digital nomad work is nomads' tendency to consider what they do in terms of their portfolio of projects rather than in terms of businesses or professions.[14] This framing of work as a portfolio of projects that may simultaneously encompass entrepreneurship, freelance work, and even dedicated employment differs substantially from the sequential movements depicted in most accounts of international careers.[15] Consistent with this framing, most nomads resisted defining themselves through their businesses, professions, or occupations. Instead, they preferred to represent themselves as people whose work transcends traditional categories. We now turn to the role of the digital nomad community in supporting such varied work needs.

DIGITAL NOMAD WORK IN A PLACE-BASED COMMUNITY: FOUR FUNCTIONS OF A NOMAD HUB

As they build and maintain their new lives and work identities, digital nomads seek a variety of contacts with others who can psychologically and financially sustain them. These contacts are most readily available in nomad hubs, place-based communities where large numbers of digital nomads gather. Everyday working for digital nomads is, in part, a performance, and nomad hubs provide the stage. Whether taking time out from working by the pool in their rented villa to upload a picture of their "office of the day" to social media, ostentatiously opening their laptop during breakfast at a café, or smiling as they wipe the sweat from their brow in a crowded, hot, coworking space, digital nomads frequently engage in activities that explicitly remind themselves and others of their identity. An obvious sociological referent to explain such performative working styles is Erving Goffman's[16] classic dramaturgical model that analyzes individuals' presentations of self. Goffman argued that individuals engage in performances, presenting themselves to others, aiming to control others' impressions of them, and even creating mutually reinforcing performances by tapping into societal rules. Congruent with the concepts of self-presentation and performance, nomads adopt specific interactional norms according to their goals. For instance, in chapter 3 we described the digital nomad norm of accelerating intimacy by telling stories about their personal journeys—complete with private, emotional details—to people they have just met. This practice allows digital nomads to advance their personal and career goals by strengthening their connections quickly.

Goffman argued that much of the performance of everyday life is *inauthentic*: a "veneer of consensus is facilitated by each participant concealing his own wants behind statements which assert values to which everyone present feels obliged to give lip service."[17] In contrast, most nomads whom we met viewed their performances as highly authentic expressions of their "true" selves. They rarely spoke of their multiple motives or admitted to presenting idealized versions of themselves. We attribute this to the fact that, in Bali, nomads' like-mindedness has reached a critical mass.[18] Assured that those around them share their values, nomads view Bali as a place where they can more authentically enact their identities without fear of rejection. Indeed, nomads see their lifestyle choices as emblematic of their desire to escape the inauthentic world of Goffman's performances that, in their view, are dictated by social norms, organizational hierarchies, and laws.

This is not to say that *we* believe that all nomad work performances are authentic, but in contrast to Goffman, most nomads seemed to us—in both their expressed thoughts and observed behaviors—to be trying to better align their lives with their ideal values of freedom, sharing, personal development, positivity, and minimalism. In an effort to push back on nomads' presentations of themselves as authentic, we would often suggest to them that some individuals' performances appeared to be inauthentic. For instance, we would point out that individuals who stage pictures of themselves meditating and then post them on social media with captions like "in the moment" are arguably not "in the moment." In response to such confrontations, most nomads would acknowledge our perspective but then gently disagree by saying that rather than criticizing them, we should respect nomads' efforts; they were simply trying to "manifest" a new reality for their lives. Laurence, the American fashion entrepreneur whose words open this chapter, captured many nomads' feelings of leniency toward others pursuing reinvention: "I respect anyone's hustle that's willing to come to Bali and take a chance, *especially* if they don't know exactly what they're gonna be doing."

In the remainder of this chapter, we focus on four work-related functions of digital nomad hubs, which we label *varied environments for work, social support, employment markets,* and *igniting entrepreneurship.* These functions represent the manifestations of nomads' values toward the domain of work. These functions cannot just exist anywhere: they develop when significant numbers of digital nomads come together to create a place-based community. Once they come into being, the functions draw nomads to a hub, providing the inflow necessary to sustain the digital nomad community in the face of ongoing transience. As these functions strengthen, they enable digital nomads to perform and sustain their new lives and identities.

Varied Environments for Work

It should come as no surprise that having traveled thousands of miles to gain what they view as the necessary freedom to attain their desired work lives, digital nomads make conscious and careful choices about their daily work environments. As with larger concerns about location, nomads' choices about work environments always begin with the question of *where* to work. At home in one's villa? Alone in a café? In a social coworking environment or in a more isolated one? In the coworking space's main area or in the quiet section? With a humid but inspiring rice paddy view or in the more sterile comfort of air-conditioning?

With the natural beauty of Bali all around them wherever they work, many digital nomads' day-to-day choices about work environments are governed more by their beliefs about the benefits and drawbacks of the social side of work. As nomads, they are invested in the freedom to shift their work environments, and they want to take advantage of it. Therefore, digital nomad hubs must provide a variety of work settings. Although prior research has shown that working around others can trigger feelings of threat and competition,[19] digital nomads have a far more positive view of working in the presence of others, as long as they are surrounded by the *right kinds* of people.

Accordingly, we begin by describing the ways in which varied work environments provide *social energy* to nomads, an important dimension of nomad hubs. Additionally, we show that digital nomads recognize their need to balance social energy with productivity and require self-discipline to sustain their lifestyles, so we also discuss the *accountability* mechanisms that constitute a second important dimension of hubs' varied work environments.

Social Energy

Digital nomads travel to hubs to be with their peers and in search of something that seems intangible—a feeling of social energy around work. They are excited to be surrounded by others who are crafting new lives as digital nomads, and they desire to be with people who want to talk about their work aspirations. But why must they travel abroad to do this? When we proposed that they might find similar social energy in the many coworking spaces that have been popping up at home, digital nomads repeatedly emphasized that Bali's social energy is incomparable. They explained that they had already tried coworking in creative class cities, but without the sufficient numbers of like-minded people, those experiences never came close to Bali.

In chapter 2 we briefly introduced the basic features and mechanics of Bali's coworking spaces.[20] But for a place to attain Bali's reputation as a primary nomad hub requires more than fast internet and open floorplans. As Nik, the marketer from Siberia, explained:

> That's the problem with cities, actually. You probably noticed that coworking spaces in a big city is [the] same as [an] office [that] people used to have, but for freelancers. Same working time, but people go to [a] coworking space instead of [an] office. They sit down and get [the] job done but don't talk to each other. They are really productive, but they don't talk to each other.

Many digital nomads echoed this sentiment and described coworking spaces in their home cities as little more than surrogate offices designed to look like start-ups. They found that coffee, snacks, and hot desking[21] do not equate to social energy. Nomads told us that at home, coworking spaces are largely filled with people who have very little in common and seemed unmotivated to interact in any meaningful way. For instance, at coworking giant WeWork, 40 percent of members are employees of large companies, and this category of coworking space users is the fastest growing segment of WeWork customers.[22] Even when digital nomads acknowledged that some coworking spaces back home had facilitated connections from time to time and the owners had attempted to encourage community-building,[23] they pointed out that these were hollow versions of Bali's social energy as a nomad hub. For instance, Caleb, a thirty-five-year-old marketing consultant whom we first introduced in chapter 1, described how the social energy at his favorite coworking space, Dojo Bali, differed from coworking back home in Australia, where he felt he was surrounded by the wrong people and remained in an environment that was largely similar to an office:

> When you work in a coworking space in Australia, it's like an office. . . . The thing that happened to me was that I was originally coming to Bali for two months, and within three days of coming to Dojo I was like, "I'm moving here," and that's pretty much changed everything for me. As soon as I got to Dojo I realized the quality and the talent of the people that were there compared to what the coworking spaces were like in Melbourne, and the networking opportunities that were available. Because in Melbourne—I was in Melbourne for six months before I went to Bali—I would go to *all* the events. I would go to all the meetup things. I'm a networker. The networking thing in Australia was

nowhere near as effective. There're some high-level people in Melbourne, obviously, but I suppose when you work at Dojo, it's like living in a share house, and you get to know people really well. Whereas if you're going to a once-a-month meetup you get to meet people and have a chat with them for five or ten minutes, but you don't really get to establish much. It takes a long time to develop that relationship. I came to Bali, and within three days, I'm like, "The quality of tech people is fucking amazing, and I'm going to live here because there's a lot going on here. It's attracting the *right* people."

Metaphors abound for describing the atmosphere of Bali's coworking spaces: "university," "share house," "crazy incubator," "clubhouse," "magical place," and "creative community." No matter which imagery or comparisons are offered, coworking in Bali is emphatically *not* like an office. Nik described feeling inspired by the social energy and cohesion of the people there:

It's really strong in terms of community-building. It's like a huge bowl of minds, like you make soup in. Whatever you put there, it would grow, perform, take place, like a crazy incubator. The second parallel is [that it's] like university for those who are in their 30s, and it feels exactly this way. We learn, we have fun, we work, and we stay together.

Although the digital nomad community's social energy is most concentrated in its coworking spaces, the size and density of Bali's nomad population means that such energy is also found in cafés, at parties and meetups at various locations, and even on the beach or on the street.

In all of these settings, conversations tend to revolve around the question "What are you working on?" Asking people about their work, professions, and occupations is considered to be rude in many cultures, in part, because it is seen as judgmental, reductive, and perhaps even dehumanizing. In addition, when off the clock and in a social setting, work talk can be perceived as bragging and threatening, or else boring and an indicator that the speaker is no fun or is only interested in networking. However, the opposite is true in Bali's nomad universe. Many nomads told us that the expression "What are you working on?" is a welcome greeting and a standard conversation starter. It fuels the fire of storytelling that drives so much community intimacy. To test this norm, we enacted it ourselves in Bali's coworking spaces.

For instance, we purposefully asked this question one day when we were at Kumpul,[24] a coworking space in the southeastern beach town of Sanur. There, on full display, was the start-up ambiance that captivates coworking space designers and their nomad consumers. An aspirational pillow in the lobby namechecked the usual Silicon Valley icons: "Steve, Bill, Mark, Me."[25] We sidled up to a white male in his fifties wearing a T-shirt advertising his business. He told us he is an expat and resident nomad in Bali, and he was happy to exchange contact information with us and tell us all about his trash removal business, which he also views as a social enterprise. We soon realized that our question was almost like a secret handshake. We then asked our question to two Indonesian men working on a transportation app, two Dutch programmers working on projects for infrastructure at the coworking space, and eventually the owner of the coworking space—who invited us to dinner with his family and staff. Repeating this routine at other coworking spaces, and even in cafés, we observed again and again that digital nomads are highly receptive to engaging with strangers and are eager to answer the intrusive question "What are you working on?"

Although all of the nomads we met responded positively, those who were newer to the lifestyle were especially excited when we inquired about their work. Paul, the marketer and entrepreneur, had been in Bali for two years at the time of our interview. He explained that even though he continued to reap benefits of social energy in the community, coworking spaces were especially important for new arrivals: "Perhaps, it depends on where you are in your journey. Particularly if you are a new person coming into this world, you couldn't wish for a better place than Hubud." The social energy in Bali's digital nomad community communicates that people are eager to meet and help others in a meaningful way.

Accountability

As thrilling as nomad hubs' social energy is, digital nomads are always concerned with "getting shit done," meaning being productive and meeting goals.[26] Because productivity and sociability sometimes conflict and nomads must rely on themselves to be accountable, they constantly reevaluate their work process, including whether their environment is benefiting them. In fact, many nomads told us that they alternate their work sites between coworking spaces and other locations (e.g., cafés, villas, and outdoor spaces with Wi-Fi) because coworking spaces are social to the point of being distracting and interrupting workflow. For instance, Belinda, a German freelancer and entrepreneur whom we introduced in chapter 3, told us: "There is so much going on that a lot of people come to you and maybe interrupt you." Similarly, Nadine, a forty-one-year-old Australian entrepreneur whose quote opened the book, said: "I think a lot of people find that they can't get a lot of work done if they go to the coworking space *every day*." Vance, a freelancer and entrepreneur from England whom we introduced in chapter 1, agreed that coworking spaces sometimes interfere with productivity. He attributed the distraction to the community fluidity, saying that newer nomads, or honeymooners, are "high-energy and excited . . . and they can impact the work culture, *reduce* the work culture."

Indeed, self-discipline is a shared trait among successful digital nomads. Just as some people who telecommute or work from home offices struggle to be productive while away from traditional work environments, some nomads find that they are unable to cultivate the necessary work habits in Bali. Barb, the start-up CEO who is now based in Bali, explained that some people are temperamentally incompatible with the lifestyle and fail to adapt to their new freedom:

> There're two sides to it, for sure. I've had to let a couple people go from my team that just didn't—couldn't—handle it. They couldn't handle the freedom. . . . Yes, you can work any time you want. However, we still have an expectation of deliverables.

To successfully work independently, digital nomads create accountability rituals to keep them on track in the absence of everyday structures common to offices back home. At first, we found it paradoxical that these freedom-loving nomads would choose to embrace accountability. However, Vance explained that nomads' accountability measures are self-imposed, which makes them more tolerable: "Obviously, there's no structure apart from the one that *you* impose upon yourself, so there's no direct accountability, necessarily."

Not only are nomads eager to impose accountability structures upon themselves, but they seem to relish talking about their routines and "life hacks" (i.e., efficiency and productivity tricks). Oscar, from chapter 1, described a strategy that some nomads use for creating accountability without succumbing to the distractions and expense of commercial coworking spaces:

> I used to have a villa, and I would invite people over because I had good Wi-Fi, and I would create a coworking space at my home. I had a glass table off to the side, and I would have everyone write what they were intending to accomplish that day. You show up, you declare what you are doing, and you do it.

Similar to research that shows the health benefits of group exercise,[27] nomads believe that working alongside others who are similarly striving for new lives will enhance their motivation and help them to accomplish more. In other words, they actively cultivate an audience for their day-to-day work.[28]

Another example of such self-imposed measures can be found in more formalized accountability groups. For instance, among her many gigs, Dara, a forty-three-year-old American "emotional intelligence coach" quoted in chapter 1, told us that she runs well-attended weekly accountability breakfasts at one of Bali's coworking spaces. In addition, one of Dara's income sources is group coaching. She holds six-person sessions in Bali that last an intensive four weeks, and there she blends accountability structures, business coaching, and wellness to develop clients' self-awareness and "accelerate" their businesses as well as their personal lives.

She is not alone. Demand for accountability services is robust, and even the most frugal nomads are willing to pay for help to keep them on track when they have decided to "level up."[29] By broadcasting their goals in front of nomad peers—usually people with whom they have no previous or current work connection—nomads hope to attain the accountability benefits of more conventional work structures but without the hierarchies and competition these often entail.

Knowing that nomads prize productivity and sometimes critique certain coworking spaces that are too social, Bali's coworking spaces are often designed to promote flexibility—balancing nomads' needs for both interaction and focus. For instance, coworking spaces usually have designated "quiet" zones, and nomads usually respect these boundaries. Though we did observe people initiating conversations during the day in the main working areas, we also noticed that common areas are mostly quiet during the peak working hours. During these times, nomads are less likely to start conversations unless they are in the café areas and in-between spaces, such as hallways, lobbies, and kitchenettes.

While some digital nomads are generally loyal to a single coworking space, many have taken advantage of the fact that memberships are monthly and that costs vary according to the number of hours purchased. Digital nomads enjoy experimenting with coworking spaces, moving back and forth, and even buying part-time memberships to more than one coworking space at a time so they can achieve a change of scenery, expand networks, or complete a specific task. For instance, many loyalists of the Outpost coworking space admitted that they sometimes work at Hubud, which is located just one mile away. This flow of people across different spaces, whatever their preferred environment, is a major feature of Bali's coworking culture.

Social Support

One could analyze all digital nomad hub functions through a lens of social support, but we have reserved this term for two nomad hub functions that directly help individuals to access knowledge related to professional or personal growth. We call these *everyday helping* and *skill shares*. In chapter 3 we detailed how digital nomad culture encourages the expression of values and creates community intimacy through a ritual that we labeled *telling your story.* In *everyday helping,* digital nomads take information that they glean from telling each other their stories and then use it to connect community members who need help to those who can provide it. In *skill shares,* digital nomads participate in brief, formal workshops to listen to presenters tell their stories, offer their support to presenters through their active participation, receive support in the form of an opportunity to learn something new, and explore together with the presenters and their fellow attendees options in the realm of personal development.

Everyday Helping

It is hard to overstate the degree to which the digital nomad community focuses on giving and receiving instrumental or tangible support. Nomads come to Bali to isolate themselves from the outside world, which leads them to seek and give support locally with others whom they see as like-minded. Brandi considers herself to be an expert on coworking. She estimates that she has visited thirty-five coworking spaces around the world and now works for a coworking space in the United States. She told us that she thought Bali's digital nomads had established an especially strong helping culture:

> For some reason, Bali and Hubud are different [from other coworking locales], and I don't know why, and I don't know if it's the tectonic plates,[30] or the woo-woo, or what it is.
>
> Q: The woo-woo?
>
> The spiritual thing, but it feels different in Bali. It feels different to be there. It feels different to be around people who are there, and I think somehow whatever the owners of Hubud did when they created it, they created a community unlike any other that I've ever seen. . . . The community there—because it's such a small town—all we have is each other. Whenever something happens—you fall off your scooter, you get dengue, your credit card's compromised, whatever—every single person rallies around you and helps you out, and I haven't seen that in any of the other coworking spaces [outside of Bali].

Crucially, for cash-strapped nomads, most forms of everyday helping are *unpaid.* The fact that digital nomads offer and receive so much support for free, with no strings attached, is one of the most compelling aspects of the digital nomad community. Grace, an American public relations freelancer whom we first introduced in chapter 1, told us about a friend of hers who was paying for business advice until Grace admonished her, saying: "No, no, no. You can get all of that advice for free in the Hubud community." Given that nomads value sharing, it is easy to find helpers who are genuinely interested in one's work and success. As Grace noted:

The minute you share, so many people come and check up on you. People that met me when I first got here, they'll [now] say, "Hey, that project? How's it going? Do you need anything with it? I can introduce you to someone." And it's like, "Wow! You remember."

In addition, Belinda explained her satisfaction with the *quality* of advice and contacts: "I'm actually able to work here with people who are real experts in their field, or they know people who can help me. It's quite nice." Pressed for a specific example, she quickly offered a story about someone who helped with marketing her business: "Yesterday I had a chat with someone who taught me how to run sales funnels through email." While some might argue that this kind of information on sales funnels is widely available and not worthy of such praise, Belinda told us that her new contact went above and beyond to encourage her and help her move her business forward. For instance, he coached her on sales funnel timing strategies, used his free time to conduct a quick analysis of her website data to help her optimize it, and then told her exactly what next steps she should take to move closer to getting customers to actually purchase her product. Belinda said that beyond the knowledge and new skills she gained, she was especially grateful that she learned that her timing was off and she was wasting effort on tasks that were too far ahead. Now, armed with new direction and a more effective timeline, Belinda will be less likely to chase away clients with a sales strategy that is too aggressive relative to her product's stage of development. She said she now feels empowered to meet the required preliminary milestones for her business before moving on to the later-stage tasks. All of this boosted her motivation, increased her feelings of efficacy, and strengthened her nomad bonds and identity.

Generous spirit aside, one reason that digital nomads embrace the act of providing everyday help is that they receive reputational rewards. Vance explained: "Coworking spaces generate a sense of helping each other and sharing things. . . . In a place like [this] you kind of know what everyone else is doing, so that it creates a desire to do things *together* and be very nice to everybody because everyone comes without any kind of social support." Even people who are very focused on their own productivity and who are hustling hard to make their own work projects successful are willing to devote time to helping others and sharing their knowledge for free. For instance, Rebecca, a Canadian technology and marketing freelancer mentioned in chapters 2 and 3, said she believes strongly in the nomad helping ethic. Though confident, articulate, and eager, Rebecca struggled to harness her many interests and talents and find a unifying brand and sustainable source of income. Even so, she told us that she dedicates between three and nine hours per week to helping others for free.

Laurence, the fashion entrepreneur, clearly articulated digital nomads' dominant positive philosophy around helping: He told us that he helps others without the expectation of any quid pro quo. Having launched a successful (and ongoing) social entrepreneurship venture in high school, Laurence went on to graduate from an Ivy League university and worked as a business consultant for a Fortune 50 technology firm. He is clearly advanced in his business knowledge even though he is still in his twenties. Consistent with other experienced nomads, he knows that help is not symmetrical. Perhaps affected by the Balinese belief in karma, he reported that he finds it personally rewarding to assist and mentor others in the community:

I have a feeling that it comes around, and it works out well. I would rather put more out and give more to others and know that I'm not going to end up with nothing. I don't need an even amount back, necessarily. If I'm helping someone for forty-five minutes on something, and it makes a huge difference to them, that makes me feel really good, and I'm happy to do that.

As Laurence suggests, more experienced nomads typically give more help than they get. Yet they continue to help for the emotional benefits and to stay connected to the energy provided by those who are new to the nomad lifestyle.

Skill Shares and Performative Self-Improvement

A *skill share* is a one- or two-hour group session, typically held at a coworking space, in which one member of the community teaches some particular aspect of their expertise to others without cost or obligation. As one of the digital nomad community's most revered work rituals, the skill share is both a formalized opportunity to learn a new skill and a chance to perform the personal development value so crucial to nomads' identities. In Bali it is possible to attend skill shares almost every day, and this possibility plays a role in digital nomad lore. For instance, one of the legendary success stories at Hubud that people shared with us over and over was about a young man who came to Bali with a strong entrepreneurial spirit but with few practical skills. He joined Hubud, attended every event for months to learn online business skills, and then launched what is now a highly successful online business selling custom "Wanderer" bracelets,[31] sustainably made by local Balinese craftspeople. Nomads especially enjoy the bracelet styles that mark the coordinates to places they have traveled.

In Bali's coworking spaces, skill shares come in two varieties. The first category is the personal development presentation. The second is a presentation of a more traditional professional skill. We attended six skill shares (three personal development, three professional skills) across four coworking spaces during our fieldwork (one in 2016, and the remaining five in 2017). We audio recorded four of these events after getting presenters' permission. In this section, we describe a personal development skill share in detail in order to explain how skill shares enable community social support beyond their function of knowledge transfer. At this event, twenty-five men and women were crowded into Dojo Bali's conference room for a one-hour skill share on the subject of "fear," which promised that the audience would "learn tools to create more opportunities in your life and business by relating differently to fear." As with so many events in Bali, we are invited to close our eyes, put our bare feet on the ground, and "come into our own space."

The speaker was Cheryl, an American woman who appeared to be in her twenties, wearing jangling bracelets and a printed romper. Well-known in nomad circles that focus on coaching, Cheryl told us that she wanted the atmosphere to feel sacred and spiritual, as well as empowering, practical, and entrepreneurial. Cheryl first took some time to tell her story about being the child of an alcoholic and not living up to her parents' expectations and then gave a short lecture on biological aspects of fear. Next, she asked us to pair up for an experiential exercise. She directed us to write down three of our own fears and then share these with a random person sitting next to us (and specifically, *not* with a person we already know).

One might question the wisdom of asking strangers to share their deepest fears in a brief workshop with no follow-up on their well-being. Nevertheless, Cheryl urged us not to give in to our inhibitions and instructed us to open up about our potentially traumatic experiences. Given her relatively young age, we suspected that Cheryl may have exaggerated her level of expertise in the bio promoting the event. In it, she claims that she worked with Silicon Valley Fortune 500 companies, is a "yoga therapist," that she "escaped" the world of academia, and that she is the founder of a social movement/business that promotes coaching, workshops, retreats, and speaking engagements that offer compassionate leadership, mindfulness, stress management for Millennials, turning fear into an entrepreneurial tool, and biological aspects of fear such as the "gut-brain connection." Crucially, the attendees surrounding us did not appear to share our skepticism and were busy pondering and scribbling their answers.

One of us was paired with a young Danish woman who moved to Bali with her boyfriend to start a business. She listed these fears: (1) she will fail at making their business work; (2) she will be too homesick for her family to sustain the digital nomad lifestyle; and (3) she will be bitten or mauled by the stray dogs that roam around in many less developed countries. She shared these in the larger group session, but Cheryl made no effort to specifically address her fears. Instead, she recited the platitudes that we had become familiar with from talking to nomads. These are found in many best-selling business and self-help books, especially those by Brené Brown that advocate vulnerability and courage and those by Marianne Williamson that address readers' fears of inadequacy and "imposter syndrome."[32] At the close of the event, participants applauded and thanked her as they exited.

After the session, we approached Cheryl and learned that, as we suspected, she misrepresented her advertised credentials and expertise. We learned that her relevant knowledge about fear comes down to the fact that she has experienced fear and has read self-help books about women's empowerment. Unfortunately, we were not surprised. At three of the skill shares we attended, presenters seemed to have limited training on the subjects of their talks, but nevertheless, nomad audiences enthusiastically and unquestioningly received them.

We were perplexed. As far as we could tell, skill share attendees were mostly middle-class, college educated, and seemingly capable of interrogating presenters' credentials, claims, and materials. Yet we found nomads and event organizers were surprisingly uncritical of presenters. When we questioned them privately about this, most nomads essentially criticized *our* logic and worldview. They argued that by construing skill shares narrowly as the sharing of skills, we were missing the main point of their value to the community. To digital nomads, skill shares provide opportunities for telling one's story, receiving support from the presenter and giving it back to them, and exploring together in the domain of personal development. Importantly, digital nomads argued that these functions were separate from and, perhaps, more important than any actual skill sharing in a particular session. Instead, they talked about the larger function of skill shares, which is to "draw the community together." As Vance told us, the fact that nomads are free of obligations opens up their availability to take a risk and spontaneously attend a range of skill shares, many of which are outside their wheelhouse:

> Let's say there's a skill share on a Wednesday night at Hubud. Because you don't have the same obligations at home, like the lawn or the mortgage or whatever. Because you don't have those things, you can just go—even if it's not something for you—just to see friends and socialize afterwards.

Nomads also cautioned us about our "biases" about knowledge and expertise. They emphasized that knowledge and wisdom can come from unexpected places and people, and told us that they had, at one point or another, learned valuable things at these events and from local people with almost no formal education. Several nomads either implied or directly told us that we were too focused on conventional, Western, and institutionalized ideas of knowledge acquisition and transfer, and suggested that as academics, we were too invested in gatekeeping of expertise and formal schooling as a means of education.

What we learned from attending and discussing skill shares is that nomads approach them as much through the more general lens of promoting community intimacy as through the narrower lens of learning. Thus, even when skill shares are incompetently executed from the perspective of providing facts and insights into their advertised topic, they can be well received as long as they provide a showcase for telling one's story, giving and receiving support, and collectively exploring the terrain of personal development, all of which create feelings of intimacy within the community.

Local Employment Markets for Remote Work: A Nomad Underground Economy

As workers and business owners, digital nomads can only sustain their lifestyles if they are able to generate ongoing income. The nomadic lifestyle cuts off access to many traditional, place-based networks that workers might use to find employment and that business owners might use to find employees. As we noted earlier in this chapter, nomad hubs supply a place-based forum for matching work to workers. Below, we explain that nomads tend to treat these talent markets as an underground economy even when much of their activity is legal. We also discuss how digital nomads negotiate the acceptance of their professional knowledge within these employment markets.

Employment Markets

I can be kicked out of the country at any point in time. I'm not technically legal. I am legally allowed to be here, but I'm not legally allowed to make any money here. So it's good that I work online, but I can't promote myself. I can't advertise myself, which makes it tricky.

Maddie, thirty-two-year-old Australian freelance marketer

One of the most secretive and controversial aspects of the digital nomad community is the questionable legality of a community of Western expats, almost all of whom are on short-term tourist visas, busily networking to find employment and start businesses. Nomads' paranoia runs deep with regard to discussions of visa issues, as do their misunderstandings about Indonesian law. Immigration rules regarding tourist visas suggest that many digital nomads may be able to do their work while in Indonesia for a short period.[33] However, nomads fear that Indonesian immigration officials inconsistently apply the law, and many nomads worry that this could lead to arrest or deportation if they work too openly.

In chapter 2 we noted that nomads exercise caution when posting in online forums to solicit work. This careful approach also extends to in-person activities. When we were conducting our fieldwork, we had to fill out paperwork at our various rental residences. The first time a local host asked if we were in Bali for work or for tourism, we said, "Both." Frowning, she shook her head and corrected us, instructing that the correct answer is always "vacation."

Among nomads, stories abound about immigration crackdowns in coworking spaces. Several nomads told us about a raid at one of the nomad coworking facilities in which members were temporarily deported. Barb, who was there when it happened, explained:

> Sometimes they do raids, and usually, it's someone that tips them off, so we think it's someone in that neighborhood who was like, "There's all these foreigners wandering around the neighborhood. You should probably check them out." But what's funny is, I already had the one visa you can have in Bali. It's called a KITAS. It's $3,500 [US] per year to have it. It's quite expensive. . . . I had that, but I was away. I was actually in Europe and the UK for six months, so I was away from Bali for half a year. I had to go through that visa process again, and I was on a business visa. A business visa does not allow you to work in Indonesia. You're there for "a workshop." Like, you're not working and making money there. So I had that, but they came in. Obviously, we were all on our laptops. It doesn't matter if we were checking social media or whatever. Then they asked for all our passports, and we were detained for a week in the immigration office and interrogated. We thought they were going to be deporting us, where we all had to go back to our home country, and we couldn't come back to Indonesia for at least a year, maybe even five years. But we didn't do anything bad. We just had the wrong visas. Everyone was on a different situation. So that's one thing that's a challenge for anyone that decides to pursue this life. Like, get the right visa.

Visa problems are not exclusive to Bali's digital nomads. For instance, some told us about mundane situations in Thailand that could result in refusal of entry or deportation. These problems and circumventing them are popular subjects in nomad social media groups. To us, immigration law enforcement against digital nomads appeared to be relatively uncommon, as evidenced by the fact that Bali's coworking spaces operate in the open, mostly without incident, and one can find expats brazenly typing on their laptops in many locations. Indeed, Barb's dismissal of concerns that nomads are violating their visas (i.e., they are not doing "anything bad") may be interpreted as a display of unexamined privilege, especially given the current historical context of Western nations pushing back against immigration because of its perceived negative impact on citizens' employment and quality of life. However, recounting immigration difficulties is an almost obligatory aspect of the nomad storytelling ritual, so it looms large in their minds. Ultimately, the result of nomads' fears about soliciting and doing work as short-term visitors is that, regardless of the actual legality of their work status, they behave as if their employment markets are an underground economy.

Given that remote workers are wary about visa enforcement, we assumed nomads would not dare to solicit work *in person*. However, coworking spaces function as active employment markets for digital nomads. The community fluidity means that newcomers are always in abundance, and Bali's coworking spaces actively encourage networking between newcomers and longer-term members. Because most coworking spaces have few Indonesian members, and most expats in nomad hubs can easily recognize one another as expats, digital nomads regard face-to-face employment markets as relatively safe. Nik extolled the virtues of networking in Bali's coworking spaces, saying: "In terms of networking—a friend of mine said she could go for a coffee, like fifteen meters away, and she would come back an hour later because she met someone there, and then they [would] have projects together, just because [of] one hour." Many others confirmed that Nik was not exaggerating. Paul told us that he had started two businesses with digital nomads whom he met at Hubud. Another nomad admitted that "probably 30 percent" of his work is locally based, and we even spoke to one nomad who said that she could probably earn all of her income locally but chooses not to because "the internet gives me like, *so* many more possibilities."

When we directly asked about efforts to solicit work while in nomad hubs, some nomads were vague and seemed worried about admitting visa violations to us. However, we witnessed people getting jobs this way, and in the course of interviews and conversations, many nomads told us about jobs they had attained from local networks. For instance, one digital nomad entrepreneur told us that he keeps tabs on the talent pool of locally available nomads at the coworking space. He told us that he routinely hires freelancers he meets there, and then he actually walked us through his process, which he said was made possible by the digital nomad community norm of rapid intimacy:

I can talk to five different people about one project at [my coworking space]. I can literally go over to someone and go, "Hey, I've got some work for you. Can you do this for me?" And then I'll go to another table and go, "Hey, I've got some work for you. Can you do this for me?" And then someone will come up to *me* and go, "Hey, I've got some work for *you*. Can you do this for me?" So basically, we're able to collaborate in the exchange really easily.

Thus, digital nomads are aware of the underground employment market and its importance for sustaining their lifestyle. Coworking space membership takes up a large portion of many nomads' budgets (i.e., sometimes as much as their housing), but the employment markets found there make the expense more defensible. Still, the employment market only works to the extent that digital nomads can somehow signal their skills to one another. We turn next to this process.

Negotiating Expertise

In chapter 2 we described Bali as a magical place that allows outsiders substantial latitude to reinvent themselves. Nomads' values for freedom, positivity, and personal development mean that individuals can tell almost any story about who they are, and at least publicly, fellow nomads will say, "Well, okay. Maybe so." As we discussed above in relation to skill shares, digital nomads apply lenient standards because they believe that the benefits of remaining positive and optimistic outweigh the benefits of being critical. However, maintaining this attitude of leniency is complicated by the need to negotiate expertise in employment markets. Whether they are selling their own skills or seeking to hire others, digital nomads face the challenge of how to balance their desire to stay positive while getting their fair share in employment transactions.

Despite the risks and potential for scams, digital nomads' value for freedom from conventional social structures, coupled with their desire to pivot (i.e., change the direction of) their own skills toward new applications, leads them to be suspicious of traditional credentials. In expressing their views on expertise, nomads frequently cite *4-Hour Workweek* author Tim Ferriss, who popularized the conception of expertise as simply knowing slightly more about a topic than the person with whom you are communicating. This influential view of expertise as *a situation in which a peer knows as little as one more thing than the average audience member about a domain*[34] allows Bali's digital nomad community to recognize a broad variety of claims to knowledge. Indeed, many nomad entrepreneurs told us that they discount traditional credentials and favor active demonstrations of knowledge when deciding whom to hire. However, Nadine, an Australian entrepreneur and former attorney, explained that one of her greatest challenges has been hiring for her rapidly growing business. She considers herself to be very discerning and expressed frustration about nomads who misrepresent their skills, knowledge, and work ethic. She believes that many digital nomads have learned that they "can easily pretend to be something you're not" and that "most people can't tell the difference."

All of this suggests that as individuals seek to gain work from their nomad social networks, they face the challenge of how to *show* others that their claims of expertise are genuine. Although it is an imperfect barometer, digital nomads widely believe that presenting a skill share is an important tool for cultivating and showcasing one's reputation as an expert. Indeed, when well executed, skill shares can lead to paid work and higher status within the community. As Hubud co-founder Steve Munroe put it: "That's just sort of the culture we've created here—that if you're coming [here], one of the most effective ways to engage with community and to get connected is by *giving* an event. Not just attending them, but actually by sharing something." To illustrate how a skill share might be leveraged by a presenter to gain employment, we provide an example of a professional skill share we attended in which the presenter clearly and, in our view, successfully negotiated his claim of expertise.

The skill share started at 5:00 PM on a Monday. Forty-one people were sitting in uncomfortable wooden chairs, ready to listen to Caleb (introduced in chapter 1), perhaps Bali's most recognized expert in search engine optimization (SEO)—the art and science of improving website rankings in internet searches. Web traffic for businesses, and the resulting business volume, depends on pages reaching the top of a search, so SEO is a critical part of contemporary digital marketing efforts.[35] Within Bali's digital nomad community, as well as the larger international digital nomad SEO community, Caleb is widely respected but is also considered a bit of an arrogant know-it-all, partially because he violates some positivity norms by being much more cynical than the average nomad. However, this personality trait is often laughed aside as an eccentricity because the nomads consider him to be a legitimate expert and community leader. In a subculture that subscribes to the principle of "fake it 'til you make it," Caleb appears to deliver real performance. In addition to running his own agency, he founded a popular SEO Facebook group and an international digital marketing conference. The crowd awaiting him is buzzing in anticipation for the skill share, which offers concrete lessons in data-driven content marketing that nomads could conceivably use to generate an income stream sufficient to sustain their lifestyles.

We watched as Caleb and his business partner, Wanda, a German woman in her mid-thirties, commenced the hands-on workshop. They previewed the ambitious meeting agenda and encouraged everyone to log into Google AdWords on their laptops to follow along. Over the next hour, they taught the basic framework for how to properly conduct SEO, including explaining how and why current practices have changed over time, how new techniques differ from the old, and then stressing the importance of staying current with best practices to ensure professional-quality work. The information was overwhelming but so comprehensive that the audience left feeling empowered, as if we could actually go out and do this. A half-hour "AMA" session followed, during which Caleb urged: "Ask me anything!" The audience was highly engaged and appreciative of the opportunity, with many audience members furiously taking notes. At the close, instead of being burned out and eager to pack up, the group exploded in applause.

Nomads view skill shares as important learning and community-building events, but also as opportunities to negotiate claims of expertise. Caleb's skill share provided us with an example of how an event might accomplish these goals. At a beachside dinner after the session, Caleb admitted to us that his motivation for presenting skill shares is not only to altruistically share knowledge with the community but also to acquire business contracts and recruit potential employees to his agency. In fact, he proudly informed us that all of his employees are digital nomads whom he met at his coworking space. Caleb's case illustrates the fact that the digital nomad community does, in fact, use place-based employment markets, contrary to what the local laws try to discourage and what many say about the harmlessness of digital work to local employment markets.

With such importance attached to peer-to-peer exchanges, lenient attitudes about expertise can create risk in digital nomad employment markets. As we described earlier, nomads often responded negatively when we would question a particular speaker's credentials. However, similar to Nadine's story above, others reported that they had been so impressed by skill share presenters that they eagerly hired them, but then found that the so-called experts could not deliver on their professed skills or promised value. Thus, nomads are cognizant that their relaxed attitudes about expertise come with costs as well as benefits.[36]

As a place where individuals attempt to reinvent themselves as independent from traditional work structures, Bali's digital nomad community is highly entrepreneurial. This entrepreneurial spirit animates everyone from remote employees trying to invent new lives to individuals who are actually starting businesses. Entrepreneurship even represents a way to showcase one's skills to others while still seeking more traditional work. To illustrate this point as well as the more pervasive role entrepreneurship plays in the digital nomad community, we turn to this final function of the digital nomad hub.

Although the place-based social benefits of working around others in Bali's digital nomad community help nomads who are remote workers and freelancers, much of the community activity is geared toward promoting, encouraging, and supporting entrepreneurship as a path to sustaining the nomad lifestyle. The steady flow of newcomers who are caught up in the excitement of the honeymoon stage means that everyone in the community is exposed to fresh stories, and more experienced nomads get to find new audiences with whom to share their own stories. This leads to surges of ideas exchanged among people from different countries and with a variety of perspectives and skills. A prominent outcome of all of this sharing is to ignite entrepreneurship within the digital nomad community.

Though many nomads come to Bali with entrepreneurial aspirations, others develop these aspirations only *after* arriving and experiencing the community's intense exchanges of ideas. For instance, earlier in the chapter, Lani noted that she did not initially intend to start her own business, but her thinking "evolved" in the presence of so much entrepreneurial activity and support. Even Carol, who works remotely as an employee of a recruiting company and who expressed great loyalty to her boss, said she is beginning to catch the entrepreneurship bug: "I'm not an entrepreneur *right now*, but maybe that's something I will be doing later."

The Kauffman Foundation, a leading US nonprofit organization dedicated to promoting entrepreneurship, has asserted that entrepreneurship support requires an ecosystem with policymakers, investors, researchers, lawyers, bankers, and accountants as the key helpers.[37] One part of such ecosystems is the *incubator*,[38] an organization that typically provides a carefully selected set of entrepreneurs with access to space, capital, and experts (e.g., venture capitalists, accountants, and lawyers) targeted to the businesses' specific needs for a period of two to three years.[39] However, the selectivity needed to justify such long-term investments necessarily excludes many would-be entrepreneurs. Importantly, many such incubators focus on businesses with significant growth potential in order to convince other ecosystem participants to invest their time and resources.

Although Bali's digital nomad community *is* a supportive environment for entrepreneurship, it differs in some important ways from this typical ecosystem model. Bali's digital nomad community is open to anyone, its high fluidity means that most individuals stay no more than a few months, and most of its entrepreneurs are seeking only to start businesses to support themselves and do not have aspirations toward the high growth needed to attract investment capital. None of the supporting roles on the Kauffman Foundation list described above are significant players in Bali's digital nomad community. In fact, other than its coworking spaces, Bali's digital nomad community is mostly devoid of larger institutional forces.

This absence of traditional ecosystem components has disadvantages. For instance, many nomad entrepreneurs would benefit from specialized support tailored to their needs. Moreover, Bali's coworking spaces' lightly curated, peer-to-peer learning approach may be inefficient for helping any particular set of businesses because it is dependent on who happens to be around at any given time rather than on the needs of a particular set of entrepreneurs. Instead, Bali's digital nomad community supports entrepreneurship through entrepreneurship-specific programs and events that repeat frequently and are highly celebrated by community members. Entrepreneurial nomads whom we met often talked about two kinds of events that aim specifically to ignite and encourage entrepreneurship: *masterminds* and *Startup Weekend*.

Masterminds

A *mastermind*[40] is a gathering of people who are interested in entrepreneurship and who try to help each other solve business problems.[41] Although private, members-only masterminds exist in Bali and elsewhere, these groups are generally geared toward more established entrepreneurs, often require members' businesses to have established substantial revenue (e.g., $5,000 US per month), and tend to charge membership fees that render them too expensive for new entrepreneurs.

In contrast, Bali's digital nomad community leverages its fluidity and rapid intimacy to democratize the mastermind concept through "open" sessions in which nomads are not screened out based on their success levels. Individual digital nomads organize many of these events. For instance, Tessa, the American digital marketer and remote employee first introduced in chapter 1, co-organized a monthly meetup called "Girl Boss, Wine, and Mastermind" that was held at different locations each month. Although Bali has long been known as a woman-friendly destination, its digital nomad community expands the sphere of women-focused events beyond the traditional health and wellness domains to encourage and encompass entrepreneurship and being a "girl boss."[42] Leveraging the talents of the many women drawn to Bali for a variety of reasons, such events help to counter the hypermasculine, "brogrammer" atmosphere that pervades many tech, start-up, and entrepreneur spaces, materials, and groups around the world.[43]

Coworking spaces also sponsor open mastermind events. For instance, when we attended masterminds at Hubud and Dojo, we observed nomads at all stages of business development ask for community help with solving a business problem. The meetings are organized around three questions: "What are you working on?" "What's working?" "What do you need help with?" Thus, the agenda encourages participants to tell their stories and ask for help. Community members provide support in the form of empathy and business advice, and the group jointly explores how to make nomad entrepreneurship successful.

Ned, a bearded American programmer and photographer in his late twenties, provided an example of the business problems often presented in masterminds. Ned designed a new type of strap that stabilizes cameras against photographers' wrists, but he still needed to make a prototype and knew that to reduce costs he had to outsource the work to a contract-based manufacturer. After his pitch to our group of ten, the ideas immediately flowed, beginning with help offered by a thirty-something e-commerce entrepreneur from Denmark, who asked if he had considered sourcing in China. Along with responding to Ned's immediate concerns, several people demonstrated their desire to help him by recommending a marketing strategy in which he would distribute prototypes to get endorsements from social media influencers.

Another day, we heard a presentation from two twenty-somethings, one from Germany and the other from Canada. They had met in Bali and were launching a dating service but were struggling with two problems. First, they needed help marketing their business on a large scale. Second, over the past year they had obtained user emails for a sales funnel but had no idea how to monetize the funnel without annoying users. The coworking space's room was jammed with fifteen attendees, including digital marketers, e-commerce entrepreneurs, developers, coaches, and photographers—mostly single people who were their target market. At some point, the founders admitted that their web presence was just a landing page requesting visitors' email addresses. One attendee offered this opinion: "In order for this to work you need a website, a single site with pictures, a mock-up." Soon, everyone was enthusiastically debating the business's market size, potential niches, growth, and future direction.

Most of the business problems presented in the masterminds we observed were similar in that they dealt with early-stage entrepreneurs' technical problems. However, on occasion, nomads would request help with people-oriented issues. For instance, Mike, a former New York finance employee, was having problems with a financial technology start-up. Mike, still dressed like a Wall Streeter with a short haircut, clean shave, and crisp, preppy polo shirt, stood out in the room full of scruffy, casual nomads. Though Mike's product was nearly ready, he needed advice on hiring a marketer and wanted to know whether he should offer to make the new hire a co-founder so the person would have more "skin in the game." We anticipated that the group would have a cool reaction toward Mike, viewing him as a conservative outsider mismatched to Bali's rebel vibe. We were wrong; the group eagerly embraced him, bombarding him with suggestions.

As the enthusiastic participation in Bali's masterminds indicates, the digital nomad community devotes energy to entrepreneurship with the explicit purpose of inspiring others to share their knowledge and discover their own entrepreneurial talents and passions. In contrast to the world's many exclusive, closed, and expensive mastermind groups,[44] many of Bali's digital nomad masterminds are inclusive, open, and either free with a coworking membership or available for the price of dinner. By observing someone with limited business experience explain an idea and receive validation and help, other community members feel a sense of empowerment and wonder. These sessions also illustrate a nomad paradox— the community enthusiastically gives and receives support and provides challenging and useful feedback, but simultaneously, nomads adhere to an ethos of positivity and eschew any naysayers.

We now to turn to an entrepreneurship event that combines social energy, social support, and employment markets in an extended format: Startup Weekend.

Startup Weekend

In just 54 hours, you will experience the highs, lows, fun, and pressure that make up life at a start-up.

-Startupweekend.org

It was a hot, humid Sunday afternoon, but the energy was high in Dojo's main room. In just a few minutes, Startup Weekend's final pitch session would begin. The culmination of two days of intensive work, the program began on Friday evening when seventy-six individuals from twenty-nine countries formed into eleven teams. The only requirement to participate was the price of a ticket. The theme of this edition of Startup Weekend was Bali tourism, and each team developed its own business idea, ranging from an Airbnb-like platform targeting digital nomad customers, to an agritourism website, to proposals to improve trash handling and reduce plastic bottle use in Bali.[45]

Participants worked to develop and test their start-up ideas by creating websites, sourcing products, talking to potential customers and distributors, and even launching a test version of a product. True to digital nomads' working community norms, participants spent a great deal of time networking, eating meals together, and even participating in an hour-long guided meditation. The last event was the final pitch session in front of a crowd of fellow attendees, friends, and supporters from the community as well as a panel of judges, including a local business coach, an investment professional, the founder of a pet-friendly travel website, and a Balinese entrepreneur who makes and sells personal care products. A few groups huddled around laptops tweaking their presentations until the last minute. Others mingled, continuing to indulge in the favorite nomad pastime of telling each other their stories.

Startup Weekend is a worldwide phenomenon, claiming events in 150 countries. Organizers hope to connect aspiring entrepreneurs and help them to learn about starting a business. Ambitiously, they do this by placing them in a hands-on situation where they must start an actual business in the course of one weekend.[46] Bali's version of the event, organized by Hubud but held at Dojo during the time of our fieldwork, is an eagerly anticipated occasion within the digital nomad community.[47] We participated in the event, and our team, "Bali Bottle," developed an idea to address the environmental problems that are partially caused by, but also interfere with, tourism in Bali. Our business plan was to reduce plastic bottle waste by convincing eco-conscious hotels to provide guests with reusable water bottles and filling stations. Team members, who chose a team to join after hearing leaders pitch their ideas, included a French computer programmer, marketers from Bulgaria and England, and a Balinese real estate entrepreneur. Our leader was an American who teaches at Bali's famous Green School, a non-profit, private school founded and run by expats. It is well known for its innovative, environmentally focused curriculum, and it attracts wealthy Westerners (and even celebrities) seeking an alternative education for their children.[48]

After the pitches, we all celebrated with drinks and dinner on the roof of a nearby hotel. In the end, the digital nomad community judges announced that the winner was the team that presented a plan for a digital nomad housing service rather than one of the projects aiming specifically at Bali tourism. We agreed that the winning project best met the scoring criteria[49] for the event, but several attendees grumbled that it also symbolized the digital nomad community's priority to serve itself over contributing to the local community.

Bali's Startup Weekend provides learning, employment networking, community-building, and a big dose of social energy in a novel work situation—starting a business from scratch in just two days. Startup Weekend aims to teach people how to start businesses and promote a general culture of entrepreneurship, reinforcing digital nomads' values for freedom and personal development. Events like Startup Weekend also serve digital nomads' employment markets by helping nomads select business partners and vendors. Throughout the weekend, nomads perform and demonstrate their skills while working with their team. The team's final presentation to the entire crowd is an opportunity to showcase members' individual capabilities to judges and peers. Startup Weekend also offers connections to successful, longer-term nomads who may now spend less time in coworking spaces. Many of these more successful nomads still attend major events like this one, volunteering as mentors, networking with sponsors, assessing new talent, and staying connected to the social energy of the digital nomad community.

The novelty of joining a team of strangers for two days to start a business is highly appealing to digital nomads, who believe strongly in the importance of serendipitous events (i.e., "saying yes" to experiences that put them in contact with new people). Nicole, a twenty-six-year-old digital marketer from Paris, spontaneously attended Startup Weekend with a friend while visiting Bali as a work tourist. She told us that Startup Weekend introduced her to people who seemed both driven to be entrepreneurs and who could provide her with resources. Now she too is an entrepreneur and digital nomad:

> We go into Hubud, and there was Startup Weekend starting in two hours, and they have two spots left. At that point, I was starting to be interested in start-ups, but I was more interested in being on holiday, so I'm like, "No. Let's go to yoga." Eventually, [my friend] convinced me, and we took the last two spots. It was three guys pitching an idea, and we joined their team. . . . We worked with those guys, and then we became friends with them, and eventually, it's a long story, but out of the three, there were two Swiss guys, and they're now the partners in my company.

Despite success stories like Nicole's, the rapid-fire process of Startup Weekend more often does not result in the birth of an ongoing business.[50] At the Startup Weekend afterparty, we spoke to an experienced nomad who had just participated in a team with mixed results. He said that he liked his team's idea, which was actually his own idea, and was pleased that he had envisioned a way to pivot it in a new direction that had more potential to succeed. However, he felt disappointed by his teammates' low skill levels. When asked if he planned to continue working with any of his Startup Weekend team members, he actually laughed, "No. I don't think so." This sentiment that the community attracts many individuals whose competence is suspect, echoed by other highly skilled nomads in various settings, highlights the tension inherent in the open, inclusive environment of Bali's digital nomad community. With such low barriers to joining this working community, the most successful nomads have to carefully balance meeting *their* needs for a social, place-based experience of nomadic working with providing support to newcomers, many of whom may be floundering. Although they enjoy newcomers' energy, experienced nomads are mindful of the challenge to control social exchanges to experience that energy without allowing it to disrupt their own work goals.

CONCLUSION

Bali's digital nomad community is, first and foremost, a *work* community. Its unique value is to support a kind of avant-garde of working life in the new economy wherein individuals seek out creative ways to reclaim the opportunity to work according to their own values—an opportunity that they feel they were denied in their former lives back home.

As individuals reinvent their work identities in the company of like-minded others, Bali's digital nomad community encourages and aids their experimentation. But just as important to the community's draw and success are Bali's magical and practical dimensions, which we discussed in chapter 2. In particular, Bali's cost structure allows individuals access to the critical resource of *time* for personal, social, and business development. However, Bali's reduced resource pressure is not exclusively positive. As we noted, individuals may waste their time working with people who have positive attitudes but few skills, or they may be diverted on costly detours by accepting guidance from others with questionable expertise. Moreover, reduced resource pressure may encourage some to spend more time experimenting with identities and businesses that may yield little in terms of fulfillment of their more tangible goals.

As noted in chapter 3, digital nomads' preeminent value is *freedom,* and the community's raison d'être is to support this pursuit. Unsurprisingly, this thirst for freedom figures heavily into nomads' descriptions of what it means for them to succeed at work. Drea, a marketing professional and writer introduced in chapter 1, gave a definition of success that many others echoed: "The freedom to choose what I'm going to do at any moment in time."

When we pressed digital nomads to explicitly talk about their financial goals, most declined to reduce the discussion of freedom to earnings but rather talked about money in terms of ways it furthers their larger freedom-related goals. Estelle, a Canadian web designer whose views on minimalism we noted in chapter 3, started her first business in high school. Then, in college she outsourced her work-study job making presentation slides to a gig worker in Pakistan so that she could focus on more profitable free-lance design work. Now in her early twenties, she has already put together a significant resumé at a time when many of her peers at home are just beginning their first jobs. Our family spent a lot of time with her, and her favorite subject about work was how it was tied to freedom and money in broader terms—how work affects her larger goal of feeling long-term happiness and fulfillment: "I did a livestream about this in Ubud. I decided that my decisions were going to be made on sustainable happiness. I just want to be happy and build things. I want to own something that I build. I think that success is financial freedom and that location freedom is also really important." Ultimately, the path to such freedom seemed for most nomads to involve some form of self-employment. As Neil, a twenty-eight-year-old remote-working programmer from Denmark, put it: "My plan is certainly to become self-reliant economically as soon as possible. I like working at [my job], but in the long term that's not gonna take me where I want to go. . . . I want to have complete control over my time."

CHAPTER 5

Stages of Nomadism: Honeymooners, Visa Runners, and Resident Nomads

In the introduction, we classified digital nomads according to their lengths of stay, identifying three groups whom we termed *honeymooners*, *visa runners*, and *resident nomads*. Researchers have long categorized migrants according to length of stay.[1] Moreover, one of our first digital nomad informants alerted us to the fact that nomads' adjustment concerns tend to vary, depending on how long they have been in Bali. In this chapter, we bring these categories to life through extended vignettes of particular individuals. Unlike in typical sampling, we selected these individuals specifically for their potential to illustrate multiple themes from the book. For instance, Pauline, a honeymooner nomad, experienced many aspects of work and life in creative class cities that Millennials and younger people perceive to be particularly dissatisfying. Lucy, a visa runner, exemplifies how some skilled professionals leverage Bali's fluid, intimate community to transition to a new life of freelancing. Lorelei and Norman, resident nomads, provide an example of the pursuit of self-reinvention through entrepreneurship. The fact that all these individuals' prior lives were concerned with creative class work helps to explicate digital nomadism as a phenomenon of the new economy.

PAULINE: THE HONEYMOONER NOMAD

Digital nomads' fluid communities require a steady stream of newcomer energy to remain viable, and honeymooners—those who are new to a location and have stayed less than the sixty-day maximum on a tourist visa—are a reliable source of that energy. In digital nomad hubs, it is easy to identify nomads who are in the "honeymoon" stage, some of whom are entirely new to the nomadic lifestyle. Honeymooners are visibly and audibly bubbling with excitement about learning novel things, meeting like-minded people, and doing work on their own terms with views of pools and rice fields instead of being walled into cubicles with fluorescent lighting. A typical nomad newbie arrives with an over-packed or under-packed piece of luggage and a laptop, planning to travel to several locations in Southeast Asia, not yet realizing that a hectic travel schedule can cause burnout and interfere with work momentum. Honeymooners' eagerness extends to many novel experiences, including food, languages, cultures, friends, and work challenges.

Pauline, a twenty-eight-year-old New Yorker, arrived in Bali in August 2016. Two months earlier, she had quit her job in the music and advertising industries. We first spoke to Pauline in Ubud, just after her arrival. At that time, she was still getting her footing and trying to make friends and work contacts. Similar to many other nomads who vary their work locations, we would run into Pauline at nomad haunts both in Ubud and in the beach area of Canggu. One Sunday evening we decided to attend a music event in Penestanan, a village beloved by in-the-know expats who seek to avoid the tourist-filled central Ubud area in favor of life with locals and longer-term nomads. While we wandered down a narrow, dark, and winding path surrounded by lush bamboo, confused about how this route could ever lead to a public gathering place, we encountered an open-air restaurant called Yellow Flower. It was packed with expats who were eager to partake in this spot's first-rate vegetarian buffet.

We saw Pauline dining with a nomad friend from Puerto Rico, and she jumped up to greet us. As nomads do, we spontaneously dropped our plans, and they pulled up two chairs for us to join them. Over a meal of salads, soup, noodles, rice, tofu, corn fritters, and dessert, all for just $7.50 US, Pauline updated us on her life. Months later, we would spend even more time with her as co-participants in Startup Weekend. This is her story.

Early Life and Career Aspirations

Like so many nomads we met, Pauline's early life included formative travel experiences. Her father is French, and her mother is American, but they divorced when she was five, and her mother moved to the southern United

States. Though Pauline spent much of her childhood based in the New York City metropolitan area, she explained, "My dad is French, so I grew up traveling between the US and France."

A graduate of a small liberal arts college, Pauline majored in communications and also became increasingly interested in music. Knowing that she would need to be an ambitious self-starter to build a music-related career, she used her time in school to secure contacts that would lead to a job in the industry. Pauline's family is more privileged than most nomads, but she also took great pride in her efforts to be financially independent from them. She said that while others moved home and took advantage of family connections, she graduated from college and quickly secured entry-level work in a music advertising firm:

> They put me through college, so they were going to cut me off when I graduated. That's what they did with my siblings, so I negotiated with them. My brother went into consulting. My sister? My dad helped her out [by using] his contacts, and I was like, "I'm doing this on my own. I don't have any contacts in music. All the contacts I'm making are the ones that *I'm* making, personally. It's such a hard industry to break into. I know that I can do it, so just give me six months." So, I got a job in five. [laughs]

The Dream: A Creative Class Job in a Creative Class City

Aware that she is part of the often-reviled generational cohort called the Millennials, we noticed that Pauline had a habit of acknowledging Millennial clichés when speaking with us. Stereotypes of stigmatized people usually feature marginalized groups (e.g., members of minority ethnic groups, poor people, and those who are mentally ill or incarcerated), not middle-class Millennials. However, the popular media depict Millennials as plagued by major character flaws: they are alleged to be coddled, needy, lazy, delusional, entitled, narcissistic "trophy kids" who are unwilling to pay their dues.[2] Such character trait–related stigmas can be deeply discrediting, even for individuals who are part of a relatively privileged group.[3] Millennials were the largest segment of the labor force in 2018,[4] but they are often ridiculed and scorned as workers—warned that they should lower their standards for meaningful work, stop expecting that their first job will be their dream job, and refrain from job-hopping and asking colleagues and bosses for special privileges.

Diverging from such views of hard-to-manage Millennial employees, Pauline said she was appreciative, motivated, and excited just to be working in the music business. Even if the actual job as an assistant was less than ideal, she took every opportunity to demonstrate her potential and worth to her boss, colleagues, and the company's clients:

> I got so lucky. It was with a big advertising agency, and I got hired to be the assistant of the head of their music department, and our client was [a Fortune 100 financial services firm]. I didn't want to be an assistant, obviously, but I just saw it as such an awesome opening. . . . And yeah, I was mostly in the office, but I got to travel a lot with that team. I went to London, L.A. a bunch of times, other places in the Northeast, and I just really made myself indispensable to that team, and it was great. . . . I did that for over two years.

Pauline was patient as she waited for a promotion, but when a new opportunity with more challenging work eventually presented itself, she jumped at it. Pauline described her "dream job" at a firm that ran a thriving advertising agency as well as a music, culture, and lifestyle magazine:

> It was everything from scouting artists for endorsement deals, signing these partnership deals with artists, managing the relationships, finding sponsorship opportunities for the brand in music, managing those relationships. Obviously, day-to-day client stuff, doing sneaker collaborations with artists, and [extending] to what they're playing in [the client's] stores.

Though Pauline was excited to have more responsibility and a job in the music industry, her work satisfaction soon plummeted when she experienced problems with her new boss. As Pauline explained it, her supervisor's flaws were numerous: she failed to demonstrate appreciation for employees, refused to praise their work, and had a bad habit of micromanaging. Even though the company was new and had very young employees, Pauline described the workplace culture as creating an atmosphere of indignity.[5] Though Pauline respected the company, her boss seemed intent on creating conflict:

> So [the company] was great, but I had a psycho boss who made the experience horrible for me. . . . I started when I had just turned twenty-five, and she was maybe, had just turned thirty. She was young. It was a very young company, but she hated me, and she set out to make my life miserable from the day that I started. . . . Her communication was very, very brash, very harsh, and she did micromanage. On emails, she would just email me off to the side, and be like, "Why did you say it like this?" and give me these long emails, kind of ripping me apart. She wouldn't give me the freedom to have my own voice in what I was doing. . . . She was critiquing everything—how I handled myself on phone calls, my emails, my communication with the client.

In addition to the lack of autonomy over even the smallest tasks, Pauline said that her boss forced her to adhere to unreasonable budgets and imposed unnecessary restrictions that showed a lack of trust:

> My spending when I would go on trips? It was terrible. . . . She would just give me budgets that wouldn't work. Like, when I would go to L.A., which was really often, she gave me a $10-a-day meal budget, food budget. . . . It was bad, and the budget that she would give me for my accommodation was so low. So, I basically worked my way around it. After my first trip to L.A., which was horrible, and I was staying at this super-dodgy hotel, and I was starving—I was like, "I'm not doing this again." So, I found this badass Airbnb [laughs] that was under the accommodation budget. Then, I used the extra money for food, and I could keep food there. So, then she tried to tell me I wasn't allowed to Airbnb. I was like, "No. This is nuts." It was just sad. So, it was terrible because I loved the work I was doing, but the office environment was horrible.

As Pauline grew more dissatisfied with her work environment, she realized that she was burning out. She and her colleagues often commiserated about being underpaid and overworked, and they confided in each other about suspicions that they were victims of managerial abuse:

> They were working me nights and weekends, and not giving me the days back. I was just overworked, beyond stressed out by my work environment, just not happy, surrounded by people who were complaining a lot at the office. I was complaining a lot, which I just don't like to do. . . . I think, also, the anxiety of emails. I would get maybe 150 emails a day. I remember doing the math one day, and being like, "Wow." And my boss, she would say, right in the beginning, she would rip me apart. She was like, "Regardless of whether it's the weekend or not, if you get an email from a client, you have to respond within two hours." People were being so severely underpaid, and just worked to the bone. . . . They just hang your job over your head constantly. I remember that the first few months were really bad, and then it gradually got better, but they would never say that you did a good job, or they would never say thank you or anything.

Similar to the many Millennials who tend to favor open and frequent communication with supervisors,[6] Pauline tried to address her work concerns with her boss. Unfortunately, she did not get the response she was hoping for:

> There was never any positive reinforcement. . . . I just felt like I was doing a horrible job. You know? I had no idea. So, I went to talk to [my boss]. I said, "I just feel like everything I'm doing isn't right and that there's no positive reinforcement," and she literally said, "Your paycheck is your reinforcement."

Eventually, Pauline's poor relationship with her boss led to a showdown, and after almost two years on the job, Pauline was fired. She said that she knew that the termination was coming but felt relieved rather than distraught: "I had been planning an exit anyways. It was actually great. As I said, I was getting so burned out." Although she was not yet ready to leave New York permanently, her burnout began a process that would ultimately lead her to say goodbye to all that.

Waking Up from the Dream: A Gradual Process

Many nomads expressed disdain for the "busy trap"[7] that dominated their old lives in creative class cities, where a workaholic lifestyle is seen as a status symbol.[8] Pauline also tired of the hamster-wheel mentality: "The thing about New York is it's kind of like the battle of the busiest. It's like, 'Oh, you're so busy. No, *I'm* so busy.' It's kind of a competition." Yet even though job loss is routinely rated among life's most stressful events,[9] Pauline found that breaking free of the "busy" mentality proved to be the greater challenge. She wanted to use her unexpected freedom to take a break, but the idea of a "vacation"— staying in one place, even a beautiful place, and "doing nothing"—did not appeal to her: "I like to work. I like to always be progressing. If I just went to Hawaii, and just sat on my butt I'd be like, 'What am I doing?'" After deciding on a more open-ended form of travel to several locations, Pauline confronted the reality that she needed a source of income to sustain her until her trip. Fortunately, the job market provided immediate validation of her skills and worth: "After I got fired I actually got a job freelancing right away. I got fired on Wednesday, and I was hired on the spot on Monday . . . and I was making triple the amount of money I was making [before], so it was great."

Research on young professional expats has shown that they view themselves as a part of a global network society,[10] a cosmopolitan class of people who are like-minded in their regard for and attainment of international social and cultural capital.[11] These professionals feel a *privilege* of mobility even if they lack the wealth often associated with international travel.[12] Pauline had some savings and a small income stream. She planned to make the most of it by traveling to inexpensive places and living in shared housing:

> I was renting my apartment on Airbnb all the time. I was traveling for work a lot, so every time I traveled for work I would rent it, and then . . . I got $5,000 when my grandmother passed away, so I had kind of budgeted.

Refreshed and motivated after her trip, Pauline returned to New York with a clear sense of how to improve her life:

My plan was to go back to New York and freelance. . . . That's where all my contacts are. . . . I had this revived energy after traveling, where I knew so much more about myself, and I felt fucking badass—like, "I just traveled the world by myself for eight months. I can do anything." And I knew that I had skills . . . and I was also, at that point, connecting with so many other entrepreneurs and freelancers because that's what I wanted to do. . . . I didn't want to get a full-time job. I was like, "Hell no! I am not being stuck in an office again. My experience at [my last job] traumatized me, and I am not doing this again."

Despite her desire to freelance, Pauline was constantly hustling to find work. Although many seek autonomy, a flexible schedule, and freedom from an office, the job instability and work-related stress can take their tolls on freelancers' health and well-being.[13] Some have argued that the knowledge economy has reduced employment stability, which has led independent contractors like Pauline to take on stress-inducing risk and uncertainty.[14] Pauline decided that the remedy might be to travel again, but this time she would do so while also *working* as a digital nomad.

Although recent research emphasizes the new economy as a precarious place where companies are "loath to hire new employees into regular positions,"[15] Pauline's skills and networks allowed her to have a different experience: "While I was freelancing, I was getting a lot of job offers." Supporting this, she relayed the details of desirable job offers from prestigious companies. Even though she enjoyed her time as a freelancing digital nomad, she soon returned to New York to accept another full-time position. The job, which offered her a prime role with a music tech start-up, seemed like a perfect fit. However, the company was far less organized than it had appeared from the outside, and Pauline quickly realized that taking the job was a mistake:

> I was so miserable, and I was going home crying. I looked like crap. I would meet up with people who I respected—other entrepreneurs, freelancers who were doing so well— and they were like, "Are you okay? This is not the Pauline that I know." My energy was so low. I wasn't depressed, but I was so drained. I couldn't get to the point of depression because I knew that there's a solution to this, which is to not be here.

Then, on a weekend trip with a friend, Pauline developed the idea to start a business using her music and advertising expertise: "That was an aha moment. . . . I went back [home] and quit [my job]."

We pointed out to Pauline that she seemed to have done what most people would have advised: have an employment backup plan. She told us that freelancing and travel had ruined her ability to tolerate office life:

> When I was freelancing . . . I was like, "Well, if this doesn't work out, at least I can always go back to what I was doing before." . . . I had the contacts. I have the experience. I can

get a job. I used that as a fallback plan, and then I did it, and I was like, "Oh, my God. I can never do this again."

Becoming a Digital Nomad

Pauline, like many digital nomads we observed, had become steeped in *enterprise culture*, a neoliberal discourse that reconstructs the self and culture using capitalist language about markets, customers, brands, and management.[16] Embracing a self-styled entrepreneurial identity,[17] Pauline aspired to transform herself into a businesswoman and gain a new self-conception that, ironically, seemed impossible to achieve in New York City. The question was no longer whether she would become an entrepreneur but where she would do it.

> I was like, "Okay, so now where am I going to go?" [laughs] But I was really at peace with it because I had some money saved up. I knew I was over New York. I was like, "I can't do this. I can't be in New York. It's not my place right now." I was like, "I want to be in a very nurturing environment. I want to be in a place where it's beautiful, that's balanced, where there are other people like me, other entrepreneurs, other people who have gone against the grain, where I can live well for the amount of money that I have." I am not going to be feeling inspired, and great, and wanting to start my company if I am living with my parents.

Having stopped in Bali during her previous travels, Pauline was aware that the island had become a digital nomad hub. As a tourist, she had heard about Hubud, attended a talk there, and found the coworking space to be inspiring: "Hubud was awesome. It was great to see people working but also being here in Bali." Upon returning to New York, Pauline convinced a friend who had just quit her Los Angeles job to meet up with her in Bali. This time, she had something more than travel in mind. There, they would each work on their own start-up project:

> Once it kind of came into my mind, it was like there was no question that's what I'm doing. . . . And I literally left a month later from making that decision. . . . I knew that Hubud was it because so many entrepreneurs were there. The plan was to come here for three months. Very soon after, I realized that's not enough time. I just knew this was the path. I'm just getting so much done.

After coming to Bali, Pauline enrolled in a customized course through a local university in order to build skills relevant to her new business. She also worked hard to get the most out of the digital nomad community, especially at Hubud. Through making contacts there, Pauline located her first test client. Within a short time, she realized that Bali could be an affordable and hospitable base to relaunch her work life:

> When I first got here, and I went to my first Hubud event—just like two months ago . . . it was all about these people who had left corporate environments and started their own journey and their own businesses, and I was just feeling so at ease. It was like, "Oh, my God. It's so nice. I don't have to explain myself to anyone here. Everyone's in the same boat. Everybody's doing the same thing in a way." It's so good that you're in such a supportive environment, and everyone's willing to help out in any way they can, but it's also funny, because you're like, "Am I not special anymore? Is my idea not good?" Because there's so many other ideas that people are doing, too.

The fact that Pauline began to question the quality of her ideas reflects the emergence of a larger goal: to rediscover her creative identity. Pauline told us that she has since come to regard herself as a creative person, a new identity that she has actively cultivated along with her move into entrepreneurship. We were surprised to learn that back in New York she did not feel creative, especially since she worked in what most would consider a highly creative job—programming music for advertising clients. Pauline explained that the creative class hierarchy is especially rigid and visible in New York's music industry. Her contact with talented musicians and artists—what Richard Florida has called the "super-creative core"[18]—set a high bar for creative identity. Although she had no intention to become an actual musician, entrepreneurship provided a new sense of freedom, control, and creative challenge. When we asked if her new business was her passion, she enthusiastically said yes, but also emphasized that it *must* generate income to be a success.

When we last saw her, Pauline still had a long way to go toward realizing her dream business, but she had already transformed into a happier, more peaceful person. As of this writing, Pauline lives in Singapore with her boyfriend. In 2019 she once again accepted a job with a music-related technology start-up. However, her experience in a senior role at this new company in Singapore has been much more positive. Indeed, she told us that she has enjoyed a rare combination of "start-up life, flexibility, and having a hand in really creating something, while also joining the industry I love and missed after leaving NYC." She wrote to us that she is still working on her business, but it is "my side hustle": "There is so much less pressure to make [it 'big'] and I can have more fun with it now. Phew!" Still a nomad at heart, though, Pauline also wrote of a new project with her side business programming music for a major luxury hotel in Mexico, and that she and her boyfriend are "always looking for the next thing. We're thinking of our future steps—maybe in Africa. We want to be in a vibrant, developing culture."

Pauline's story emphasizes the factors that push individuals into nomadism, as well as the starts and stops as they struggle to leave home and begin the process of reinventing their lives. In the next section we turn our attention to nomads who have gained a foothold and are working to make this lifestyle a sustainable, longer-term choice.

LUCY: THE VISA RUNNER NOMAD

I found myself coming here initially for six to eight weeks, and then I just never came back after that. I mean, I've been back to visit, but loads of things happened after I arrived. I just stayed.

As we first described in the introduction, a visa run is a short trip out of the country for the purpose of renewing one's entry visa.[19] We use the term *visa runner* to describe nomads who decide to make such a trip in order to extend their stay. Although two months may seem like a long time for a traditional tourist, it goes quickly for digital nomads who are trying to establish new work lives, income streams, and routines. They feel the clock constantly ticking and are hard on themselves about reaching their goals within specific time frames. Despite its inconveniences, Bali has proven to be a "sticky" place, with most people whom we met staying longer than they had planned. Thus, visa runners are a large and important segment of the digital nomad community. They balance honeymooners' excitement with resident nomads' location expertise. Compared to honeymooners, visa runners make more focused contributions to Bali's digital nomad community. Armed with as much enthusiasm as the honeymooners but in possession of more local knowledge, higher levels of work momentum, and more extensive social capital, visa runners organize many local events and help acclimate the honeymooners as they adjust to Bali and nomadism.

Lucy is very well known in the nomad community, and getting to know her is easy. She exudes fun, with a loquacious, disarming, and mischievous sense of humor that is instantly endearing. For instance, Lucy thought it was hilarious that she got her newest tattoo at the weekly "Tacos and Tatt Tuesdays" event at a local digital nomad haunt. At thirty-three years old, she has come a long way from her stylish flat in chilly London working for celebrities and downing a bottle of wine every night. Without a hint of makeup and seemingly disdainful of fashion trends, Lucy has a slender yogi build, brown shoulder-length hair, and freckled skin; she's usually found in her simple uniform of a gray tank top and black shorts. As a freelance videographer with strong professional skills, Lucy quickly found a path to sustaining her new life. Similar to other nomads who have succeeded as freelancers, the intensity of her old life both prepared her for success in Bali and made the move seem necessary.

Before Bali: On Autopilot and without a Purpose

Lucy's life in London stands in stark contrast to the one she has cultivated in Bali, showing the importance of both place-based and situational factors in pushing and pulling digital nomads into the lifestyle. Back in London, Lucy had a life and career that many would envy. She began her career working in "reality" or unscripted television, and at first, she was content: "In the early stages, when I was young, I quite liked it because I was fresh out of university, and I was working [on] all these big shows. At the time, it was just fun because I didn't care, and I didn't have a lot of responsibility [other than work]."

Eventually, the novelty and excitement of simply landing jobs and succeeding in a creative career began to diminish. Realizing that she had just taken one opportunity after another, moving from contract to contract without taking the time to figure out what she wanted to do in the long term, Lucy began to actively search for more fulfilling work: "I definitely moved away from that [reality shows] quite consciously after I'd been in the industry for three or four years because I didn't want to be around that stuff that's so soul-destroying. It's such a manipulative industry if you take part in it." Yet even as she moved into other forms of video content, she continued to resent that she was directing her creative energies toward projects that conflicted with her personal values:

It wasn't that I wasn't getting to be creative. It was the fact that I felt like the purpose for what I was doing didn't feel good. I was working for this channel. We secured sponsorship by [an international beauty care company], so I was basically making content for [them]. I'm making these videos, which started out being—like, of course, they're always to make money—but it started out being for entertainment's sake. . . . I was basically selling makeup to teenage girls, which is exactly *not* what I wanted to be doing. I'm a minimalist who doesn't believe we need to spend this money on clothes and makeup and stuff like that, and there I was selling makeup to teenagers.

As her career priorities changed, Lucy also began to realize that London's creative class lifestyle was holding her back:

In London I was drinking a lot. If you spend any time in the UK, you know what the drinking culture is like. In the city that drinks the most, in the industry that drinks a lot, in the group of friends that drinks a lot, I was probably the worst out of everyone. . . . It would come in phases, but I would be drinking to the point of blacking out a couple times a week, and to me, that wouldn't be that weird.

Similar to many other digital nomads, Lucy's changing work goals were a catalyst to transforming other facets of her life:

> I decided I wanted to quit the job I was doing. God, it had taken me such a long time to work up the courage to leave—not because I was scared about leaving, [but because] I was worried about what I was going to do. . . . I definitely had this plan [that] I was going to do video in a different way.

Although her employer tried to retain her ("I handed in my notice, and they basically said, 'Do whatever you want. Work wherever you want. Work from home. We just don't want you to leave'"), she had lost the motivation to stay in her job. Then, just like Vance, one of our London informants who found out about digital nomadism while at a coworking space there, Lucy became inspired when she came across some marketing materials for a Bali soft-landing program:

> I sat in a coffee shop, not really working, and I saw this thing called "Tribewanted." ... There's one in Bali, and the idea is that you're with people who are working on projects, and you come out, and work together, and share skills and whatever, and meet at Hubud a couple days a week. Anyway, I saw that and was like, "I think I want to go do that."

With a new plan and a little bit of savings, Lucy quit her job and left for Bali.

Lucy's Healthy and Happy Nomad Lifestyle

When we first met her, Lucy was living in an open-air villa in Bali:

> It's kind of like a retreat space. They have a yoga shala and pool, a main house, and some self-contained apartments. It's also the kind of place where there's people living here for a week, or two weeks, or three weeks, and there's a couple of people here who are here long term. I'm here for six months at least. I just signed a six-month contract.

To understand her new nomad life in Bali, Lucy insisted that we attend her favorite event, one she rarely misses: ecstatic dance. Ecstatic dance, which many nomads had recommended to us, requires courage. Dancers attend this drug-free and alcohol-free event at The Yoga Barn to have fun and create a feeling of freedom, empowerment, and connection. Talking is prohibited, but people silently dance as if they are in a nouveau-hippie-style club. We were surprised to learn that it occurs on Sunday mornings. Though some go to the Friday night version of ecstatic dance, we went on

Sunday because it was marketed as "family day." We were curious about this because very few expat spaces in Bali are child-friendly.

On the Sunday we arrived, hardly any children were there, though we did see a couple dancing while their baby nursed, protected by noise-canceling headphones. We lined up with more than a hundred enthusiastic expats, all wearing wristbands and awaiting admission. This event almost always sells out, so people arrive early for a ticket. We saw a Netflix production team filming, so excitement may have been especially high. Even on a Sunday morning, on family day, and with everyone sober, it was a sexually charged environment. Dancers of all ages made exaggerated eye contact, grinding, gyrating, and seducing to the sounds of drumming and trance music at what looked to us to be an exhibitionist dance party.

As expected, we saw Lucy, clad in yoga shorts and sports bra, sweating and dancing to thumping music. She immediately introduced us to her friend, laughing as she told him, "They're professors writing a book about me." We clarified that we were writing about digital nomads, and he frowned and said, "There is nothing *digital* about this place." We found this comment amusing, as we watched him dance to a laptop playing electronic music. Lucy explained that while digital nomads are focused on self-reinvention through work and earning money in new ways, spirit-seekers often want to distance themselves from this group. Lucy, straddling both worlds and retaining her cynical British wit, could not resist a dig at the spirit-seekers: "There is a big difference between the digital nomad entrepreneur scene here and the more spiritual side of this community. My [spirit-seeker friend who] I was out with last night? He's just a dude who doesn't have a job who's just been discovering himself and the world for the past year."

Lucy left us so she could continue dancing, eager to take advantage of every minute of this experience that brings her so much joy. Yet even though she has not fully embraced Bali's spiritual fringe, Lucy reflected that she has become tolerant of alternative spiritual practices that she does not personally endorse:

> I've become so much less cynical about this kind of stuff since I came here. . . . If someone would say, "Oh, you're a Libra. Oh, that's because you're a Libra," I'd *have* to tell them that I thought astrology was complete shit and have to explain *why* it was. . . . Now, not only am I like, "I wouldn't say that," [but] I also wouldn't *think* that, and even though I'm still not one for astrology, I'm just so open to the possibility that there's so much in all of these things.

Remote-ivated: Facing the Learning Curve of Digital Nomad Work

As much as Lucy has embraced Bali's opportunities for individual trans-formation, she chose to become a visa runner because of its digital nomad community. Far from London, surrounded by like-minded others, Lucy has seen her personal life flourish and has gained work direction and satisfaction. Perhaps, most important, she has found the nomad hub to be a sustainable income-generating opportunity. As a result, Lucy has rekindled a love of her craft.

In chapter 4 we noted that many digital nomads continue to do the same kind of work abroad as they did in their old lives. Although Lucy initially questioned whether she would find freelancing videography work that would sustain her and feel meaningful, she soon learned that her skills were in high demand. This has presented two major challenges: managing the mix of projects she accepts and controlling her workaholic tendencies.

Digital nomads tend to conceive of their work as a portfolio of gigs and projects. This means they have both the burden and privilege of managing that portfolio. Lucy still pursues highly compensated work to pay the bills, but now she rejects work that conflicts with her values. In addition, finding herself flooded with offers, she specifically reserves time to create videos for projects that closely *align* with her values. For example, Lucy enjoys working for charities and businesses that benefit Bali: Balinese children who need money to pay for school, Indonesian disaster relief, and local anti-plastic environmental campaigns.

However, Lucy has also found that working in alignment with her values often translates into accepting contracts from smaller clients and that these more fulfilling projects can interfere with her larger, better-paying jobs. The fact that she charges less than her usual fee for charitable work means that she needs to carefully consider how to fit in smaller, purpose-driven jobs between her more lucrative gigs:

> At the moment, I'm wrapping up things for people, stuff I filmed, little jobs. It's half a day's work or a day's work and at a reduced rate. I need to finish that, and I can't finish it because I've got bigger jobs, and I'm doing video for a [big] Kickstarter campaign, which is a more typical thing that I do. That was a five- or six-day shoot, a seven- or eight-day edit.

This leads to Lucy's second problem: time. By carving out more time for meaningful work, she has not met her original aspiration to work fewer hours. Though it was obvious that Lucy is proud that she now uses her professional talent to bring visibility to causes that are close to her heart, she lamented, "I don't have time for [a passion project]." She has fantasized about taking a month-long break from work to focus on cultivating a different interest or passion, but, she said, "That month never comes because I'm always working."

Lucy said she is working toward making time for herself by controlling her workday to fit her natural and preferred rhythms of "early to bed, early to rise." As a honeymooner, Lucy was swept up by the excitement of finding like-minded community at Hubud. As a visa runner, she has started to use coworking spaces to manage her competing desires for social contact and productive, focused work. Lucy feels a specific sense of interactional freedom at Hubud: she can use her discretion to choose whether or not to be distracted:

> I think I've always enjoyed having colleagues, and that's always been a big part of most jobs that I've done, and I've always been really lucky where I've worked. I just got on with people really, really well. But sometimes, working with people *directly* can affect your friendship with them in some way, and it's really, really nice that I get to have all these colleagues that I work *beside* every day, but I don't have to work *with* them. Some of them I do work with. . . . I just really enjoy *that* aspect of it. There's just always stuff going on there. . . . It feels like I have all the social benefits of going into work and all that social side of it, but I don't actually have to work *with* anyone.

Interestingly, when we conducted observations at Hubud, our experiences were similar to Lucy's. We observed Hubud's social aspects but also found that the main working space was sufficiently quiet for us to concentrate.

Lucy explained how her coworking routine helps keep her schedule consistent, but she still struggles to lower her total number of working hours:

> I tend to go into Hubud at seven [in the morning], four days a week . . . until about two, and then pick up a laptop and do a couple hours over the weekend. I'm trying to get to a point where I'm working from seven 'til two, three days a week, and the rest of time I'm supposedly not doing anything.

Although Lucy exhibits a self-driven work discipline, she told us that she rejects the idea that maximizing efficiency produces the best work outcomes, especially for creative people. For instance, Lucy seemed proud that she made a spontaneous choice to rearrange the entire previous workday so that she could spend time at a friend's house, having coffee and talking. She has learned to loosen up some of her old work habits, grant herself freedom from the grind, and allow herself time to socialize—all of which have stoked her creativity.

Same Work Identity but Now Freelancing and Networking Abroad

Unlike many digital nomads we met, Lucy has no desire or need to create a completely new work identity, to pivot her skills to something entirely different, or to become an entrepreneur. She is experiencing creative fulfillment simply by using her skills on some jobs that agree with, or at least do not contradict, her values, and by controlling her time and workload. This puts her on a different path from digital nomads who feel the need to craft and perform completely new work identities. She poked fun at some nomads' tendencies to create lists, check boxes, and broadcast their lofty goals:

> They're like, "This is my bucket list, and I'm going to put this bucket list on the internet, and then tick it off publicly to show I did all this cool shit. I'm gonna have a 20K month, and I want to have a podcast on the Top Ten in iTunes, and I want to visit ten countries this year."

Like all freelancers, Lucy still needs to make work contacts. She admitted to us that coworking spaces are not just for finding community and meeting work goals; they are for securing work contracts. Because Lucy conducts video shoots on location in Bali, and some of her work may be considered illegal in Indonesia, she must keep a low profile when online: "I can't post on Facebook: 'I'm a videographer. Do you need one?'" When we asked how she obtains freelance contracts, she explained:

> Work-wise, it tends to normally be [that] I'll be in Hubud, I'm getting a juice or coffee, and then I'll talk to someone, and [they'll] be like, "Oh, I need video," or "I know someone who needs a video." Or, I'll just be in there, and just put a tripod up next to the camera, [and] someone will come up that day and be like, "Do you do video? I need that," or "I know someone who needs that."

She also articulated the role of social media in finding work in Bali, telling us that while she might typically gain fifty Facebook friends in a year in London, "It seems like an average to gain here is like, 400 or 500." At the same time, Lucy admitted that she has a freelancer's eye for making useful contacts: "They're not all friends. Some of them are people who are trying to promote something. . . . I usually accept because maybe they'll want me to make a video."

Although securing work as a freelancer abroad presents challenges, some aspects of working in Bali are much easier when compared to London, or what Lucy calls "the real world." With its lax regulatory environment and tourism economy, Lucy can work in Bali without the bureaucratic processes typical at home. For instance, she explained that a video shoot back in Europe requires tons of paperwork for government permits that allow her to shoot on location:

> There's just no way in [Europe] I could do the type of [projects] that I do [now] because you have to jump through so many hoops to even make something there. . . . This woman

is coming over from Mexico, and she said, "I heard you are good." . . . We're going to film next week—without all this red tape and forms and stuff that you need when you work in the real world. . . . Here, you don't.

With her strong and stable professional identity, Lucy has found ways to thrive as a freelancer in Bali's digital nomad community. We end our portrait of Lucy by considering how she has come to regard this transient community as "hers."

"New Best Friends": Embracing the Fluid and Intimate Community and Social Distance from Home

When she was new to the digital nomad scene, Lucy experienced doubts about living in a place where the community members are so transient. During her honeymooner period, still a cynic, Lucy was constantly comparing herself to others, questioning everyone's motives, trajectories, and the soundness of their choices, including her own:

> When I was dealing with worrying about should I be going, or should I be staying, sometimes I didn't like hearing people say, "Oh, now I'm going back to Vancouver in a few weeks," or "I'm going back to New York in a few weeks," because I'm not.

Some visa runners and resident nomads admitted to us that they hesitate to invest too much time in getting to know honeymooners, as many of them leave within a month or two. Yet in chapter 3 we noted that digital nomads tend to view the benefits of fluidity (e.g., supporting values of freedom and exposure to new arrivals' energy) as outweighing the costs of having friends constantly leaving. By the time Lucy had decided to renew her visa, she had already learned about and accepted the fluidity of the digital nomad community. We asked whether she felt ambivalent about befriending honeymooners, but she said: "I don't think I'm like, 'Oh, I don't want to be friends with you because you're going to be gone in three weeks.' I don't think that goes through my head. Consciously, it certainly doesn't." Instead, Lucy believes that transience is a legitimate pathway to intimacy. She has made new best friends by opening up to people who are at all stages of nomadism, and she appreciates that people in the community automatically understand her choices and are not invested in her returning to "normal" life:

> There's just this constant stream of people going in and out, so if you're someone who makes friends easily—and it's easy to do it here—it's almost like it's done for you. These

people are just presented to you as new friends all the time. You don't even have to try. . . . It's almost like I felt like they are my best friends after two days because they already knew about me, and I've already got to know them, and it's just easy.

Lucy says that the community fluidity makes Bali's coworking spaces special. They are sites of reunions with old friends and are places where owners, managers, and members are intentional about encouraging new relationships. This is another aspect of what distinguishes coworking in nomad hubs from the experience of interacting with work colleagues in a company or sitting alongside others in a traditional coworking space or coffee shop within a busy Western city: "The other thing about Hubud—it's not like you're going into a company, and you're the new person. Everyone's different degrees of new. . . . Not like [it is] in London."

However, similar to other digital nomads, Lucy's embrace of the new community has further weakened her ties to home: "I don't miss my family, to be honest." We were surprised to hear this, but she explained her reasoning. First, Lucy's parents are healthy, so she does not feel concerned about them needing her as a caregiver: "I tend to be more in touch with them when *I* need something from *them*. I don't feel like they really need anything from me, and they would quite happily not hear from me for a couple months." Second, as much as she loves them, Lucy said that her parents epitomize the clichéd portrait of reserved Brits—averse to expressing strong feelings and unable to meet Lucy's emotional needs.

Even in an era of constant communication via texting and video calls, most digital nomads decrease the frequency of their contacts with people back home. When we asked Lucy about her London friends, she explained the ways in which digital nomadism creates *social distance*, a perceived remoteness or lack of intimacy, from people back home:

> I do miss some close friends, but not as much as I thought that I would. . . . I think we all—people who come here and do this long-term—you just feel this disconnect with your friends back home, and then you start to feel way more connected with your friends here. Then, you feel elements of—people are jealous of the stuff that you're doing.

She went on to provide an example of her feelings of social distance and mentioned a mutual acquaintance of ours. The woman, a life coach, lives in Bali, and she had recently authored and released a book: "She was saying, with her book, she feels like she's had so much more support from people [in Bali] since she left [her country] in the three years . . . than she's had from what she *thought* were her long-term friends."

In addition to the basic ways in which spatial distance from home creates social distance, Lucy thinks that nomadism triggers negative feelings from people back home, which further weakens social bonds and increases detachment from family and friends. As another example of how nomadism creates discord with loved ones, Lucy explained that she has tried to stay connected with people back home, but she has found that her friends have reacted in one of three ways. The first response has been disinterest, as some friends simply no longer relate to her. The second was jealousy. After all, the decision to become a digital nomad occurs within a larger context of social comparison and self-evaluation, made worse by social networking sites. When nomads actively post photos and status updates boasting of their healthy lifestyles and adventures, they risk alienating friends back home who are comparing their own lives to those of their nomad friends. Lucy's friends have made disapproving and skeptical comments, so she has learned to tread lightly. However, she has found that it is difficult to maintain authentic bonds with old friends while avoiding talking about nomadism or Bali.

A third reaction Lucy has noticed is resentment. Sometimes, her friends complain about their lives, framing her new life as "lucky" and thereby denying her a sense of accomplishment or agency:

> You have to be careful. Say you've come here, and you're literally having the most amazing life, and you've gone from this job that—yeah, it might have been fun—but it was kind of soul-destroying in terms of the hours and the amount of money and the amount I was working. A huge part of me living here is healthy lifestyle and the weather. That's massive for me, and you see your friends *not* doing that, and then people say, "Oh, you're so lucky to be there," or "How are you doing this?" . . . I think they just assume that I'm really lucky, or I don't know what they think, but I don't think they think that *I've* created this myself and worked for it.

Lucy is especially offended when friends imply that digital nomadism is only working for her because she is rich, entitled, or fortunate:

> I didn't have much. I just lived really cheap, but I think that you want to say to people, "You can do this as well." Like, "Here, I'll help you. Show you how to do it." Like, "No matter what relationship you're in or what job you think you can't leave. You can. You just don't realize it. It's not going to be easy." You kind of want to say that to them and help them, but you also don't want to be lecturing people and saying, "I think my life's better than yours, and you should do what I do, and then you can be happy like me," because people can really interpret that as being judgmental. It doesn't come from that place. . . . I've tried to have this conversation with friends. People interpret that as saying that we think they're leading boring lives that they should change.

Like most digital nomads, Lucy greatly objects to her friends' negative thinking, complaining, lack of agency, and their seeming unwillingness to confront their own paralysis about their problems. Digital nomads often want to evangelize and empower others to live in a way that will make them happier. Though soul-searching conversations are the norm in Bali's self-selected digital nomad community, these kinds of discussions often go over poorly with outsiders who see themselves as entrenched in their work and family lives back home. In this way, the expected social distance that often comes with a move to another country is exacerbated by friends from home who no longer relate to nomads' new lives and worldviews and actively display disinterest, jealously, and resentment.

Visa runners like Lucy are transitioning from experimenting with work tourism to making it a longer-term lifestyle:

> I'm definitely becoming a long-term person. I can see there's a difference between people who have been here [for] years, people who come and go, and people who spend half the year here . . . I was kind of like, "Shit. Everyone's leaving. Everyone's going home, and I don't want to." I was like, "Why do I not want to go?" And I can't explain it, but I just don't.

As of mid-2020, Lucy is still in Bali. In our final vignette, we describe the experiences of those who decide to stay long-term.

LORELEI AND NORMAN: RESIDENT NOMADS

For those who become captivated by the digital nomad lifestyle, the pressing question becomes, "How can I sustain this?" Our interview data and the membership statistics provided by coworking space managers led us to conclude that most of Bali's digital nomads are highly transient, and almost all of them move on to other locations within a year. However, a subset of digital nomads stays for far longer. *Resident nomads*—those who have been based in Bali for over a year and have no immediate plans to leave—have come to understand the benefits of mostly working from a single nomad hub. They still cherish the novel experiences and inspiration that come from international travel, but staying put has actually led them to have more time that truly feels "free."

Applied to digital nomads, the word "resident" requires qualification. In general, resident nomads spend about eight to nine months of the year in Bali and then travel back home and to other countries in the summer months and at the end of the calendar year. Despite their long tenure in Bali, resident nomads remain very attached to their identities as nomads. Insisting that they remain true nomads at heart, nearly everyone in this category expressed to us their intent to leave Bali permanently at *some point*.

In fact, several times, as we talked to people who had been based there for years, we would imply that they appeared to *live* in Bali, but they would reply by doubling down on their claim that they are true location-independent nomads, an identity that signals an embeddedness in the lifestyle and communicates a level of trust and credibility within a digital nomad hub.

Lorelei, age thirty-three, and Norman, age thirty-six, are from the same western European town. The couple moved to Bali in 2014 and have been based there ever since. We conducted separate interviews with each of them and spent time with them in Bali. One particularly sweltering day, Lorelei spotted us in a raw vegan restaurant near our rented house, and she seemed so excited to reunite and meet our three-year-old daughter that she spontaneously abandoned her table to join us for hours. Another time, we made plans for them to come to our small villa. On a rainy night, we all sat around a table in our sheltered outdoor kitchen while our children slept inside. In true nomad fashion, instead of a bottle of wine or a six-pack of beer, they presented us with a gift of several one-liter bottles of fresh coconut water sold by a local Balinese family.

Still in our own honeymoon phase, we were in awe of Bali's indoor-outdoor housing style and were eager for them to see our place. They humored us, but then showed us photos of their large, luxurious hillside villa, the kind for expats who sign long-term leases and who have no children likely to fall off scenic cliffs and destroy white linens. Lorelei explained their decision to stay in Bali: "We just agreed to a long-term lease, which would be eight months renting a house." We laughed at their characterization of an eight-month lease as "long-term," but we understood why they thought this level of commitment was so momentous. Such a contract is unthinkable to the many digital nomads who have nominal savings, have few long-term plans, or get antsy when staying in one place for more than a month.

Before Bali

Norman and Lorelei's route to Bali, though unique in some ways, was similar to that of many other nomads in that it has involved personal struggles. Norman's parents both died of cancer by the time he turned eighteen, and after a time of aimlessness, Norman connected with an international spiritual community run by an Indian guru. He has since come to conclude that "the Center," as he calls it, had many cult-like features. Still, Norman recalled that his time in the group was not all harmful. He actually developed talents and learned skills that paved the way for his current success. For instance, he traveled to participate in and lead meditations, learned graphic design skills to develop marketing materials for the programs, and found he had a natural talent for connecting with people as he persuaded employers to hire him for jobs. Soon, he harnessed these skills and talents into a side business as a marketing consultant. But after living in London for four years while employed in a branch of the Center, Norman had tired of working for both the Center's businesses and his marketing clients. He had also become disenchanted with London's cultural obsession with intense work, wealth accumulation, and materialism:

> I still valued money, and I would have liked to have made more, but it wasn't a goal because I had enough. . . . I would have never sacrificed my time for the money. My time was much more valuable—my meditation time, my ability to just take a month off and go somewhere. . . . I could feel it creeping in a little bit in London, like, "Oh, they're making this much a year. What kind of a job do I need to get to make that?" But the moment I would realize what it would take to make that kind of money, [I'd] be like, "Oh, forget about that. I'm never ever going to go be somebody's bitch."

Becoming distanced from the Center, Norman turned to a self-help book by a motivational speaker, who is also a self-proclaimed visionary and a consultant known for a popular TED Talk and book about the makings of great leaders:

> I was getting inspired by Simon Sinek—you know, "finding your why."[20] He's a marketer, and he wrote a book—*Start with Why*. Sinek basically goes into a whole thing with how to start with "why" and the vision-driven business. "What do you want to contribute to the planet?" Have *that* be a main driver on everything else.

Contemplating his options, Norman decided that it was time to fully disengage from the Center: "I wasn't as happy as I used to be, and I knew I needed to make a move."

Unlike Norman, Lorelei's early years were more conventional. After earning a master's degree in anthropology, she began searching for a PhD dissertation project: "At that time, science was the only thing I could think of as a career or what I *really* wanted to do." Her struggles began when she failed to receive funding to conduct her research. On a whim and with little to lose, Lorelei considered a teaching career. A school immediately hired her to teach biology and physics to students between the ages of ten and fourteen. Initially, she enjoyed it, but she soon realized that her values conflicted with elementary and middle school teachers' socialization responsibilities:

> Since I have this strong background in social sciences and questioning our norms all the time, it's very hard to step in and teach students things I don't believe in. I don't subscribe to most of the things we get taught.

Lorelei's comments about the values mismatch between herself and mainstream educational systems were echoed by three other former teachers during our fieldwork. Bert, a former teacher who happens to be from the same country as Lorelei though they do not know each other, had a similar perspective on how the bureaucracy of the teaching profession made him choose to leave. Although he developed a successful pedagogy that was appreciated by students and parents, he ran afoul of other teachers, who began to unite against him. He told us, "Either I would have to go on the fighting path . . . [or o]therwise, I would have to give in to the system. But then I chose to leave the system." Now a parent of three small children, his new worry is about teachers and school systems indoctrinating them: "Having seen the other side of school—like, the conference room and the teachers—I'm thinking, 'Would I say yes to having my kids under the supervision of someone who, personally, I don't respect for their worldview, for their mindset, for their rigidity?'" Such mismatched values help to explain why nomads did not simply seek out new professions at home.

Alongside her frustrations with teaching, Lorelei continued to struggle with her lingering academic aspirations. For Lorelei, the lack of funding and increased stress translated into thoughts about spirituality and philosophy as she searched for meaning in what was happening. On this search for self-discovery, she concluded of her PhD that "it just didn't want to happen": "You're in your late twenties, and the only idea you have is *science*, and all you get is rejection, and I lived for that. . . . My only friends were colleagues. . . . Then, I decided, 'Okay. This is enough. I need to find another way.'"

Things began to change when Lorelei and Norman met at a holiday party in their hometown and hit it off immediately. After "doing a relationship trial run" for a month on vacation in Vietnam, they decided to move to Bali to sort out the next steps for their lives. Although they chose Bali in part because Lorelei had obtained some research funding for a project in Indonesia, she knew by this point that research was likely not her future. As she thought about her many struggles to launch a career, she also noticed her increasing attraction to a less conventional lifestyle:

That's how the Bali story starts. . . . I was in a café, and I read this magazine—a really beautiful magazine of alternative lifestyle and yoga and the green movement—and I remember reading it and saying, "This sounds like my people."

Recovery and Reinvention in a Nomad Hub

During their first months on the island, Lorelei and Norman connected to Bali's expatriates. Lorelei quickly found friends in the spiritual expat community and began to change her mindset from that of a tourist into someone making a long-term change. Having recently left the Center, Norman "liked the whole vibe" of Bali because it reminded him of the positive aspects of living in a spiritual growth community but with the added features of a digital nomad hub. He was especially intrigued—if also a bit intimidated—by the new entrepreneurial horizons found within the coworking spaces: "I remember I would start going to workshops [at Hubud] and stuff, and that was pretty interesting, but I remember it feeling like it was expensive, and we couldn't afford it because there was only so much that we could spend every month."

While Norman searched for an entry point to leverage his marketing skills and entrepreneurial interests, Lorelei was on the verge of abandoning academia, the source of career and personal identities:

> I had a huge crisis in the meaning of my life. What should I do next? I was very restless and had a huge urge to create and to do meaningful stuff, to figure it out, to have a plan, to know the way, to *work*. . . . I started a blog, but I kept questioning: "What am I doing? What does that lead to?"

Barely making ends meet, the couple was paying their expenses with credit cards and the remains of Lorelei's graduate school stipend. They knew that if they wanted to transition from the experimental honeymooning stage to the more committed step of visa running, they had to find a new income stream. Though Norman still felt insecure about his lack of college credentials and formal training, his work experience during his last year in London prepared him for freelancing. In addition, Lorelei felt encouraged by the digital nomad community. For instance, when she described her skills as limited, they would push back and present counternarratives that empowered her. Soon, Lorelei began rising to their challenges and started to reimagine her work experiences, talents, skills, and career options. For instance, Lorelei told us that she came to realize that as a graduate student, she had actually created content and branding for a large e-learning project. Together, the couple pooled their skills and pursued freelance digital marketing work as a path to a sustainable income.

To "launch" their agency, Norman and Lorelei put out the word that they were "open to do stuff"—a typical signal within Bali's underground digital nomad employment market that one is looking for work and is ready to hustle. As discussed in chapter 4 and above in Lucy's story, digital nomads frequently draw on the community as an employment market. They tapped their Bali networks to secure gig work that would pay the bills, hoping that larger projects would follow. Before long, Norman and Lorelei were building websites for both digital nomads and members of Bali's expat spiritual community.

After a "couple of months" of "just getting by," Norman and Lorelei met Natalia, a successful digital nomad entrepreneur in her forties. Originally from the Middle East, Natalia owned two software businesses and was launching another. Norman told us that she became their key client: "We branded that and did a whole thing for her, and we got along quite well. She's her own kind of character—a little older than we are, but there are elements where we connected." Lorelei told us: "That was a good thing to challenge my belief system: 'Am I ever to make money here?' It's possible."

"Getting Serious": Committing to Entrepreneurship

During their first year in Bali, as Lorelei and Norman engaged in personal transformations, became visa runners, grew their networks, and engaged in more freelance work, they gradually saw the island as a base from which to live their new lives. Bali's constant influx of newcomers provides fresh narratives about the shortcomings of corporate and conventional life and injects the community with the encouragement to continue to seek sustainable freedom from it. New people are always arriving, eager to tell their stories of escaping traditional work organizations and seeking to explore new ways to create an alternative work life. Like many Europeans, the couple said that their home societies tended toward negative views of entrepreneurship, so they were captivated by expats who seemed optimistic and committed to starting their own business:

> We had two friends over, and they were in their fifties, around fifty, fifty-five, something like that, and [there are] so many people like that here who take time off to do some healing work. . . . They were talking about how they were running out of money, and they would need to find a stream of income soon. One of them—she was actually quite [a] successful businesswoman—she said, "But I'm not going to work for anyone anymore." And the other one said, "Yes. Me, too." And I got scared when I listened to their conversation. I thought, "Well, actually, me, too." But those decisions, they can be a huge driver and a huge motivator to get serious about stuff.

For those who are ready to commit to changing their career path, Bali's digital nomad community provides a nurturing atmosphere to figure it all out. Lorelei explained how the supportive, entrepreneurial culture oriented toward freedom, in combination with the personal development ethos of letting go of the past, began to transform her entire mindset and clarified her sense of purpose, her priorities, and her trust in her own intuition and judgment:

> What I learned here in Bali is to start listening to life's feedback. If there are too many no's, then don't do it. Go for the yes flow. Really, follow the yes. There is a lot of satisfaction in that. I don't know if you are meant to do something . . . but what I do know is I want to be happy. That, I know for sure. And also, I want to have a positive impact on people and on the environment if I can, so I'm working towards that. That's enough. How, and what I do, it is in second and third place.

Armed with a new mindset and a focused purpose, the couple was keen to say yes when Natalia approached them with an opportunity related to Amazon dropshipping. The three of them began discussing the benefits of owning a business tied to a physical product, including the prospect of earning passive income (a nomad aspiration mentioned in chapter 4). As they began brainstorming ideas and identifying consumer needs, they all agreed that they had noticed that Bali expats and tourists often complained about Bali's scarcity of natural personal hygiene products. They found this unmet market need to be especially surprising because Bali has a significant yogi and vegan community and most Balinese engage in and believe in medicinal uses of coconut, tree oils, herbs, and plants.

Believing they would be able to solve a consumer problem, the team gained the momentum to take action. Natalia offered seed funding using the classic entrepreneurial mechanism of credit card debt.[21] Natalia had identified a high-quality online course to teach them about this type of business, but it was scheduled to start soon so they had to decide fast:

> She asked us to take part in an Amazon course that we can use as a launchpad. . . . We had like, twenty-four hours to decide because the deadline for the course was approaching, and we needed to set up for that, and she had received a credit card from American Express offering her $10,000 interest-free for a year.

Norman now reflects on this time of fast-paced risk-taking as evidence of the couple making heart-driven decisions and the power of timely, serendipitous meetings that only happened because the couple placed themselves in the right place and among the right people.

Norman explained the nuts and bolts of the business's progression as the team transitioned from bootstrapping to turning a profit:

> We did everything properly the way we learned in that Amazon course. . . . We didn't pay for any advertising. We didn't pay for any media. We just called a couple of friends and sent them messages like, "Can you buy this and give us a review?" and people did

that. . . . We showed up on page one [on Amazon] within seventy-two hours, and we had our first ten reviews, and we got traction and organic traffic, and people started "liking" us, and we've seen exponential growth ever since. . . . This year we started paying ourselves. There's money coming out of it right away, in under a year.

Lorelei and Norman's case shows how nomads may first leverage a supportive community in order to obtain freelance work and then use it to pivot into entrepreneurship. As orders increased, Norman and Lorelei stopped accepting freelance marketing work so they could focus on their new business. Yet their greatest sense of achievement is that they have proven to themselves and others that it is possible to make a living from a business that is in harmony with one's personal values. Norman explained: "Basically, we just used what I've been preaching to other people as a way of doing business: being honest, being sincere, paying people a little more than they expect, making sure everybody's happy—customers, suppliers." As a result, their products have a high proportion of five-star reviews on Amazon, a feat that may help their products to continue to garner attention in Amazon's vendor ranking system.[22] Thus, Lorelei and Norman have leveraged Bali's digital nomad hub to reinvent themselves as values-driven entrepreneurs.[23]

Norman and Lorelei represent one side of a significant split we observed among digital nomad entrepreneurs: the desire to make money while having a positive social impact on the world. This view is not entirely free of the feel-good utopianism espoused by tech entrepreneurs even in the face of significant criticisms.[24] For instance, when we asked what kind of social impact they would ultimately like to have, Norman summarized a familiar digital nomad agenda of "empowerment programs," teaching "entrepreneurial thinking," and "learning your way out of the hamster wheel." Echoing a common view among these socially conscious nomads, Norman told us that money "has an energy aspect." Norman's view is that money, when it flows as a *byproduct* of one's motivation rather than the origin of it, can enable scaling of a positive vision to larger audiences.

On the other side of this split among digital nomad entrepreneurs, many individuals were completely self-focused and discussed their goals only in terms of freedom, money, and productivity. For instance, we met Amazon sellers who had no attachment to the products that they were selling, some who did not personally believe in their products, and some who were selling services and products that appear to deceive people in some way. Norman agreed that many people get caught up in the dream of being rich and having passive income, such as the many followers of *The 4-Hour Workweek* who say that they believe in the minimalist philosophy but are actually using it as a means to retire at a young age and live an upscale life of leisure and travel.[25] Much as Lucy signaled her disapproval for materialist goals, Norman voiced strong opinions on the perils of being driven primarily by money:

> Doing something *for* money? Very often, I feel like there's a very fear-driven aspect. Like, if someone tells me they need a million dollars to feel successful, I'm like, "Dude, I know once you hit that goal you'll need ten million because you're still empty, and that's not going to change anything." I've met enough people like that. They say by thirty they've got to do A, B, C, D, and they hit that goal by twenty-nine, and that feeling that they were after—of security and safety and comfort, confidence, and success—never comes.

Distancing themselves from this group of nomads, Norman told us that money is "not a good motivator." By building their business on products and business practices in which they believe, Lorelei and Norman now aim to make money from something that fits their ethical worldview.

Based in Bali: An Intentional Choice about Where to Live

The freedom to choose and vary one's location does not preempt the desire to have a long-term base—what non-nomads might simply call a home. The right place, where magic, practicality, and like-minded community come together, can facilitate personal transformation in alignment with one's values. For Lorelei and Norman, Bali has delivered, with the result that they now see the island as essential to their lives and their story. Yet for digital nomads, location is a choice; the whole point of leaving home was to craft a life on their own terms and *not* to surrender to circumstances. Norman and Lorelei firmly believe and repeatedly told us that their new sense of well-being is no accident. Rather than passively accepting cultures and structures that run counter to their beliefs, they have worked hard to create lives in accordance with their values. As Norman told us: "That's something I learned from my mother: to really learn to arrange things the way I want them rather than surrendering to the circumstances. . . . Some people say, 'Just give it a couple of years,' and I'm like, 'Hell, no. I won't work there for three days if it's uncomfortable.'"

As they elaborated on their decision to remain in Bali, Lorelei and Norman admitted that they sometimes long for the familiar things they left behind and have not ruled out returning home someday. Asked about the negatives, Norman and Lorelei freely spoke of their ambivalence about home and the social distance they feel from people who can no longer relate to them:

This is a huge topic for us. There are a lot of negatives, costs of the lifestyle. . . . I feel that I lose some connections back home, and I lose that rootedness of being in [Europe], which I loved. I love my country and people, but at the same time, I'm a living criticism of their lifestyles. I would not advise anyone to stay in a job they don't like. Because life is precious.

Yet even as they debated long-term plans, Lorelei restated her commitment to maintaining the lifestyle for now: "For me, it's not a choice. It's just the path that I'm on."

Though their path began with hardships, Norman and Lorelei believe that adversity has led to their current successes and has helped them to appreciate how far they have come. As they look to the future, Lorelei said she finds strength in the fact that many skeptics back home have come around and validated their choices:

I think that's a great gift I got in [Europe] last year. We were only there for five weeks, and some people said, "You're still kind of normal, and you're not crazy and all spiritual now." I don't know what they thought. This year we came back, and we were kind of perceived as a success story because we have an amazing life, we are happy, and it's very real, and it's not in any way fake, and people can see that. And now *they* are asking to travel.

CHAPTER 6

Conclusion

In Search of Freedom, Community,

and Meaningful Work

Ln this book, we have described digital nomadism as a radical self-reinvention movement for those who believe that creative class cities and jobs have failed them. We have observed that digital nomads have strong work identities, but they have become so frustrated with the confining and disempowering norms in their home societies that they believe that their best option is to exit. We have followed their choices to reinvent themselves in the company of like-minded others in digital nomad hubs such as Bali, and we have observed their creation of a new kind of community, one focused on attaining and sustaining individual freedom in the company of like-minded others. In this final chapter, we contextualize key observations and offer some thoughts about what our study of digital nomads may reveal about the future of community and work.

OVERSELLING CREATIVE CLASS CITIES AND JOBS

Richard Florida's 2002 book, *The Rise of the Creative Class: And How It's Transforming Work, Leisure, Community, and Everyday Life,* was a bestselling and optimistic manifesto about the growth of the creative economy and the future of cities that are intentionally designed to attract and satisfy a needed population of knowledge workers. Florida proposed that creative class cities would provide skilled people with a place to unlock their creative potential. In this story, individuals would choose to move to cities that match their tastes and values. There, they could thrive at work, at home, and within a community of striving peers who share their interests and passions. Their lives would be rich and fulfilling, and their cities would flourish, becoming even greater engines of innovation and desirable places that continue to attract and retain diverse and talented citizens.

Though many have challenged Florida's core arguments about catering to creative class workers as a strategy for boosting urban and regional economies, this topic is not the concern of our book.[1] Instead, we asked questions about the toll that creative class cities and jobs take on the very citizens and workforce who are said to be benefiting the most. We have shown that the promise of creative class jobs in top-tier cities has been oversold. Specifically, our informants report that (1) creative class cities are expensive, and the cost of living is outpacing wage growth; (2) the culture of creative class cities is a toxic mix of materialism, busyness, and workaholism that leaves little time and energy for personal growth, to invest in relationships, or to take advantage of the much-promoted urban amenities; and (3) the actual creative class work is often unfulfilling, taking place within organizations that routinely subject employees to indignities and rob them of autonomy over both their work and their lives.

Today, cities are pitted against each other as they compete for corporate investments in facilities. In the same ways that city leaders have attempted to lure sports teams to cities by building new stadiums and arenas,[2] they now woo corporations with tax incentives, property tax abatements, and land and transportation deals.[3] Even struggling cities go to absurd lengths to compete for creative class firms and jobs, despite evidence that the benefits of such competitions accrue mainly to the corporations and not to the broader population.[4]

In addition, cities compete to attract skilled workers. Although best known for his claims about the role of the creative class in the economic regeneration of cities, Florida also argued that place matters for creative workers as individuals.[5] Just as aspiring creative professionals are encouraged to relentlessly build their own skills,[6] they must ask themselves: "Who's your city?"[7] Skills in hand, the most ambitious (and arguably, privileged) among them move to creative class cities in pursuit of top jobs.

Living in those cities, however, our informants found themselves disappointed. Digital nomads disagree with conventional wisdom that creative class cities are full of stable communities of creative professionals that will offer them well-being, life satisfaction, healthy relationships, and paths to achieve their goals. As several nomads who formerly resided in cities like New York, London, Paris, Melbourne, and Brussels pointed out, a major disadvantage of creative class cities is that like-mindedness is rare and not necessarily found at the office or in one's neighborhood. Furthermore, people are too busy and too spread out across the metropolis to easily connect on a regular basis. In addition, creative professionals often work long hours in the office while also being mobile and likely to move away. Digital nomads *do* desire the amenities available in creative class cities, but they observed that their lifestyles there allowed little opportunity to take advantage of them. Hence, digital nomads reported that they see few benefits of long-term residence in creative class cities.

Given the centrality of work to the identities of creative professionals, concerns about jobs and communities almost inevitably come together in creative workplaces. It is no secret that many creative individuals are idealistic and that they dream of living in a place where they can find happiness and secure meaningful work. What has been neglected is what a poor job cities and organizations have done in providing these outcomes. As we noted in chapter 1, digital nomads were disappointed with the content of their jobs back home. This lack of meaning is problematic because it undermines creative individuals' ability to feel that they are part of a work community of like-minded people. As Liam, a veteran of two leading global technology companies, explained it, tech companies employ talented people to do tedious, "awful stuff" and then try to make up for it with a positive work environment.

Like the cities where they operate, creative class employers seem to have equated culture—that "positive environment"—with a slate of perks. These much-promoted perks are intended to keep workers in the office continuously (e.g., free on-site gyms and massages, Ping-Pong and foosball tables, arcade games, and complimentary food at "campus" cafés). But free food and incentives to stay at the office for longer periods of the day do not constitute culture. This substitution of perks for vibrant culture (e.g., values that support dignity, respect, autonomy, growth opportunities, creativity, realistic workloads, and work-life balance) has only increased nomads' sense of alienation and their desire to break bonds with the status quo. Our research provides a key lesson for cities and organizations: culture is not reducible to the mere provision of generous perks and amenities, whether in the form of gentrification and bike paths or free food and nap pods.

Overall, we conclude that the overselling of creative class cities and jobs has, at the very least, left many with expectations that are significantly out of step with reality. Far from blaming Millennials for these inflated expectations, our research has led us to believe that civic leaders, economists, public intellectuals, corporate executives, and the mainstream media as well as parents, teachers, and career professionals have all done their part to build a vision of a utopian creative meritocracy where the best and brightest will live side-by-side in diverse, yet harmonious communities dedicated to fulfilling humans' innovative potential.

Perhaps young people must share some blame for buying into the overly optimistic vision of the creative class, but we doubt that their willingness to believe in the vision that has been so aggressively marketed to them is the result of any systematic, generational fault. The shortcomings of creative class cities and jobs, acute as they were to our informants, did not constitute the sole basis for their departure. Rather, it was the way that these conditions interacted with their desire for freedom and community that led them to seek an exit.

FREEDOM AND A NEW KIND OF COMMUNITY

When people experience large gaps between their expectations of work and its realities, they come to dislike their jobs and try to leave within the first few years of employment.[8] Similarly, the digital nomads we met and interviewed reported a mismatch between their expectations about creative class cities and their lived experiences of them, which led to generalized disillusionment and despair about their futures there. However, instead of hoping for a transformative change by aiming narrowly for a better job or a different city in their home country, digital nomads took a more extreme path. Why?

We conclude that the answer has to do with both freedom *and* community. Whereas prior generations of workers may have prioritized security and benefits above all else, digital nomads reject this inclination, in part, because they doubt that such a path guarantees them happiness, fulfillment, or even protection from economic hardship. Instead, their dissatisfaction initiates a search for freedom. They have come to believe that freedom, in the long run, offers their best hope for controlling their own lives and accomplishing whatever kinds of meaning and balance appeal to them over time. For some, the goal is to have periods of time when they feel their work is making a difference in the world. For others, the struggle to work independently is inherently meaningful, especially as they learn, grow, and triumph over the obstacles that come and go. Overall, nomads at all stages of the lifestyle are thoughtful, reflecting on their lives and finding personal meaning in their own efforts to cultivate a life outside of the constraints imposed on them back home.

Understanding that freedom is hollow unless it is shared, digital nomads use their freedom to realize their dreams of engaging with a like-minded community. Demographers who study migration—complete changes in residence including a readjustment of community affiliations—recognize that it is not random; rather, it is patterned and selective.[9] The decision of digital nomads to migrate around the world separates this group from the many Millennials and disaffected cubicle workers who stay put and would never consider moving to another city, let alone to another country without a secure job. Beyond demographic variables such as ethnicity, class, age, and family status, digital nomads also share values that distinguish them from their non-nomadic peers. Digital nomads' selective migration results in digital nomad hubs that offer homophily (i.e., social segregation of like-minded people). This, in turn, helps them to rapidly develop intimate network ties, even in highly transient places. In these hubs, digital nomads can find the kinds of people and institutions that affirm and support their evolving identities and goals.

Despite their online work and claims of "location independence," we learned that digital nomads reject any suggestion that the internet is a substitute for offline, place-based community. In large part, nomads have moved thousands of miles from home with the intention to join a place-based community, and they recognize that their strongest ties are to people around them with whom they are in frequent, in-person contact. Further reinforcing the ecology of nomad hubs is the fact that nomads' spatial distance from home is accompanied by increased *social distance* from home. In practical terms, digital nomads' social obligations to family and friends from home are mostly eliminated when they live abroad. Thus, nomads rely on their networks in hubs to meet their residential, work, community, social, spiritual, and recreational needs. This further intensifies the sense of community found in hubs with homogenous clusters of expatriates, causing these hubs to flourish, remain vibrant, and draw in new members. Thus, the digital nomad phenomenon supplies evidence that place-based community still matters and even has primacy in the modern era of online communities and with a population that is especially immersed in the world of digital technology.

As much as digital nomads value place-based community, they dispute the claim that it requires a stable population within a locality. As we discussed in chapter 3 and throughout the book, the fluid, intimate community of digital nomad hubs challenges traditional understandings of strong connections between people. Although the digital nomad lifestyle weakens person-based ties in the traditional sense (i.e., wherein long lengths of residence in one location increase the strength of social ties),[10] it does not weaken nomads' general desire for and action toward fostering strong relationships. In contrast to the traditional focus on how the population stability of *individuals* within a single geographic location creates stronger community ties,[11] digital nomad communities leverage stability in the *types* of people who are drawn to a place. Even as the actual population churns, this stability in the types of arrivals maintains the subculture's essential character and institutions.

Digital nomads accept rapid, frequent, and large fluctuations in the strength and composition of their network ties as normal, realizing that relationships will wax and wane as people come and go. Rather than focusing on maintaining strong ties to the same individuals across time and distance, digital nomads seek to initiate and rapidly develop new, place-based ties to other like-minded individuals who can meet their current relational needs. For the digital nomad community, it is this version of stability, rather than the retention of a specific group of individuals remaining in one place over many years,[12] that is critical to a specific place thriving as a nomad hub.

One of the reasons that nomads are so accepting of transience in digital nomad hubs is their shared value for freedom. Without a doubt, one of the most striking features of digital nomads is their unique melding of community and freedom. Nomads normalize and accept fluctuations in community engagement because they understand that the main purpose of a digital nomad community is to support individuals in their pursuits of personal goals. Although such attitudes may seem inauthentic, superficial, transactional, and even insular to outsiders, digital nomads' shared value for the primacy of individual freedom leads them to regard these relational strategies as entirely reasonable, and indeed, expected.

"DIGITAL NOMAD" AS A SOCIAL IDENTITY

Although digital nomads are extremely individualistic and exhibit few impulses toward collective action, they do share at least one hallmark of social identification: the preference to associate with others whom they view as members of their "tribe."[13] Research on younger expatriate employees finds that they spend most of their discretionary time with other expats.[14] Similarly, digital nomads are mostly drawn to other digital nomads. Aside from the few individuals who went out of their way to develop deeper connections to the Balinese locals, we rarely observed digital nomads who interacted with Balinese people as full peers (outside of service-related roles).[15] Moreover, digital nomads largely actively avoided more conventional tourists. A partial exception to this pattern concerns Bali's spiritual expat community. Many nomads come to Bali intentionally seeking spiritual experiences, and many others inadvertently chance upon such experiences because of the omnipresence of spiritual culture there. As a result, digital nomads whom we met often had connections with expats who were in Bali solely for spiritual purposes. Yet, on the whole, most nomads stated that their main reason for moving to Bali was to experience life in a concentrated digital nomad community with the hope that it would move their work lives forward.

In addition to spending most of their time within the digital nomad community, another way that nomads reinforce their new identities is by distancing themselves from people who seem to be indifferent, skeptical, or averse to nomad values. For instance, when we asked nomads about plans to return to their home countries, most told us that the longer that they live nomadically, the less they relate to people back home. Unlike traditional expatriate employees who often tether themselves tightly to their Western lives and conceptualize their futures in terms of rotations between required stints abroad and return trips to their home countries,[16] digital nomads do not pine for home and the friends and relatives they left behind. In chapter 5 Lucy described how the rapid expansion of her networks as a digital nomad led her to feel more connected to the like-minded people she was meeting in Bali, while the spatial and social distance from the UK led her to feel less connected to people back home whom she had known for years. Vance, a forty-three-year-old English freelancer and entrepreneur, echoed this view: "My family have been upset with me, and some friends have been upset with me for not being more in touch, but I think you meet so many new people in Bali, you just like, forget about everyone else." As Vance's comment suggests, digital nomads' zeal for their new identity can even lead them to "forget" their old lives, thus reinforcing their new identity.

Digital nomads view their new identities as permanent changes. Most said that they would no longer be comfortable living permanently and full-time within their society of origin. Maddie, a thirty-two-year-old Australian marketer, offered the typical digital nomad pessimism about the likelihood of finding personal growth and community in Western cities: "I feel the most enriched when I'm stimulated by a new culture or surrounded by like-minded people doing something creative, and I just don't feel like I'm getting that [in Sydney or New York]."

Even those nomads who returned to their home countries (or told us that they intended to do so) have retained a strong sense of identification with the digital nomad lifestyle, remaining on message boards, posting about their persistent feelings of longing for nomadism, and discussing the difficulties of transitioning back to conventional life.[17] For instance, we discussed an American digital nomad named Brandi in chapters 1 and 4. Brandi left a stable yet boring government job and its generous benefits package. She quit because she had come to believe that the draw of security was anchoring her to a mindless job that she hated and was stunting her personal development. Brandi's transformation from jaded government worker to digital nomad freelancer resulted in massive changes to her identity as well as to her work and life goals. Brandi began to work as a freelance writer, which became her main source of income, and she also became a certified life coach, pursued a business coaching others on changing their work lifestyle, and even started a podcast about leaving cubicle work.

However, as Brandi told us, "These are now side hustles, again." Brandi decided to "pause" her life as a digital nomad and resettle in the United States to be near her nieces. She put her digital nomad knowledge and skills into practice and accepted a full-time job as the community manager of a coworking space. Though she reached this decision after a great deal of soul searching, Brandi still feels ambivalent about it. The transition has been difficult, and Brandi continues to miss her nomadic identity and travel, but she also views her current life as an intentional choice and feels empowered to resume her nomadic life at any time.

Although Brandi's decision to resettle in her hometown was unusual among those in our sample, many digital nomads expect that their future lives will include spending some time in their home societies. However, most feel confident that a visit home is unlikely to become permanent. Lucian, a thirty-one-year-old eastern European marketer and entrepreneur who lives in Bali with his wife (who works for a Bali-based start-up), said that in a year they would return to live in Europe in order to have children and raise them in proximity to relatives. Almost three years later, they remain based in Bali, do not have children, and continue to take trips to other nomad hubs, such as Lisbon, Portugal. Similar to many other nomads who are reluctant to do anything that would curtail their freedom, Lucian also said that the couple is committed to "travel and experience the world. We don't want to settle down."

GROWTH AND SUSTAINABILITY: WHAT IS THE FUTURE OF DIGITAL NOMAD COMMUNITIES?

Before the Covid-19 pandemic, digital nomadism was growing rapidly.[18] But the phenomenon was by no means mainstream. Nothing we have observed suggests that masses of disaffected knowledge workers are racing to take the extreme step of leaving their home societies for extended periods of time. Even after the eventual passing of the pandemic that, as of this writing, is shutting down travel across the world, there remain many questions about the longer-term viability of digital nomad communities. Is the digital nomad phenomenon just a fad, or is it the beginning of a more enduring iteration of work-based community? The future of digital nomad communities obviously depends on numerous individual, economic, and geopolitical factors that are difficult to predict. However, our research suggests two proximal factors related to the nomad population that are likely to determine the viability of digital nomad communities: population flow and composition.

Whereas communities generally thrive as they reach a state of stability, fluidity is the primary engine of the digital nomad community. Without a constant churn of arrivals and departures, nomad hubs are likely to stagnate and lose the energy that attracts digital nomads and entices them to stay with the lifestyle. During our research, Bali's digital nomad community seemed primed for continued growth. However, this growth has been accompanied by an increase in crowding that may negatively affect both the economic and social dynamics of the community over time. The Covid-19 pandemic obviously resets the clock on crowding, but it is difficult to know whether the eventual waning of the pandemic will lead to longer-term changes in travel, or whether Bali's digital nomad community will soon face growth-related problems once more.

Sustainability is another concern related to digital nomads' population flows. Though digital nomads constitute just a small percentage of Bali's total number of tourist arrivals, they still contribute to the tourist impact on the environment.[19] Sustainability problems are severe and worsening on the island, as rice fields are sold off to resort developers. Tourism strains the supply of land, water, energy, and food; causes gridlocked roads; and creates large amounts of plastic and waste that are dumped on the island and in the ocean. Nomads and traditional tourists alike complain about trash-strewn beaches and plastic floating in the ocean or dumped in dried-out waterways, and they hate sitting in congested traffic for hours. If growth returns, Bali's charm may not last, especially for nomads who pride themselves on ecotourism, a love of nature, and discovering places that are hidden gems. Government officials and those who work in Bali's tourism industry are aware of visitors' complaints and are alarmed at the possibility that tourists may search for cleaner, less chaotic places, or try to find the next hidden gem to add to their bucket lists and Instagram feeds.

A second factor related to the viability of digital nomad communities is the *mix* of arrivals and departures. Bali's digital nomad community has thrived, in part, because many of its members are highly skilled. In our sample, a typical nomad is an early thirties professional with several years of work experience. This is important because such individuals are better able to quickly devise a way to earn a basic income online in order to support themselves, and they also have skills they can use to help others, making them more valuable to the community.

Nomad hubs thrive when they attract a critical mass of people who have skills and know how to market them to get work. However, research shows that freelancers who lack *distinctive* skills that match market demands are more likely to struggle to attain and sustain the income necessary for a good lifestyle in the West.[20] The lower cost of living in places like Bali suggests that digital nomadism might be especially attractive to this determined but struggling group of individuals, but what happens if people with more marginal skills begin to disproportionately populate digital nomad communities? Media coverage of digital nomadism has increased its mainstream visibility. In fact, *Forbes* featured an article proclaiming: "Once an under-the-radar trend, living the digital nomad lifestyle has become so well-accepted it's now an aspirational spectator sport."[21] With so many eyes on this lifestyle, it is, perhaps, inevitable that even more marginally skilled individuals will be drawn to digital nomadism. As discussed in chapter 4, some highly skilled nomads believe that this trend is already underway, while others think that the mix of skills continues to be well balanced and is an asset to the community.

How might digital nomad communities react to changes in the flow and composition of the nomad population? One possibility is that the community will become further niched. For instance, resident nomads' tendencies to separate themselves from the frenetic energy of honeymooners may intensify, and they may become more similar to other wealthy expat groups. Simultaneously, a trend toward further niches could create digital nomad subcommunities dedicated to new arrivals, functioning more as entry-level getaways where vendors sell pre-packaged "nomad experiences." It is also easy to imagine new niche hubs emerging that cater to specific professional domains, certain skill levels, or skill sets, and that target nomads by gender, within a specific age range, or with a certain experience level.[22]

Another possibility is that nomad communities will remain balanced as they become more enticing to highly skilled, remote-working employees. This group, with the talent to demand location independence, could create population gains to counterbalance any population growth of less-skilled nomads. Of course, it is also conceivable that skilled workers will become less attracted to nomad hubs, seeking to distance themselves from less skilled nomads whom they may see as adding little value to their own career growth. Yet currently, many nomads who are remote employees seem to enjoy the mix of people in digital nomad hubs for the same, community-based reasons that draw freelancers and entrepreneurs.

THE DARK SIDE OF DIGITAL NOMADISM

Although many generally view digital nomadism as a positive trend because it enables some individuals to find new ways to thrive amid the transactionalization of creative class labor and the oppressive aspects of creative class cities, we also observed a darker side of the phenomenon. In chapter 2 we noted that when nomads (and expatriates, in general) take advantage of the favorable economics of lower-cost nations, they engage in activities that can be viewed as exploitative of the societies in which they operate. Digital nomads largely either rejected the validity of this neocolonial critique or else rationalized it as inevitable. Still, the fact remains that the lifestyles of many digital nomads would not be possible if these individuals had not earned high wages in the strong currency of a wealthy country to then spend in a less wealthy country with low wages and a weak currency. Also, the interactions that most nomads have with locals are confined to hiring them for service roles such as drivers or housekeepers, and most nomads bargain hard to receive pricing that is below typical tourist rates. Thus, the exchanges between digital nomads and the Balinese are often only economic and transactional.

One argument against applying the neocolonialist label to digital nomads is that their income is earned elsewhere, so they neither prevent the growth of local businesses nor take jobs from local citizens. When successful, digital nomads may even create a few valuable business jobs that open new opportunities for local citizens. However, as the ranks of digital nomads swell, it is possible that more nomads may attempt to create place-based employment or otherwise work in ways that take money from locals.

The dark side also extends to the negative effects of digital nomadism on individual nomads. In chapter 4 we explained that digital nomads' distrust of traditional sources of expertise leaves them vulnerable to charlatans. Digital nomads' tendency to validate each other's identity claims, no matter how unsubstantiated, also places community members at risk, leading some to pursue identities that are neither economically viable nor healthy.

Furthermore, nomads' pursuit of individual freedom often comes at a cost of longer-term, romantic relationships and family formation. Most nomads we met were single and articulated fatalistic attitudes about long-term relationships (e.g., "If it is meant to be, it will happen") that seem at odds with their more proactive approach to the rest of their lives. Yet we noticed that in our longer interviews, many digital nomads privately admitted that they are concerned that their lifestyle will prevent them from fulfilling their ultimate dreams of lasting love and family. Oscar, a Canadian life coach, summarized nomads' romantic predicament: "People are tired of staging the same play, so they write their own script, but they forget to put other characters in, or room for other characters. So, a lot of people are living these nomadic lives, and asking why they can't find someone, but there's no room for that person."

BEYOND DIGITAL NOMADS: EVOLVING VIEWS OF MEANINGFUL COMMUNITY AND WORK

In studying digital nomads, we aimed to observe and understand a disruptive phenomenon at the edge of typical notions of work and community. What we found is that the digital nomad phenomenon offers broader insights about work and community that apply to many of us—even those of us disinclined to become world travelers.

Community has long been considered to be a result of selective migration dynamics that result in a specific place's population composition, character, norms, and styles of interaction. Place-based communities are often seen as a passive product of these population dynamics rather than in terms of agentic mobility decisions determined by cultural shifts in how we relate to jobs, technology, social relationships, and the very idea of place. Understandably, some have grown skeptical of the word "community" and of organizations and marketing experts that exploit, claim, and arguably, abuse the word. Such distrust makes sense when organizations label even the most mundane forums and the most top-down, forced sites of social interaction in this way.

Yet the nomad phenomenon shows that community remains an important priority for many, and increasingly, individuals are challenging what they view as inauthentic attempts to harness the power of the concept. For instance, as we were finalizing this book, WeWork, the world's largest purveyor of coworking space, was in the middle of a spectacular meltdown. WeWork's brand emphasized its ability to foster community so much that the word appeared 150 times in the paperwork for the company's initial stock offering (which was withdrawn).[23] In our view, the fact that WeWork got as far as it did demonstrates a demand for like-minded community at work; at the same time, WeWork's failure might be seen as an indictment of the potential to monetize such a top-down approach to community.

Businesses like WeWork operate on models of remote work that largely mirror an office setting and miss the larger possibilities to form authentic communities that change our working relationships and our relationship to work. These larger changes were very much on the minds of the proprietors of Bali's coworking spaces. One owner was unequivocal that "We're *not* WeWork" and was especially prophetic about how untenable traditional work arrangements would become:

> Coworking is a way to create a new move away from capitalism, and create a network outside of the existing network . . . Having more of a conscious revolution than having like, a fighting revolution. [There are] intelligent people coming out of big corporations going, "I want something different," and moving towards those communities can build

a more decentralized system, moving away from [the current system] because at the moment, it's not sustainable. The world's not sustainable, so having a place like this, you build a framework to create change.

Indeed, the Covid-19 pandemic has thrust workers and managers across the globe involuntarily into suboptimal, emergency remote working situations. Some people have coped by attempting to recreate their old office routines; others slowly started to use digital tools (e.g., Zoom meetings) as they waited for things to return to normal. But should we return to how things were? Looking to the future, digital nomads' experience suggests that more people and organizations might ultimately consider a different path that provides more workers with the freedom to tailor their work lives to create greater life and work satisfaction.

As we have argued throughout this book, a larger lesson of the rise of digital nomad communities is that individuals want to feel that they have volition in two of life's most important arenas: where to live and what work to do. Choices about place and work affect our incomes, our amount of free time, our social networks, and the norms and values of the people and institutions that surround us. The ability to move to a place where you want to live, that matches your preferences, and where you can pursue your goals is undoubtedly a privilege. The Covid-19 pandemic has revealed that this privilege may be within reach for a much larger number of workers in the future.

This book connects remote work to place-based community. Community researchers have focused on stability as the basis for effective communities;[24] sociologists hoping to understand growing precarity in employment have similarly focused on stability as the foundation of high-quality work.[25] Our study of digital nomads shows that stability is only one dimension of contemporary communities and work; when faced with communities and work that they do not find meaningful, many talented, work-identified individuals choose freedom over stability. In a world connected by rapid, relatively inexpensive mobility and technology, the potential meaning of this move toward freedom is greatly expanded. We hope that this book inspires others to join the conversation about changing definitions of place-based community, meaningful work, and life satisfaction in the digital age.

NOTES

INTRODUCTION

1. Nietzsche and Hollingdale (1996).
2. To protect participants' confidentiality and in compliance with Institutional Review Board training and standards, we assigned pseudonyms to all informants. Their quotations are transcriptions of taped interviews that we conducted.
3. The term "New Economy" (also often called the "Knowledge Economy") first gained wide usage in the 1990s and early 2000s as a description of how technology and innovation, particularly based on the internet, have replaced conventional industry as drivers of economic value. For definition, see, e.g., https://www.inc.com/encyclopedia/new-economy.html; https://www.investopedia.com/terms/n/neweconomy.asp.
4. Finding "your tribe" or "your people" has become a catchphrase and marketing tool among Millennials and digital natives. Various iterations of the advice that one should "find your tribe" have become ubiquitous. The general idea is that in the modern, global society, in which the internet makes people more connected than ever, many individuals still feel lonely. Thus, self-help books, health-oriented websites and podcasts, doctors, public health advocates, and, of course, businesses promote the idea that the key to health, well-being, and even career success is participation in a like-minded community. From the observation that humans have a basic craving for connection, the advice is that if individuals happen to live in a place where like-minded community is lacking, it is one's personal responsibility to be proactive and seek out the right-fitting "tribe."
5. *Eat, Pray, Love* is a 2006 best-selling memoir by Elizabeth Gilbert in which she visits Italy, India, and Bali, Indonesia, in search of self-discovery and a more balanced life.
6. We mainly developed this definition based on our conversations with digital nomads, but we also consulted media sources (see Elgan 2012; Lamarque 2015; Mohn 2015, 2017; Snedden 2013; Spinks 2015).
7. Oberg (1960).
8. "Office of the day" is a popular Instagram hashtag in which a digital nomad posts themselves working from a laptop in a desirable location that is not a traditional office.
9. Black and Gregersen (1999).
10. Gallup (2017).
11. WeWork has coworking spaces where customers can rent private offices ($720 a month in Philadelphia, for example) or get memberships to a hot desk or shared desk that can be reserved ($360), or rent a dedicated desk ($450). The spaces are largely aimed at Millennials in trendy neighborhoods in large international cities including New York City (44 locations), Barcelona, Berlin, Chicago, London, Prague, San Diego, and Amsterdam.
12. Florida (2005).

13. Park (1936); Simmel (1903); Wirth (1938).
14. Gans (1962).
15. See, for example, the work of Mary Pattillo (1999) and Elijah Anderson (1999), as well as Woldoff (2011) and Woldoff et al. (2016).

CHAPTER 1

1. Cohen (2010: 29) writes about long-term lifestyle tourists as "alienated individuals" who desire to "escape from the constraints of a perceived mundane existence and/or the anomie of Western society." Furthermore, Moscardo (2010) argues that storytelling is an essential part of the tourism experience and marketing of destinations.
2. Florida (2002).
3. Gyourko, Mayer, and Sinai (2013) describe the "ever-widening gap in housing values and incomes" in "superstar cities."
4. Cadwallader (1992). See also our discussion of Lee's (1966) theory of migration in the introduction.
5. Some people in our sample experienced a change in family structure (i.e., divorce), but they did not frame their mobility as mainly motivated by these factors. We discuss the important role of personal trauma in nomads' mobility decisions later in this chapter.
6. Cadwallader (1992); Lee, Oropesa, and Kanan (1994).
7. Bélanger (2010); Castles (2003); Myers, Slack, and Singelmann (2008); Richmond (1993).
8. Lee (1966); Massey, Arango, Hugo, Kouaouci, Pellegrino, and Taylor (1998); Pedraza (1991).
9. Haug (2008).
10. Expatriates or "expats" are individuals who have settled abroad, outside of their native countries.
11. For a review of the literature, see Baruch, Altman, and Tung (2016).
12. Baruch et al. (2016); Mahroum (2000).
13. Baruch, Dickmann, Altman, and Bournois (2013).
14. For a review of the literature, see Baruch et al. (2013).
15. Baruch et al. (2013: 2375).
16. Coulter, van Ham, and Findlay (2016).
17. Halfacree and Boyle (1993).
18. Cilluffo and Cohn (2017).
19. Gallup (2018); Spreitzer et al. (2017).
20. Barley and Kunda (2004); Osnowitz (2010). A recent Gallup report concludes that data show a "tale of two gig economies" with freelancers and online platform workers reaping greater advantages than contingent "on-call" gig workers (2018: 2).
21. Gregg (2011).
22. Hampton and Gupta (2008); Woldoff, Lozzi, and Dilks (2013).
23. Garrett, Spreitzer, and Bacevice (2017); Spinuzzi (2012).
24. Merkel (2019).
25. Mirowsky and Ross (2007).
26. Florida (2008:30).
27. Florida (2002, 2003, 2005, 2008, 2015, 2017).
28. Florida (2015).
29. Florida (2005); Peck and Tickell (2002); Woldoff, Decola, and Litchfield (2011).
30. Florida (2002, 2003, 2005, 2008); Moos, Pfeiffer, and Vinodrai (2018).
31. Storper and Scott (2009).
32. Florida (2017).
33. Lerner (2008).

34. Woldoff, Morrison, and Glass (2016).
35. Amabile and Conti (1999); Probst, Stewart, Gruys, and Tierney (2007).
36. Wirth (1938).
37. Castells (1977).
38. Beauregard (1986).
39. Researchers have increasingly acknowledged that some places have cultures that cause psychological distress and affect mood, self-concept, health, and illness (Fitzpatrick and LaGory 2003; Hanlon and Carlisle 2009; Marmot and Wilkinson 2006).
40. The City refers to the City of London, the London financial district where the Bank of London and Stock Exchange are located.
41. According to the Trades Union Congress (2018), annual commuting time has been rising in the UK, with Londoners taking the longest time to get to and from work (one hour and twenty-one minutes per day).
42. Sassen (2014).
43. Nap stations in London, such as Pop Pods Ltd., Podtime, Casper Sleepmobile, and Pop & Rest Nap Bar, host customers from local offices who pay by the hour to rest or sleep.
44. Autor (2014); Beaudry, Green, and Sand (2014).
45. Ibarra (1999); Reid (2015); Tierney (2015).
46. Deloitte (2015); Reid (2015).
47. Deloitte (2018).
48. Bidwell, Briscoe, Fernandez-Mateo, and Sterling (2013).
49. Cappelli and Keller (2013); Spreitzer, Cameron, and Garrett (2017).
50. Torpey and Hogan (2016).
51. Scholz and Schneider (2016); Scholz (2017).
52. Gill (1999).
53. Amabile (1988).
54. Csikszentmihalyi (1997).
55. Mainemelis (2001).
56. Parker, Van den Broeck, and Holman (2017).
57. Alsop (2008); Marston (2007); Myers and Sadaghiani (2010).
58. Bidwell et al. (2013); Hollister (2011); Spreitzer et al. (2017).
59. Kalleberg (2009).
60. Many practitioners and scholars have written about the clinical and diagnostic uses of terms like stress, crisis, and trauma. We refer to these terms in a more general way, noting that one individual may view a specific event as a minor stressor, while another may have a more traumatic reaction and experience it as a crisis (Corcoran and Roberts 2000).
61. Pearlin (1989).
62. Robbins and Wilner (2001).
63. Robinson, Wright, and Smith (2013).
64. Robinson, Wright, and Smith (2013).

CHAPTER 2

1. Gittleson (2014).
2. https://en.wikipedia.org/wiki/List_of_Indonesian_islands_by_population, retrieved July 23, 2019.
3. https://www.retalkasia.com/news/2017/12/06/balis-economy-2017-q3-overview/ 1512555803.
4. This statement is based on a June 4, 2018, search using the Google Trends "topic explore" for the search term "digital nomad," with the parameters set to worldwide searches from the last five years. At the time, Bali ranked as the number-one-related topic. As of June 18, 2019, it was ranked in the top three for related queries and the top four for related topics.

5. Lee (1966); please see our discussion of Lee's theory of migration in the introduction.
6. Gieryn (2000).
7. Brown-Saracino (2009); Gotham and Brumley (2002).
8. Aronczyk (2013); Kavaratzis (2004).
9. For examples of cities' competition for tourist dollars, see Judd and Fainstein (1999).
10. Cohen (1984).
11. Lin, Pearson, and Cai (2011).
12. Teaching English abroad is also a transition step to becoming a digital nomad, especially for those who are younger and less experienced.
13. Kavaratzis (2004); Sevin (2013).
14. Heller (2017).
15. Sevin (2013).
16. Sevin (2013).
17. Pine and Gilmore (1998).
18. Indrianto (2005).
19. These numbers are from Indonesia's 2010 Census (Badan Pusat Statistik 2010).
20. There are no official figures on the size of the work tourism population. We based our estimate on the self-reported turnover and membership figures of Bali's largest coworking spaces (Dojo, Hubud, Kumpul, and Outpost). We note that some work tourists do not use such spaces, but we have no way of tracking their numbers. We also attended a brainstorming session at Hubud in 2017 where a roomful of digital nomads who specialize in marketing to other digital nomads estimated that about 50,000 people knowingly identified as digital nomads online as of 2017.
21. Plunkett (2018).
22. Homes are surrounded by high walls, include shrines of intricate carved stone and Hindu statues, and entrances are adorned with offerings and incense placed in banana leaves.
23. See, for example, Goclowaska, Ritter, Elliot, and Baas (2019).
24. Cohen (1972) captured aspects of novelty-seeking travelers in his typology of tourists, which featured organized mass tourists, individual mass tourists, explorers, and drifters.
25. Self-help literature, which often extends to popular business books, has popularized the use of the verb "manifest." It suggests that individuals have control over their fate through positive thinking, that it is almost impossible to be successful if one does not mentally visualize goals and positive outcomes, and that such visualization creates self-fulfilling prophesies. The most famous example of this is the "law of attraction," popularized in the book "The Secret" (Byrne, 2006).
26. In 2019 the New York Times featured an article on the "new sobriety," also called "hip sobriety," an industry and social media phenomenon popular among Millennials, complete with mocktails, sober dance events, podcasts like "Sober Curious," and websites like "The Sober Glow" (see Williams 2019).
27. See Robinson (2018).
28. A banjar is a neighborhood in Bali and is also its smallest form of government. Men in Balinese families are representatives at meetings and handle cultural, religious, social, and administrative aspects of the community.
29. As we mentioned in the Introduction, Elizabeth Gilbert's popular book, Eat, Pray, Love, along with the movie inspired by it, takes place partially in Bali. It popularized Bali as a place of inspiration to a broad audience in the West.
30. Stephen King wrote about his writing productivity technique that entails setting a minimum daily word count. He actually wrote, "I like to get ten pages a day, which amounts to 2,000 words. That's 180,000 words over a three-month span, a goodish length for a book—something in which the reader can get happily lost, if the tale is done well and stays fresh" (King 2000: 149).

31. See Lau (2000).
32. Fezehai (2018).
33. See Singleton (2010) for a discussion of the rise of "health club types of yoga," and the rise of more "gymnastic" Western "body culture" yoga techniques.
34. Pollan's 2018 book, *How to Change Your Mind*, was one of the *New York Times Book Review*'s ten best books of 2018. In it, Pollan describes his own use of hallucinogenic drugs, as well as their history, and spiritual and medical benefits.
35. Kuta is the site of the two bombings in Bali. The 2002 nightclub attack killed 202 people, including 88 Australians. The 2005 bombings in a resort area called Jimbaran killed 20.
36. Steve Munroe, a co-founder of Hubud, shared that monthly membership was approximately 300 as of May 2017. After the merger of Hubud and Dojo in 2019, memberships (other than day passes) provide dual access to both spaces and are not specific to one or the other.
37. Prices for coworking at Hubud in 2017 ranged from $20 US for a day pass to $275 per month for unlimited access. These prices actually decreased in 2019 following the merger of Hubud and Dojo. As of July 2019, membership costs ranged from $16 US for a day pass to $206 per month for unlimited access.
38. We retrieved these monkey population figures on July 23, 2019, from monkeyforestubud.com, the official website of the Sacred Monkey Forest Sanctuary.
39. According to 2017 data, Indonesia as a whole has low English-language proficiency, although it does rank higher than Thailand (Education First 2017). Proficiency is uneven across the region and is higher in Jakarta and Bali, where people are considered moderately proficient.
40. Zhang and Peltokorpi (2015).
41. Davies and Hoath (2015).
42. https://www.gapurabali.com/news/2019/01/30/balis-tourism-numbers-exceed-targets-2018/1548819004, retrieved July 23, 2019.
43. Bird, Osland, Mendenhall, and Schneider (1999: 164).
44. Cohen (2000).
45. Ferriss (2007).
46. Although not the pioneers, coworking spaces have been active in this market, particularly as other companies have failed. As of July 2019, Dojo and Outpost each offer live-work options.
47. Tourist guide books refer to these services as "notorious" and assert that "cartels" control them (Rough Guides 2017).
48. https://bostonstartupsguide.com/guide/boston-coworking-spaces-roundup/, retrieved August 2, 2019.
49. The Balinese drink bottled water, and we never observed any practices in our fieldwork to give us any concerns about water.
50. Although there is some fluctuation, data generally show strong and continuing tourist interest in Bali. See, for example, https://www.statista.com/statistics/976842/foreign-tourist-arrivals-numbers-bali-indonesia/, retrieved February 10, 2020.
51. Davies and Silviana (2018).
52. Mullis (2017).
53. Mullis (2017).
54. Mullis (2017).
55. See, e.g., Cohen (1972).
56. Due to our large database of contacts, we had a sense of what various things should cost that was undoubtedly superior to that of most new arrivals in Bali.
57. Rough Guides (2017).
58. Cohen (2017).
59. Costa (1998: 317, 321).

CHAPTER 3

1. Wellman (1979: 1201).
2. Park, Burgess, and McKenzie (1925).
3. Tönnies (1957 [1887]) and Wirth (1938) are classic examples of such a conceptualization.
4. Putnam (2000).
5. Janowitz (1967).
6. Hunter (1974); Keller (1968); Tilly (1973); Wellman (1979).
7. Gans (1962); Wellman (1988).
8. Suttles (1972); Wellman (1979).
9. Florida (2002, 2003, 2005)
10. Florida (2003: 5)
11. Wellman (1979).
12. Wellman (1979).
13. Rainie and Wellman (2012).
14. Sampson (2008: 310).
15. Fischer (1982).
16. McPherson, Smith-Lovin, and Cook (2001).
17. The total number of digital nomads is unknown, though the population is growing rapidly (Mohn 2017). We spoke to several digital marketers who target this group, and they estimated that, as of mid-2017, there were roughly 50,000 to 70,000 individuals worldwide who fit the category. We conducted a Google search on August 9, 2019, exploring the topic "digital nomad" and the result showed consistent growth in use of the search term throughout the last five years.
18. Fischer (1982: 216) also wrote about the freedom to form allegiances around "new interests," and described urban dwellers as drawn to freedom from obligations. He wrote: "Voluntary kinship—for example not feeling obligated to visit one's uncle and aunt every week—is debilitated kinship.... [U]rban ideology ... endorses such freedom from obligation" (Fischer 1982: 83).
19. Oyserman, Coon, and Kemmelmeier (2002: 5).
20. Tiessen (1997).
21. Amabile (1996).
22. See Oyserman et al. (2002).
23. See Oyserman et al. (2002).
24. Wellman and Wortley (1989).
25. See McGee (2005) for a summary of the rise of self-help culture and its relationship to the experience of work.
26. Ferriss's (2007) book was known to all of our informants and had been read by most. In it, Ferriss popularizes the idea of living more luxuriously by earning money in US dollars online and using this work to finance traveling and living in less expensive locations around the world. We return to the influence of Ferriss's ideas in chapter 4.
27. Author of the book *Eat, Pray, Love*, which documents a woman's personal development journey that culminates in Bali.
28. A popular self-help author and personal development guru.
29. A popular self-help author and book.
30. This terminology is used by personal development practitioners. For example, see https://www.tonyrobbins.com/mind-meaning/are-you-stuck/.
31. Adler and Kwon (2002).
32. Portes (1998: 7–8).
33. Hunter (1985).

34. See https://www.pewresearch.org/fact-tank/2019/04/25/trends-in-international-public-opinion-from-our-global-indicators-database/.

35. Carver, Scheier, and Segerstrom (2010).

36. Crant (2000).

37. Groth (2012).

38. Covey (1992).

39. Covey (1992).

40. This reference is to Bridgewater Associates, a hedge fund managed by founder Ray Dalio with his philosophy of "radical transparency," which he has shared with the public through his book *Principles: Life and Work* (2017). Radical transparency has become popular among businesspeople who identify with rebellious, nonconformist, and disrupting management perspectives in the corporate world. Radical transparency advocates argue that secrecy creates atmospheres of distrust and disengagement, and progressive companies should use an honest approach to empower workers, increase fairness, and improve happiness within organizations.

41. Elon Musk is a South African technology entrepreneur and engineer, known for co-founding Tesla, PayPal, and SpaceX. He is admired by many because he uses his wealth for projects that are intended as for-profit businesses but that he and his followers believe will also have positive social impact.

42. https://www.nytimes.com/2019/09/10/style/oh-behave.html.

43. Carrigan (2015).

44. Stillerman (2015).

45. Kondo (2014).

46. Bourdieu (1984).

47. Veblen (1899/1994).

48. For instance, note the incidence of such far-flung locations on annual lists like that of the *New York Times*, https://www.nytimes.com/interactive/2019/travel/places-to-visit.html.

49. Cf. Nishi et al. (2015).

50. See Turner (1969) for an anthropological discussion of the importance of rituals for managing transitions, especially detaching from an earlier point of stability to a more ambiguous one or from an ambiguous one back to a stable one that requires adherence to customary norms.

51. See Hermanowicz and Morgan (1999).

52. "Why am I leaving Bali, for now?" https://hubud.org/blog/live/why-am-i-leaving-bali-for-now/, retrieved July 8, 2018.

53. Pedersen and Rytter (2018).

54. Pedersen and Rytter (2018).

55. "A computer program designed to simulate conversation with human users, especially over the internet." Lexico.com, retrieved September 1, 2019.

56. Artificial intelligence.

57. Granovetter (1973: 1361).

58. Granovetter (1973); Wirth (1938).

59. See Granovetter (1973).

60. Perry-Smith and Shalley (2003).

61. Florida (2002: 286).

62. See Putnam (2000).

63. Cf. Granovetter (1973).

64. Sprecher, Treger, and Wondra (2012).

65. Collins and Miller (1994).

66. Barrell and Jourard (1976).

67. See, for example, Branson (2011), Ferriss (2007, 2010), and Robbins (2007).
68. Cf. Granovetter (1973). Wellman (1991) summarizes dimensions of intimacy as "three related characteristics of strong ties": (1) a voluntary investment with the ties with a sense of the relationship being special, (2) frequent interactions in multiple social contexts over a long period of time, and (3) a sense of mutual support. Our view is conceptually more consistent with that of Granovetter (1973), who focused on what he called "mutual confiding." Yet similar to Wellman (1991), nomads also clearly view all of their relationships as voluntary and seem to view many of them as special. Finally, the dense social networks we observed in Bali meant that frequent interactions in multiple social contexts (e.g., coworking spaces, cafés, grocery stores, and events) were normal. During our fieldwork, we frequently ran into the same individuals multiple times within a day or two and in different locations. Hence, digital nomad intimacy contains aspects of both Granovetter's and Wellman's views.
69. Recent psychological research supports this practice, suggesting that unacquainted individuals who share unusual experiences feel greater closeness with each other (Min, Liu, and Kim, 2018).
70. Fischer (1975).
71. Simmel (1903).
72. Cf. Wellman (1979).

CHAPTER 4
1. Durkheim (1893/1933).
2. Ferriss (2007).
3. See Barley and Kunda (2004); Duffy (2017); Gregg (2011); Osnowitz (2010).
4. As we noted in chapter 2, language such as "manifested" suggests a sense of control over one's fate and a belief in positivity or an "abundance mindset."
5. Buffer is a company that makes social media management software for companies.
6. For a review of definitions of alternative forms of labor, see Gallup (2018) and Spreitzer, Cameron, and Garrett (2017).
7. Gregg (2011); Kalleberg (2009); Ravenelle (2019).
8. We acknowledge that some freelance professionals call themselves entrepreneurs. Our goal is simply to distinguish meaningful types of employment among digital nomads.
9. The word "unicorn" is used to describe the explosive growth start-ups that venture capitalists highly prize.
10. Lifestyle entrepreneurs generally cannot attract external investors because external investors seek investment returns, and these require growth to generate. Thus, external investors prefer to fund business owners with high growth goals.
11. De Stefano (2015).
12. Digital nomads view Chiang Mai, Thailand, rather than Bali as the primary hub for those who consider dropshipping to be their main business.
13. Grant and Stober (2006).
14. Cf. Barley and Kunda (2004); Osnowitz (2010).
15. Baruch, Dickmann, Altman, and Bournois (2013).
16. Goffman (1959).
17. Goffman (1959: 9).
18. Cf. Fischer (1975).
19. For a review, see Seitchik, Brown, and Harkins (2017).
20. As we noted in chapter 2, the four major coworking spaces at the time of our fieldwork were Hubud, Dojo Bali, Outpost, and Kumpul.

21. Hot desking is the practice of multiple people in an office or coworking setting working without an assigned desk but instead using a single shared workstation or any open surface, and not necessarily working next to the same people each day.

22. https://qz.com/1687299/wework-ipo-reveals-that-40-percent-of-its-members-work-for-companies-with-500-plus-employees/, retrieved October 7, 2019. Indeed, all of these criticisms seem particularly applicable to coworking giant WeWork which, as of this writing, was reeling from investors' realizations that it may be primarily understood as a purveyor of office space with a high-risk business model (see https://venturebeat.com/2019/09/30/wework-withdraws-its-ill-fated-ipo/, retrieved October 7, 2019).

23. See Garrett, Spreitzer, and Bacevice (2017) for an example of Western coworking spaces that have fostered a sense of community.

24. In the Bahasa language, "kumpul" means "together." Since the time of our research, Kumpul has closed its location in Sanur. As of October 2019, Kumpul operates facilities in Denpasar and Seminyak.

25. Referencing Apple's Steve Jobs, Microsoft's Bill Gates, and Facebook's Mark Zuckerberg.

26. The phrase "getting shit done" is the language used by many Millennial business coaches and is also found all over the internet in the form of hashtags, memes, YouTube videos, and blogs.

27. Yorks, Frothingham, and Schuennke (2017).

28. Cf. Seitchik et al. (2017).

29. "Leveling up" is a gaming term that refers to progressing to the next stage of a game or skill.

30. Indonesia is located between several tectonic plates, making it susceptible to earthquakes and volcanic activity.

31. www.wandererbracelets.com.

32. Brené Brown is known for her TED Talks and Netflix special as well as several books including *The Gifts of Imperfection: Let Go of Who You Think You're Supposed to Be and Embrace Who You Are* (2010), *Daring Greatly: How the Courage to Be Vulnerable Transforms the Way We Live, Love, Parent, and Lead* (2012), and *Rising Strong: How the Ability to Reset Transforms the Way We Live, Love, Parent, and Lead* (2015). Marianne Williamson ran for president of the United States in 2019–2020, and she is also known for her activism and many spiritual books, especially *A Return to Love: Reflections on the Principles of "A Course in Miracles"* (1992).

33. What nomads commonly call "tourist visas" are technically called "visit visas."

34. Cf. Ferriss (2007).

35. https://www.investopedia.com/terms/s/seo-search-engine-optimization.asp, retrieved September 24, 2019.

36. Indeed, skill shares' uneven quality may have contributed to the growth of more traditional, fee-based training programs and conferences sponsored by Bali's coworking spaces. Still, skill shares remain the primary format for learning events in Bali's digital nomad community.

37. Kauffman Foundation (2019).

38. https://www.entrepreneur.com/encyclopedia/business-incubator, retrieved October 20, 2019.

39. Kauffman Foundation (2019).

40. Napoleon Hill popularized the term "mastermind" in his 1937 classic self-help text *Think and Grow Rich*. He described a "master mind alliance" in which individuals rely on trusted others for planning and support. Self-help and entrepreneurship have a long, and often shared, history. The types of peer-to-peer helping groups are known in the digital nomad community as masterminds, but they exist under a variety of names in more traditional business communities.

41. Location-independent entrepreneurs even have their own network of masterminds called "Dynamite Circle" that claims 950 members in fifty-six cities worldwide (http://www.tropicalmba.com/dcold/, retrieved November 2, 2018).

42. This is part of a broader trend among digital nomad women and Millennial women in general. We observed that many nomad women owned or talked about the popular book *#GIRLBOSS* (Amoruso 2014), which has since become a Netflix series. The term "girl boss" is found on girls' and women's items in the largest retailers in the United States. We have even observed the migration of this slogan in the rise of multilevel marketing and in mainstream media campaigns that urge women to be the boss, as evidenced in the Avon Corp. 2016 advertising campaign "This Is Boss Life" (https://www.youtube.com/watch?v=KWbWJ8xweUg, retrieved October 17, 2019).

43. Lyons (2017).

44. Cf. Fiset (2015).

45. https://inc42.com/indonesia/startup-weekend-bali-indonesia-winners/.

46. Startupweekend.org.

47. For comparison, we attended the final pitches and closing party for Pittsburgh's Startup Weekend, 2017. While the structure was similar, the overall event was extremely different in terms of the types of participants (US citizens who were full-time residents of Pittsburgh, mostly younger, and many of whom were in college), the types of businesses (oriented toward local markets in Pittsburgh), and the atmosphere of a loft-like incubator space. Despite Startup Weekend's goal of making entrepreneurship accessible, the incubator space where it was held, with its many "off-limits" areas of equipment for incubator members, was a reminder of the exclusionary atmosphere surrounding start-up ecosystems in the United States.

48. https://www.greenschool.org. See also https://www.nytimes.com/2017/11/13/t-magazine/bali-green-school.html.

49. Scoring criteria include the business model, the degree to which the team has validated that customers would buy the product, and the execution of a minimally viable product. See https://www.techstars.com/content/community/startup-weekend-judging-criteria/, retrieved October 18, 2019.

50. Worldwide, organizers claim that approximately 25 percent of teams continue with their project after the weekend ends (https://startupweekend.org/attendees/faq#team-continuation).

CHAPTER 5

1. For instance, decades ago anthropologist Kalervo Oberg (1960) used the term "honeymooners" in describing one of the stages of culture shock.

2. Alsop (2008); Twenge (2006).

3. Goffman (1963).

4. Bureau of Labor Statistics (2015); Fry (2018).

5. Hodson (2009).

6. Myers and Sadaghiani (2010).

7. See Kreider (2012).

8. Pinsker (2017).

9. Latack, Kinicki, and Prussia (1995).

10. Polson (2016).

11. Polson (2016).

12. Polson (2016).

13. Ertel et al. (2005).

14. Kalleberg (2009); Kalleberg and Vallas (2018).

15. Kalleberg and Vallas (2018: 16).

16. Cross and Payne (1991).
17. Vallas and Cummins (2015).
18. Some have argued that the concept of a super core, which includes cultural industries and cultural occupations, is the true creative economy rather than Florida's broader conception, which includes science, engineering, computing, and education (see Markusen, Wassall, DeNatale, and Cohen [2008]).
19. As mentioned in the introduction, digital nomads usually arrive in Bali on tourist *visit visas* (i.e., single-entry visas) that allow them to stay legally for a maximum of sixty days, after which they must go to another country to obtain an entry stamp before returning and extending their time there (see https://www.embassyofindonesia.org/index.php/visa-requirements/. Retrieved July 30, 2020).
20. Sinek's 2011 book has been a number-one bestseller in the computers and technology industry, according to Amazon.
21. Google and Airbnb were bootstrapped in this manner. Although some find it risky to start a business with a credit card, many respected businesses have been funded this way (see https://www.entrepreneur.com/article/197848; retrieved December 15, 2019; Clifford, 2017; French, 2019).
   For more, see https://about.crunchbase.com/blog/fund-startup-with-credit-card/).
22. Matsakis (2019).
23. For discussion of the factors that lead individuals toward various degrees of social entrepreneurship, see Wry and York (2017).
24. Prominent examples of professed altruism and techno-utopianism include Google's famous "Don't be evil" slogan and Facebook's corporate responses to criticisms (see Marantz 2019).
25. Many digital nomads are captivated by the "FIRE movement," which stands for "Financial Independence, Retire Early" (Kerr 2019).

CHAPTER 6

1. See Peck's (2005) critique of Florida's thesis, arguing that Florida's ideas are a version of a neoliberal policy strategy. See O'Connell (2017) for media coverage of Florida's reconsideration of the creative class thesis and the ways in which urban inequality has increased in recent years in many creative class cities.
2. See Schwirian, Curry, and Woldoff (2004).
3. Morales (2017).
4. Morales (2017); Streitfeld (2018).
5. Florida (2003, 2008).
6. Autor (2014).
7. Florida (2008).
8. Buckley et al. (1998).
9. Bogue (1969).
10. Granovetter (1973).
11. Kasarda and Janowitz (1974); Park (1926).
12. Cf. Fischer (1975).
13. Tajfel and Turner (1986).
14. Fechter (2007).
15. Often, Balinese people would be the ones to discourage more intimate, egalitarian relationships. There are several reasons for this. First, Balinese people tend to have social worlds that are quite full of obligations already. Second, many Balinese people establish boundaries with tourists because of cultural differences, fear of crossing a line that might cost them income, and concerns about tourists bringing negative attention, displaying inappropriate behavior, and falsely accusing them of a crime or behavior. Finally, Balinese

people tend to be concerned about the effects of negative karma on themselves, their families, their businesses, and their community.

16. Fechter (2007).
17. As of this writing, our follow-ups with informants from our primary sample suggest that only three nomads, all of whom are American, have returned to location-dependent, full-time employment in their home societies. Of these, one returned to a job substantially similar to the one the person had left, while the other two have made significant career changes.
18. We conclude this based on several pieces of data, including reports from our informants, information from membership at the coworking spaces we visited, online forums, and nomad websites that show increases in the number, size, and types of coworking spaces (see for example, https://www.coworker.com/search/bali/indonesia).
19. Hutton (2019).
20. See, for example, Duffy (2017) and Gregg (2011).
21. This article featured the headline "Digital Nomadism Goes Mainstream" (Pofeldt 2018).
22. For instance, some nomads reported that Bali is the preferred destination for digital nomads with high professional skills, whereas e-commerce entrepreneurs prefer Chiang Mai.
23. Laughlin (2019).
24. Kasarda and Janowitz (1974); Park (1926).
25. Kalleberg (2009); Scholz and Schneider (2016).

BIBLIOGRAPHY

Abbott, Andrew. 1997. "Of Time and Space: The Contemporary Relevance of the Chicago
    School." *Social Forces* 75(4): 1149–82.
Adler, Paul S., and Seok-Woo Kwon. 2002. "Social Capital: Prospects for a New Concept."
    Academy of Management Review 27(1): 17–40.
Alagiah, Matt. 2018. "Core Strength." *Monocle* (April): 84–87.
Alba, Richard D., and Victor Nee. 2003. *Remaking the American Mainstream: Assimilation and
    the New Immigration.* Cambridge, MA: Harvard University Press.
Alsop, Ron. 2008. *The Trophy Kids Grow Up: How the Millennial Generation Is Shaping Up the
    Workplace.* San Francisco: Jossey-Bass.
Amabile, Teresa M. 1988. "A Model of Creativity and Innovation in Organizations." Pp.
    123–67 in *Research in Organizational Behavior,* edited by B.S. Cummings. Greenwich,
    CT: JAI Press.
Amabile, Teresa M. 1996. *Creativity in Context: Update to the Social Psychology of Creativity.*
    Boulder, CO: Westview Press.
Amabile, Teresa M., and Regina Conti. 1999. "Changes in the Work Environment for
    Creativity during Downsizing." *Academy of Management Journal* 42(6): 630–40.
Amabile, Teresa M., Regina Conti, Heather Coon, Jeffrey Lazenby, and Michael Herron. 1996.
    "Assessing the Work Environment for Creativity." *Academy of Management Journal*
    39(5): 1154–84.
Amabile, Teresa M., and Michael G. Pratt. 2016. "The Dynamic Componential Model of
    Creativity and Innovation in Organizations: Making Progress, Making Meaning."
    Research in Organizational Behavior 36: 157–83.
Amador, Cecilia. 2018. "Coworking by the Numbers: Stats That Show That Coworking Is
    Dominating Office Real Estate." *Allwork.space.* Retrieved January 22, 2019 (https://
    allwork.space/2018/10/coworking-by-the-numbers-stats-that-show-that-coworking-
    is-dominating-office-real-estate/).
Amoruso, Sophia. 2014. *#GIRLBOSS.* New York: Penguin.
Anderson, Elijah. 1999. *Code of the Street: Decency, Violence, and the Moral Life of the Inner City.*
    New York: W.W. Norton.
Aronczyk, Melissa. 2013. *Branding the Nation: The Global Business of National Identity.*
    New York: Oxford University Press.
Australian Embassy, Indonesia. 2016. "Australian and Indonesian Tourists Make History."
    Retrieved April 9, 2019 (http://indonesia.embassy.gov.au/jakt/MR16_042.html).
Autor, David H. 2014. "Skills, Education and the Rise of Earnings Inequality among the
    'Other 99 Percent.'" *Science* 344(23): 843–51.
Badan Pusat Statistik. 2010. "Penduduk Menurut Wilayah dan Agama yang Dianut." Retrieved
    April 9, 2019 (https://sp2010.bps.go.id/index.php/site/tabel?tid=321&wid=0).

Barley, Stephen R., and Gideon Kunda. 2004. *Gurus, Hired Guns, and Warm Bodies: Itinerant Experts in a Knowledge Economy.* Princeton, NJ: Princeton University Press.

Barrell, James, and Sidney Jourard. 1976. "Being Honest with Persons We Like." *Journal of Individual Psychology* 32(2): 185–93.

Baruch, Yehuda, Yochanan Altman, and Rosalie L. Tung. 2016. "Career Mobility in a Global Era: Advances in Managing Expatriation and Repatriation." *Academy of Management Annals* 10(1): 841–89.

Baruch, Yehuda, Michael Dickmann, Yochanan Altman, and Frank Bernois. 2013. "Exploring International Work: Types and Dimensions of Global Careers." *International Journal of Human Resource Management* 24(12): 2369–93.

Beaudry, Paul, David A. Green, and Benjamin M. Sand. 2014. "Declining Fortunes of the Young since 2000." *American Economic Review* 104(5): 381–86.

Beauregard, Robert A. 1986. "The Chaos and Complexity of Gentrification." Pp. 35–55 in *Gentrification of the City,* edited by N. Smith and P. Williams. Boston: Unwin Hyman.

Bélanger, Danièle. 2010. "Marriages with Foreign Women in East Asia: Bride Trafficking or Voluntary Migration?" *Population and Societies* 469: 1–4.

Bellezza, Silvia, Neeru Paharia, and Anat Keinan. 2017. "Conspicuous Consumption of Time: When Busyness and Lack of Leisure Time Become a Status Symbol." *Journal of Consumer Research* 44(1): 118–38.

Bidwell, Matthew, Forrest Briscoe, Isabel Fernandez-Mateo, and Adina Sterling. 2013. "The Employment Relationship and Inequality: How and Why Changes in Employment Practices Are Reshaping Rewards in Organizations." *Academy of Management Annals* 7(1): 61–121.

Bird, Allan, Joyce S. Osland, Mark Mendenhall, and Susan C. Schneider. 1999. "Adapting and Adjusting to Other Cultures: What We Know but Don't Always Tell." *Journal of Management Inquiry* 8(2): 152–65.

Black, J. Stewart, and Hal Gregersen. 1999. "The Right Way to Manage Expats." *Harvard Business Review* (March–April). Retrieved August 4, 2017 (https://hbr.org/1999/03/the-right-way-to-manage-expats).

Bogue, Donald J. 1969. *Principles of Demography.* New York: Wiley.

Bootstrappingecommerce.com. 2018. Retrieved September 4, 2018 (https://bootstrappingecommerce.com/how-i-chose-the-niche-for-my-new-online-store/).

Bourdieu, Pierre. 1984. *Distinction: A Social Critique of the Judgement of Taste.* Cambridge, MA: Harvard University Press.

Branson, Richard. 2011. *Screw Business as Usual.* New York: Penguin.

Brewster, Chris, and Juana Pickard. 1994. "Evaluating Expatriate Training." *International Studies of Management and Organization* 24(3): 18–35.

Briscoe, Jon P., Douglas T. Hall, and Rachel L. Frautschy DeMuth. 2006. "Protean and Boundaryless Careers: An Empirical Exploration." *Journal of Vocational Behavior* 69: 30–47.

Brown, Brené. 2010. *The Gifts of Imperfection: Let Go of Who You Think You're Supposed to Be and Embrace Who You Are.* Center City, MN: Hazelden Publishing.

Brown, Brené. 2012. *Daring Greatly: How the Courage to Be Vulnerable Transforms the Way We Live, Love, Parent, and Lead.* New York: Gotham Books.

Brown, Brené. 2015. *Rising Strong: How the Ability to Reset Transforms the Way We Live, Love, Parent, and Lead.* New York: Random House.

Brown-Saracino, Japonica. 2009. *A Neighborhood That Never Changes: Gentrification, Social Preservation, and the Search for Authenticity.* Chicago: University of Chicago Press.

Bucketlistbonbshells.com. 2017. Retrieved March 13, 2017 (https://bbcourses.com).

Buckley, M. Ronald, Donald B. Fedor, John G. Veres, Danielle S. Wiese, and Shawn M. Carraher. 1998. "Investigating Newcomer Expectations and Job-Related Outcomes." *Journal of Applied Psychology* 83(3): 452–61.

Bureau of Labor Statistics. 2015. "Labor Force Projections to 2024: The Labor Force Is Growing, but Slowly" (https://www.bls.gov/opub/mlr/2015/article/labor-force-projections-to-2024.htm).

Byrne, Rhonda. 2006. *The Secret*. New York: Atria Books.

Cadwallader, Martin. 1992. *Migration and Residential Mobility: Macro and Micro Approaches*. Madison: University of Wisconsin Press.

Campbell, Joseph. 1949. *A Hero with a Thousand Faces*. New York: Pantheon Books.

Cappelli, Peter, and J.R. Keller. 2013. "Classifying Work in the New Economy." *Academy of Management Review* 38(4): 575–96.

Carrigan, Mark. "The Lure of Minimalism." 2015. *The Sociological Imagination*. Retrieved April 1, 2019 (http://sociologicalimagination.org/archives/16965).

Carver, Charles S., Michael F. Scheier, and Suzanne C. Segerstrom. 2010. "Optimism." *Clinical Psychology Review* 30: 879–89.

Cast, Alicia D., and Peter J. Burke. 2002. "A Theory of Self Esteem." *Social Forces* 80(3): 1041–68.

Castells, Manuel. 1977. *The Urban Question: A Marxist Approach*. Cambridge, MA: MIT Press.

Castles, Stephen. 2003. "Towards a Sociology of Forced Migration and Social Transformation." *Sociology* 37(1): 13–34.

Chokshi, Niraj. 2017. "Out of the Office: More People Are Working Remotely, Survey Finds." February 15. Retrieved January 29, 2018 (https://www.nytimes.com/2017/02/15/us/remote-workers-work-from-home.html).

Cilluffo, Anthony, and D'Vera Cohn. 2017. "10 Demographic Trends Shaping the U.S. and the World in 2017." *Pew Research Center*. Retrieved January 28, 2019 (http://www.pewresearch.org/fact-tank/2017/04/27/10-demographic-trends-shaping-the-u-s-and-the-world-in-2017/).

Clifford, Catherine. 2017. "How the Co-founder of Airbnb went from $25,000 in Credit Card Debt to Running His $30 Billion Company." https://www.cnbc.com/2017/06/30/airbnb-ceo-went-from-25000-in-debt-to-running-a-30-billion-company.html. Retrieved August 2, 2020.

Clynes, Tom. 2017. "Peter Thiel Thinks You Should Skip College, and He'll Even Pay You for the Trouble." *Newsweek*. Retrieved April 17, 2019 (https://www.newsweek.com/2017/03/03/peter-thiel-fellowship-college-higher-education-559261.html).

Cohen, Erik. 1972. "Toward a Sociology of International Tourism." *Social Research* 39(1):164–82.

Cohen, Erik. 1984. "Sociology of Tourism: Approaches, Issues, and Findings." *Annual Review of Sociology* 10: 373–92.

Cohen, Erik. 2017. "Towards a Convergence of Tourism Studies and Island Studies." *Acta Turistica* 29(1): 7–31.

Cohen, Natalie. 2000. "Business Location Decision-Making and the Cities: Bringing Companies Back." Washington, DC: Brookings Institution Center on Urban and Metropolitan Policy.

Cohen, Scott. 2010. "Searching for Escape, Authenticity, and Identity: Experiences of Lifestyle Travelers." Pp. 27–42 in *The Tourism and Leisure Experience: Consumer and Managerial Perspectives*, edited by M. Morgan, P. Lugosi, and J.R.B. Ritchie. Buffalo: Channel View Publications.

Collins, Nancy L., and Lynn Carol Miller. 1994. "Self-Disclosure and Liking: A Meta-Analytic Review." *Psychological Bulletin* 116(3): 457–75.

Corcoran, Jacqueline, and Albert R. Roberts. 2000. "Research on Crisis Intervention and Recommendations for Further Research." Pp. 453–86 in *Crisis Intervention Handbook: Assessment, Treatment and Research* (2nd ed.), edited by A.R. Roberts. New York: Oxford University Press.

Costa, Janeen A. 1998. "Paradise Discourse: A Critical Analysis of Marketing and Consuming Hawaii." *Consumption, Markets and Culture 1*(4): 303–46.

Coulter, Rory, Maarten van Ham, and Allan M. Findlay. 2016. "Re-thinking Residential Mobility: Linking Lives through Time and Space." *Progress in Human Geography 40*(3): 352–74.

Covey, Stephen. 1992. *The Seven Habits of Highly Effective People.* New York: Simon & Schuster.

Crant, J. Michael. 2000. "Proactive Behavior in Organizations." *Journal of Management 26*(3): 435–62.

Cross, Malcolm, and Geoff Payne. 1991/2018. *Work and the Enterprise Culture.* New York: Routledge.

Csikszentmihalyi, Mihaly. 1997. *Finding Flow: The Psychology of Engagement with Everyday Life.* New York: Basic Books.

Dalio, Ray. 2017. *Principles of Life and Work.* New York: Simon and Schuster.

Davies, Amanda, and Aileen Hoath. 2015. "The Migration of Australians to Bali, Indonesia: More Than Retirees and Surfers." *Geographical Research 54*(1): 35–51.

Davies, Ed, and Cindy Silviana. 2018. "New Indonesia Web System Blocks More Than 70,000 'Negative' Sites." *Reuters.* Retrieved July 19, 2019 (https://www.reuters.com/article/us-indonesia-communications/new-indonesia-web-system-blocks-more-than-70000-negative-sites-idUSKCN1G30KA).

Deloitte. 2015. *Global Human Capital Trends 2015: Leading in the New World of Work.* New York: Deloitte University Press.

Deloitte. 2018. *The Rise of the Social Enterprise: 2018 Deloitte Human Capital Trends.* New York: Deloitte University Press.

De Stefano, Valerio. 2015. "The Rise of the 'Just-in-Time Workforce': On-Demand Work, Crowdwork, and Labor Protection in the 'Gig-Economy.'" *Comparative Labor Law & Policy Journal 37*: 471–503.

Directorate General of Immigration. 2013. "Visit Visa." Retrieved April 17, 2019 (http://www.imigrasi.go.id/index.php/en/public-services/visit-visa).

Directorate of General Immigration. 2018. "Visit Visa." Retrieved November 2, 2018 (http://www.imigrasi.go.id/index.php/en/public-services/visit-visa).

Duffy, Brooke Erin. 2017. *(Not) Getting Paid to Do What You Love: Gender, Social Media, and Aspirational Work.* New Haven, CT: Yale University Press.

Du Gay, Paul. 1996. *Consumption and Identity Work.* Thousand Oaks, CA: Sage.

Durkheim, Emile. 1893/1964. *The Division of Labor in Society.* New York: Free Press.

Education First. 2017. "EF English Language Proficiency Index." Retrieved April 16, 2019 (https://www.ef.edu/epi/regions/asia/indonesia/).

Elgan, Mike. 2012. "I'm a Digital Nomad (And So Are You)." *Computerworld.com.* July 14. Retrieved August 4, 2017 (http://www.computerworld.com/article/2505870/mobile-wireless/elgan--i-m-a-digital-nomad--and-so-are-you-.html).

Elsbach, Kimberly. 2009. "Identity Affirmation through 'Signature Style': A Study of Toy Car Designers." *Human Relations 62*(7): 1041–72.

Ertel, Michael, Eberhard Pech, Peter Ullsperger, Olaf Von Dem Knesebeck, and Johannes Siegrist. 2005. "Adverse Psychosocial Working Conditions and Subjective Health in Freelance Media Workers." *Work and Stress 19*(3): 293–99.

Fechter, Anne-Meike. 2007. *Transnational Lives: Expatriates in Indonesia.* London: Routledge.

Ferriss, Tim. 2007. *The 4-Hour Workweek: Escape 9–5, Live Anywhere, and Join the New Rich.* New York: Harmony Press.

Ferriss, Tim. 2010. *The 4-Hour Body: An Uncommon Guide to Rapid Fat-Loss, Incredible Sex, and Becoming Superhuman.* New York: Harmony Press.

Fezehai, Malin. 2018. "What This 76-Year-Old Man Can Teach about Healing." *New York Times.* Retrieved April 17, 2019 (https://www.nytimes.com/2018/05/19/world/ what-this-76-year-old-man-can-teach-about-healing.html).

Fischer, Claude S. 1975. "Toward a Subcultural Theory of Urbanism." *American Journal of Sociology* 80(6): 1319–41.

Fischer, Claude S. 1982. *To Dwell among Friends: Personal Networks in Town and City.* Chicago: University of Chicago Press.

Fiset, Jay. 2015. "Are Business 'Masterminds' a Scam?" *Entrepreneur.com.* Retrieved January 14, 2019 (https://www.entrepreneur.com/article/253145).

Fitzpatrick, Kevin M., and Mark LaGory. 2003. "'Placing' Health in an Urban Sociology: Cities as Mosaics of Risk and Protection." *City and Community* 2(1): 33–46.

Florida, Richard. 2002. *The Rise of the Creative Class.* New York: Basic Books.

Florida, Richard. 2003. "Cities and the Creative Class." *City and Community* 2(1): 3–19.

Florida, Richard. 2005. *The Flight of the Creative Class: The New Global Competition for Talent.* New York: HarperCollins.

Florida, Richard. 2008. *Who's Your City? How the Creative Economy Is Making Where to Live the Most Important Decision of Your Life.* New York: Basic Books.

Florida, Richard. 2015. "America's Leading Creative Class Cities in 2015." *CityLab.* April 20. Retrieved February 11, 2019 (https://www.citylab.com/life/2015/04/americas- leading-creative-class-cities-in-2015/390852/).

Florida, Richard, 2017. *The New Urban Crisis: How Our Cities Are Increasing Inequality, Deepening Segregation, and Failing the Middle Class and What We Can Do about It.* New York: Basic Books.

French, Susan. 2019. "Can I Fund a Startup with My Credit Card?" https://about.crunchbase. com/blog/fund-startup-with-credit-card/. Retrieved August 2, 2020.

Fry, Richard. 2018. "Millennials Are the Largest Generation in the U.S. Labor Force." *Pew Research Center.* Retrieved October 11, 2018 (http://www.pewresearch.org/fact-tank/ 2018/04/11/millennials-largest-generation-us-labor-force/).

Galek, Candice. 2018. "If You've Searched 'My Job Is Killing Me' You're Not Alone." *Inc.com.* February 28. Retrieved November 27, 2018 (https://www.inc.com/candice-galek/if- youve-searched-my-job-is-killing-me-youre-not-alone.html).

Gallup. 2017. "State of the American Workplace." *Gallup.* Retrieved May 20, 2019 (https:// www.gallup.com/workplace/238085/state-american-workplace-report-2017.aspx).

Gallup. 2018. "The Gig Economy and Alternative Work Arrangements." *Gallup.* Retrieved January 28, 2019 (https://www.gallup.com/file/workplace/240878/Gig_Economy_ Paper_2018.pdf).

Gans, Herbert. 1962. *Urban Villagers: Group and Class in the Life of Italian-Americans.* New York: Free Press.

Gans, Herbert J. 1968. "Urbanism and Suburbanism as Ways of Life: A Reevaluation of Definitions." Pp. 34–51 in *People and Plans: Essays on Urban Problems and Solutions.* New York: Basic Books.

Garrett, Lyndon E., Gretchen M. Spreitzer, and Peter A. Bacevice. 2017. "Co-Constructing a Sense of Community at Work: The Emergence of Community in Coworking Spaces." *Organization Studies* 38(6): 821–42.

Gieryn, Thomas F. 2000. "A Space for Place in Sociology." *Annual Review of Sociology* 26: 463–96.

Gill, Flora. 1999. "The Meaning of Work: Lessons from Sociology, Psychology, and Political Theory." *Journal of Socio-Economics* 28: 725–43.

Gittleson, Kim. 2014. "Forget Silicon Valley, Meet Silicon Bali." *BBC.com*. April 23. Retrieved January 18, 2018 (http://www.bbc.com/news/business-27043778).

Goclowaska, Malgorzata A., Simone Ritter, Andrew J. Elliot, and Mattjijs Baas. 2019. "Novelty Seeking Is Linked to Openness and Extraversion, and Can Lead to Greater Creative Performance." *Journal of Personality* 87(2): 252–66.

Goffman, Erving. 1959. *The Presentation of Self in Everyday Life*. Garden City, NY: Doubleday.

Goffman, Erving. 1963. *Stigma: Notes on the Management of Spoiled Identity*. Englewood Cliffs, NJ: Prentice Hall.

Gotham, Kevin Fox, and Krista Brumley. 2002. "Using Space: Agency and Identity in a Public-Housing Development." *City and Community* 1(3): 267–89.

Granovetter, Mark S. 1973. "The Strength of Weak Ties." *American Journal of Sociology* 78(6): 1360–80.

Grant, Adam M., and James W. Berry. 2011. "The Necessity of Others Is the Mother of Invention: Intrinsic and Prosocial Motivations, Perspective Taking, and Creativity." *Academy of Management Journal* 54(1): 73–96.

Grant, Adam M., and Diane R. Stober. 2006. "Introduction." Pp. 1–14 in *Evidence-Based Coaching Handbook: Putting Best Practices to Work for Your Clients*, edited by D.R. Stober and A.M. Grant. Hoboken, NJ: Wiley.

Greenschool.org. 2018. Retrieved November 6, 2018 (https://www.greenschool.org).

Gregg, Melissa. 2011. *Work's Intimacy*. Malden, MA: Polity Press.

Groth, Aimee. 2012. "You're the Average of the Five People You Spend the Most Time With." *Business Insider*. Retrieved April 3, 2019 (https://www.businessinsider.com/jim-rohn-youre-the-average-of-the-five-people-you-spend-the-most-time-with-2012-7).

Gyourko, Joseph, Christopher Mayer, and Todd Sinai. 2013. *Superstar Cities. American Economic Journal: Economic Policy* 5(4): 167–99.

Halfacree, Keith H., and Paul J. Boyle 1993. "The Challenge Facing Migration Research: The Case for a Biographical Approach." *Progress in Human Geography* 17(3): 333–48.

Hall, Douglas T., Jeffrey Yip, and Kathryn Doiron. 2018. "Protean Careers at Work: Self-Direction and Values Orientation in Psychological Success." *Annual Review of Organizational Psychology and Organizational Behavior* 5: 129–56.

Hampton, Keith N., and Neeti Gupta. 2008. "Community and Social Interaction in the Wireless City: Wi-Fi Use in Public and Semi-Public Spaces." *New Media & Society* 10(6): 831–50.

Hanlon, Phil, and Sandra Carlisle. 2009. "Is 'Modern Culture' Bad for Our Health and Well-Being?" *Global Health Promotion* 16(4): 27–34.

Haug, Sonja. 2008. "Migration Networks and Migration Decision-Making." *Journal of Ethnic and Migration Studies* 34(4): 585–605.

Heller, Nathan. 2017. "Estonia, the Digital Republic." *The New Yorker*. December 18, 25. Retrieved January 30, 2018 (https://www.newyorker.com/magazine/2017/12/18/estonia-the-digital-republic).

Hermanowicz, Joseph C., and Harriet P. Morgan. 1999. "Ritualizing the Routine: Collective Identity Affirmation." *Sociological Forum* 14(2): 197–214.

Hill, Napoleon. 1937/2016. *Think and Grow Rich*. Wise, VA: Napoleon Hill Foundation.

Hillery, George A. 1955. "Definitions of Community: Areas of Agreement." *Rural Sociology* 20(2): 111–23.

Hodson, Randy. 2009. *Dignity at Work*. New York: Cambridge University Press.

Hollister, Matissa. 2011. "Employment Stability in the U.S. Labor Market: Rhetoric versus Reality." *Annual Review of Sociology* 37: 305–24.

Hunter, Albert D. 1974. *Symbolic Communities: The Persistence and Change of Chicago's Local Communities.* Chicago: University of Chicago Press.

Hunter, Albert D. 1985. "Private, Parochial and Public Social Orders: The Problem of Crime and Incivility in Urban Communities." Pp. 230–42 in *The Challenge of Social Control: Institution Building and Systemic Constraint,* edited by G.D. Suttles and M.N. Zald. Norwood, NJ: ABLEX.

Hutton, M. 2019. "Why Bali Is Not a Sustainable Holiday Destination." *South China Morning Post* (https://www.asiaone.com/asia/why-bali-not-sustainable-holiday-destination).

Ibarra, Herminia. 1999. "Provisional Selves: Experimenting with Image and Identity in Professional Adaptation." *Administrative Science Quarterly* 44(4): 764–91.

Inc42. 2018. "NomaStay, Hubs, and Finger Farm Secured the Top Positions at the Startup Weekend." Retrieved November 6, 2018 (https://inc42.com/indonesia/startup-weekend-bali-indonesia-winners/).

Indrianto, Agoes Tinus. 2005. "The Commodification of Culture in Bali in the Frame of Cultural Tourism." *Asean Journal on Hospitality and Tourism* 4(2): 151–65.

Janowitz, Morris. 1967. *The Community Press in an Urban Setting: The Social Elements of Urbanism.* Chicago: University of Chicago Press.

Judd, Dennis R., and Susan S. Fainstein. 1999. *The Tourist City.* New Haven, CT: Yale University Press.

Kalleberg, Arne L. 2009. "Precarious Work, Insecure Workers: Employment Relations in Transition." *American Sociological Review* 74 (February): 1–22.

Kalleberg, Arne L., and Steven P. Vallas. 2018. "Probing Precarious Work: Theory, Research, and Politics." Pp. 1–30 in *Precarious Work,* edited by A.L. Kalleberg and S.P. Vallas. Bingley, Yorkshire, UK: Emerald Publishing.

Kasarda, John D., and Morris Janowitz. 1974. "Community Attachment in Mass Society." *American Sociological Review* 39: 328–39.

Kauffman Foundation. 2017. "Entrepreneurial Ecosystem Building Playbook 2.0." Retrieved January 2, 2019 (https://www.kauffman.org/entrepreneurial-ecosystem-building-playbook-draft-2/ii-what-are-entrepreneurial-ecosystems#).

Kauffman Foundation. 2019. "Early Stage Entrepreneurship Support Programs." Retrieved January 14, 2019 (https://www.kauffman.org/microsites/state-of-the-field/topics/entrepreneurial-support-programs).

Kavaratzis, Michalis. 2004. "From City Marketing to City Branding: Towards a Theoretical Framework for Developing City Brands." *Place Branding* 1(1): 58–73.

Kawachi, Ichiro, and Bruce P. Kennedy. 2002. *The Health of Nations: Why Inequality Is Harmful to Your Health.* New York: New Press.

Keller, Suzanne. 1968. *The Urban Neighborhood.* New York: Random House.

Kerr, Alexandra. 2019. "Financial Independence, Retire Early (FIRE)." *Investopedia.com.* Retrieved December 16, 2019 (https://www.investopedia.com/terms/f/financial-independence-retire-early-fire.asp).

King, Stephen. 2000. *On Writing.* New York: Scribner.

Kondo, Marie. 2014. *The Life-Changing Magic of Tidying Up: The Japanese Art of Decluttering and Organizing.* New York: Ten Speed Press.

Kreider, Tim. 2012. "The 'Busy Trap.'" *New York Times.* June 30. Retrieved October 22, 2019 (https://opinionator.blogs.nytimes.com/2012/06/30/the-busy-trap/).

Lamarque, Hannah. 2015. "The Rise of the Digital Nomad." *Huffington Post.* June 2. Retrieved August 7, 2017 (http://www.huffingtonpost.com/hannah-lamarque/the-rise-of-the-digital-n_b_7492482.html).

Latack, Janina C., Angelo J. Kinicki, and Greg E. Prussia. 1995. "An Integrative Process Model of Coping with Job Loss." *Academy of Management Review* 20: 311–42.

Lau, Kimberly J. 2000. *New Age Capitalism: Making Money East of Eden.* Philadelphia: University of Pennsylvania Press.

Laughlin, Lauren Silva. 2019. "The Hazards of Joining WeWork's Community." *Wall Street Journal.* April 14. Retrieved February 11, 2020 (https://www.wsj.com/articles/the-hazards-of-joining-weworks-community-11565798457).

Lee, Barrett A., Ralph S. Oropesa, and James W. Kanan. 1994. "Neighborhood Context and Residential Mobility." *Demography* 31(2): 249–70.

Lee, Everett S. 1966. "A Theory of Migration." *Demography* 3(1): 47–57.

Lerner, Michele. 2008. "The New Boomtowns: Why More People Are Relocating to 'Secondary' Cities." *Washington Post.* Retrieved February 19, 2019 (https://www.washingtonpost.com/realestate/the-new-boomtowns-why-more-people-are-relocating-to-secondary-cities/2018/11/07/f55f96f4-d618-11e8-aeb7-ddcad4a0a54e_story.html?utm_term=.cc96f22268da).

Levitt, Peggy, and B. Nadya Jaworsky. 2007. "Transnational Migration Studies: Past Developments and Future Trends." *Annual Review of Sociology* 33: 129–56.

Lin, Yi-Chin, Thomas E. Pearson, and Liping A. Cai. 2011. "Food as a Form of Destination Identity: A Tourism Destination Brand Perspective." *Tourism and Hospitality Research* 11(1): 30–48.

Lippard, Lucy R. 1997. *The Lure of the Local.* New York: New Press.

Lyons, Dan. 2017. "Jerks and the Start-Ups They Ruin." *New York Times.* Retrieved November 10, 2018 (https://www.nytimes.com/2017/04/01/opinion/sunday/jerks-and-the-start-ups-they-ruin.html).

Mahroum, Sami. 2000. "Highly Skilled Globetrotters: Mapping the International Migration of Human Capital." *R&D Management* 30(1): 23–32.

Mainemelis, Charalampos. 2001. "When the Muse Takes It All: A Model for the Experience of Timelessness in Organizations." *Academy of Management Review* 26(4): 548–65.

Makimoto, Tsugio, and David Manners. 1997. *Digital Nomad.* New York: Wiley.

Marantz, Andrew. 2019. "The Dark Side of Techno-Utopianism." *The New Yorker.* Retrieved December 16, 2019 (https://www.newyorker.com/magazine/2019/09/30/the-dark-side-of-techno-utopianism).

Markusen, Ann, Gregory H. Wassall, Douglas DeNatale, and Randy Cohen. 2008. "Defining the Creative Economy: Industry and Occupational Approaches." *Economic Development Quarterly* 22(1): 24–45.

Marmot, Michael, and Richard G. Wilkinson, eds. 2006. *Social Determinants of Health.* Oxford, England: Oxford University Press.

Marsden, Peter V., and Karen E. Campbell. 1984. "Measuring Tie Strength." *Social Forces* 63(2): 482–50.

Marston, Cam. 2007. *Motivating the "What's in It for Me?" Workforce: Manage across the Generational Divide and Increase Profits.* Hoboken, NJ: Wiley.

Massey, Douglas S., Joaquin Arango, Graeme Hugo, Ali Kouaouci, Adela Pellegrino, and J. Edward Taylor. 1998. *Worlds in Motion: Understanding International Migration at the End of the Millennium.* Oxford: Clarendon Press.

Matsakis, Louise. 2019. "What Do Amazon's Star Ratings Really Mean?" *Wired* (https://www.wired.com/story/amazon-stars-ratings-calculated/).

McCarthy, Niall. 2018. "The Share of Americans Holding a Passport Has Increased Dramatically in Recent Years" [Infographic]. *Forbes.com.* Retrieved October 10, 2018 (https://www.forbes.com/sites/niallmccarthy/2018/01/11/the-share-of-americans-holding-a-passport-has-increased-dramatically-in-recent-years-infographic/#f05cc7c3c167).

McGee, Micki. 2005. *Self-Help, Inc.: Makeover Culture in American Life.* New York: Oxford University Press.

McPherson, Miller, Lynn Smith-Lovin, and James M. Cook. 2001. "Birds of a Feather: Homophily in Social Networks." *Annual Review of Sociology* 27: 415–44.

Merkel, Janet. 2019. "'Freelance Isn't Free': Co-Working as a Critical Urban Practice to Cope with Informality in Creative Labour Markets." *Urban Studies* 56(3): 526–47.

Millman, Dan. 2000. *The Way of the Peaceful Warrior: A Book That Changes Lives.* Tiburon, CA: H.J. Kramer.

Min, Kate E., Peggy J. Liu, and Soo Kim. 2018. "Sharing Extraordinary Experiences Fosters Feelings of Closeness." *Personality and Social Psychology Bulletin* 44(1): 107–21.

Mirowsky, John, and Catherine E. Ross. 2007. "Creative Work and Health." *Journal of Health and Social Behavior* 48: 385–403.

Mohn, Tanya. 2015. "Co-Working on Vacation: A Desk in Paradise." *New York Times,* January 19. Retrieved August 7, 2017 (http://www.nytimes.com/2015/01/20/business/co-working-on-vacation-a-desk-in-paradise.html?_r=0).

Mohn, Tanya. 2017. "The Digital Nomad Life: Combining Work and Travel." *New York Times,* April 3. Retrieved August 7, 2017 (https://www.nytimes.com/2017/04/03/business/digital-nomads-work-tourism.html).

Molla, Rani. 2017. "Big Companies Are Fueling WeWork's Growth." Recode.com. August 28. Retrieved January 22, 2019 (https://www.recode.net/2017/8/28/16214370/wework-coworking-fastest-growing-business-large-companies).

Moos, Markus, Deidre Pfeiffer, and Tara Vinodrai. 2008. *The Millennial City: Trends, Implications, and Prospects for Urban Planning and Policy.* New York: Routledge.

Morales, Patty Gorena. 2017. "Here's What Cities Are Offering Amazon to Host Its New Headquarters." *Making Sen$e.* Retrieved March 19, 2019 (https://www.pbs.org/newshour/economy/making-sense/heres-what-cities-are-offering-amazon-to-host-its-new-headquarters).

Moscardo, Gianna. 2010. "The Shaping of Tourist Experience: The Importance of Stories and Themes." Pp. 43–58 in *The Tourism and Leisure Experience: Consumer and Managerial Perspectives,* edited by M. Morgan, P. Lugosi, and J.R.B. Ritchie. Buffalo: Channel View Publications.

Mullis, Brian. 2017. "The Growth Paradox: Can Tourism Ever Be Sustainable?" *World Economic Forum.* Retrieved July 27, 2019 (https://www.weforum.org/agenda/2017/08/the-growth-paradox-can-tourism-ever-be-sustainable/).

Myers, Candice A., Tim Slack, and Joachim Singelmann. 2008. "Social Vulnerability and Migration in the Wake of Disaster: The Case of Hurricanes Katrina and Rita." *Population and Environment* 29: 271–91.

Myers, Karen K., and Kamyab Sadaghiami. 2010. "Millennials in the Workplace: A Communication Perspective on Millennials' Organizational Relationships and Performance." *Journal of Business and Psychology* 25(2): 225–38.

Nietzsche, Friedrich Wilhelm, and Reginald J. Hollingdale. 1996. *Human, All Too Human.* Cambridge: Cambridge University Press.

Nippert-Eng, Christena E. 1996. *Home and Work: Negotiating Boundaries through Everyday Life.* Chicago: University of Chicago Press.

Nishi, Akihiro, Hirokazu Shirado, and Nicholas A. Christakis. 2015. "Intermediate Levels of Network Fluidity Amplify Economic Growth and Mitigate Economic Inequality in Experimental Social Networks." *Sociological Science* 2: 544–57.

Nomadlist.com. Retrieved January 28, 2019.

Oberg, Kalervo. 1960. "Culture Shock: Adjustment to New Cultural Environments." *Practical Anthropology* 7: 177–82.

O'Connell, Jonathan. 2017. "This Guy Convinced Cities to Cater to Tech-Savvy Millennials. Now He's Reconsidering." *Washington Post.* Retrieved December 28, 2019 (https://

www.washingtonpost.com/news/digger/wp/2017/04/17/as-the-creative-class-divides-america-its-inventor-richard-florida-reconsiders/).

Osnowitz, Debra. 2010. *Freelancing Expertise: Contract Professionals in the New Economy.* Ithaca, NY: Cornell University Press.

Oyserman, Daphna, Heather M. Coon, and Markus Kemmelmeier. 2002. "Rethinking Individualism and Collectivism: Evaluation of Theoretical Assumptions and Meta-Analyses." *Psychological Bulletin* 128(1): 3–72.

Papastergiadis, Nikos. 2000. *The Turbulence of Migration: Globalization, Deterritorialization, and Hybridity.* Cambridge: Polity Press.

Parciany, Elizabeth Adams. 2009. "Golden Beaches & Adventuresome Wilderness: The Neocolonial Timeshare in Indonesia." *intersections* 10(2): 177–97.

Park, Robert E. 1926. "The Urban Community as a Spatial Pattern and a Moral Order." Pp. 3–18 in *The Urban Community*, edited by E.W. Burgess. Chicago: University of Chicago Press.

Park, Robert Ezra. 1936. "Human Ecology." *American Journal of Sociology* 42(1): 1–15.

Park, Robert E., Ernest W. Burgess, and Roderick D. McKenzie. 1925. *The City.* Chicago: University of Chicago Press.

Parker, Sharon K., Anja Van den Broeck, and David Holman. 2017. "Work Design Influences: A Synthesis of Multilevel Factors That Affect the Design of Jobs." *Academy of Management Annals* 11(1): 267–308.

Pattillo-McCoy, Mary. 1999. *Black Picket Fences: Privilege and Peril among the Black Middle Class.* Chicago: University of Chicago Press.

Pearlin, Leonard I. 1989. "The Sociological Study of Stress." *Journal of Health and Social Behavior* 30(3): 241–56.

Peck, Jamie. 2005. "Struggling with the Creative Class." *International Journal of Urban and Regional Research* 24(4): 740–70.

Peck, Jamie, and Adam Tickell. 2002. "Neoliberalizing Space." *Antipode* 34(3): 380–404.

Pedersen, Marianne Holm, and Mikkel Rytter. 2018. "Rituals of Migration: An Introduction." *Journal of Ethnic and Migration Studies* 44(16): 2603–16.

Pendraza, Silvia. 1991. "Women and Migration: The Social Consequences of Gender." *Annual Review of Sociology* 17: 303–25.

Perry-Smith, Jill E., and Christina E. Shalley. 2003. "The Social Side of Creativity: A Static and Dynamic Social Network Perspective." *Academy of Management Review* 28: 89–106.

Pine, B. Joseph, and James H. Gilmore. 1998. "Welcome to the Experience Economy." *Harvard Business Review*. July/August. Retrieved February 6, 2018 (https://hbr.org/1998/07/welcome-to-the-experience-economy).

Pinsker, Joe. 2017. "'Ugh, I'm So Busy': A Status Symbol for Our Time." *The Atlantic*. March 1. Retrieved October 22, 2019 (https://www.theatlantic.com/business/archive/2017/03/busyness-status-symbol/518178/).

Plunkett, Mike. 2018. "For Digital Nomads, Work Is Where the Laptop Is." *Washington Post*. July 6. Retrieved July 15, 2019 (https://www.washingtonpost.com/business/economy/for-digital-nomads-work-is-where-the-laptop-is/2018/07/06/3e146a4c-7e34-11e8-bb6b-c1cb691f1402_story.html?utm_term=.0de8bede889a).

Pofeldt, Elaine. 2018. "Digital Nomadism Goes Mainstream." *Forbes*. Retrieved March 26, 2019 (https://www.forbes.com/sites/elainepofeldt/2018/08/30/digital-nomadism-goes-mainstream/#6bce0d294553).

Pollan, Michael. 2018. *How to Change Your Mind: What the New Science of Psychedelics Teaches Us about Consciousness, Dying, Addiction, Depression, and Transcendence.* New York: Penguin.

Polson, Erika. 2016. *Privileged Mobilities.* New York: Peter Lang.

Portes, Alejandro. 1998. "Social Capital: Its Origins and Applications in Modern Sociology." *Annual Review of Sociology* 24:1–24.

Probst, Tahira B., Susan M. Stewart, Melissa L. Gruys, and Bradley W. Tierney. 2007. "Productivity, Counterproductivity and Creativity: The Ups and Downs of Job Insecurity." *Journal of Occupational and Organizational Psychology* 80(3): 479–97.

Putnam, Robert. 2000. *Bowling Alone: The Collapse and Revival of American Community.* New York: Simon and Schuster.

Rainie, Lee, and Barry Wellman. 2012. *Networked: The New Social Operating System.* Cambridge, MA: MIT Press.

Ralph, Oliver. 2017. "Lloyd's of London Bans Alcohol during Work Hours." *Financial Times.* February 14. Retrieved November 20, 2018 (https://www.ft.com/content/8de154aa-f2d9-11e6-95ee-f14e55513608).

Ravenelle, Alexandrea. 2019. *Hustle and Gig: Struggling and Surviving in the Sharing Economy.* Oakland: University of California Press.

Ray, Rebecca, Milla Sanes, and John Schmitt. 2012. "No-Vacation Nation Revisited." *Center for Economic and Policy Research.* Retrieved October 22, 2019 (http://cepr.net/documents/no-vacation-update-2014-04.pdf).

Reid, Erin. 2015. "Embracing, Passing, Revealing, and the Ideal Worker Image: How People Navigate Expected and Experienced Professional Identities." *Organization Science* 26(4): 997–1017.

Richmond, Anthony H. 1993. "Reactive Migration: Sociological Perspectives on Refugee Movements." *Journal of Refugee Studies* 6(1): 7–24.

Robbins, Alexandra, and Abby Wilner. 2001. *Quarterlife Crisis: The Unique Challenges of Life in Your Twenties.* New York: Penguin.

Robbins, Tony. 2007. *Awaken the Giant Within: How to Take Immediate Control of Your Mental, Emotional, Physical and Financial Destiny!* New York: Simon and Schuster.

Robinson, Geoffrey B. 2018. *The Killing Season: A History of the Indonesian Massacres, 1965–1966.* Princeton, NJ: Princeton University Press.

Robinson, Oliver C., Gordon R.T. Wright, and Jonathan A. Smith. 2013. "The Holistic Phase Model of Early Adult Crisis." *Journal of Adult Development* 20(1): 27–37.

Rough Guides. 2017. *Rough Guide to Bali and Lombok.* London: Apa Group.

Sampson, Robert J. 2008. "What Community Supplies." Pp. 308–18 in *The Community Development Reader,* edited by J. DeFilippis and S. Saegert. New York: Routledge.

Sassen, Saskia. 2014. *Expulsions: Brutality and Complexity in the Global Economy.* Cambridge, MA: Harvard University Press.

Scholz, Trebor. 2017. *Uberworked and Underpaid: How Workers Are Disrupting the Digital Economy.* Malden, MA: Polity Press.

Scholz, Trebor, and Nathan Schneider, eds. 2016. *Ours to Hack and to Own: The Rise of Platform Cooperativism: A New Vision for the Future of Work and a Fairer Internet.* New York: OR Books.

Schwirian, Kent P., Timothy J. Curry, and Rachael A. Woldoff. 2004. *High Stakes: Big-Time Sports and Downtown Redevelopment.* Columbus: Ohio State University Press.

Seitchik, Allison E., Adam J. Brown, and Stephen G. Harkins. 2017. "Social Facilitation: Using the Molecular to Inform the Molar." Pp. 183–203 in *Oxford Library of Psychology: The Oxford Handbook of Social Influence,* edited by S.G. Harkins, K.D. Williams, and J.M. Burger. New York: Oxford University Press.

Sevin, Efe. 2013. "Places Going Viral: Twitter Usage Patterns in Destination Marketing and Place Branding." *Journal of Place Management and Development* 6(3): 227–39.

Shaffer, Margaret A., and David A. Harrison. 2006. "Expatriates' Psychological Withdrawal from International Assignments: Work, Nonwork, and Family Influences." *Personnel Psychology* 51(1): 87–118.

Simmel, Georg. 1903/50. "The Metropolis and Mental Life." Pp. 409–24 in *The Sociology of Georg Simmel*, edited by K.H. Woolff. New York: Free Press.

Sinek, Simon. 2009. *Start with Why: How Great Leaders Inspire Everyone to Take Action.* New York: Penguin.

Singleton, Mark. 2010. *Yoga Body: The Origins of Modern Posture Practice.* New York: Oxford University Press.

Small, Mario Luis. 2017. *Someone to Talk To.* New York: Oxford University Press.

Snedden, Megan. 2013. "When Work Is a Nonstop Vacation." BBC. August 30. Retrieved August 7, 2017 (http://www.bbc.com/capital/story/20130829-when-work-is-a-nonstop-vacation).

Spinks, Rosie. 2015. "Meet the 'Digital Nomads' Who Travel the World in Search of Fast Wifi." *The Guardian.* June 16. Retrieved August 7, 2017 (https://www.theguardian.com/cities/2015/jun/16/digital-nomads-travel-world-search-fast-wi-fi).

Spinuzzi, Clay. 2012. "Working Alone Together: Coworking as Emergent Collaborative Activity." *Journal of Business and Technical Communication* 26(4): 399–441.

Sprecher, Susan, Stanislav Treger, and Joshua D. Wondra. 2012. "Effects of Self-Disclosure Role on Liking, Closeness, and Other Impressions in Get-Acquainted Interactions." *Journal of Social and Personal Relationships* 30: 497–514.

Spreitzer, Gretchen M., Lindsey Cameron, and Lyndon Garrett. 2017. "Alternative Work Arrangements: Two Images of the New World of Work." *Annual Review of Organizational Psychology and Organizational Behavior* 4: 473–99.

Startupweekend.org. Retrieved January 15, 2019.

Stillerman, Joel. 2015. *The Sociology of Consumption: A Global Approach.* London: Polity Books.

Storper, Michael, and Alan J. Scott. "Rethinking Human Capital, Creativity and Urban Growth." *Journal of Economic Geography* 9(2): 147–67.

Streitfield, David. 2018. "Was Amazon's Headquarters Contest a Bait-and-Switch? Critics Say Yes." *New York Times.* Retrieved March 19, 2019 (https://www.nytimes.com/2018/11/06/technology/amazon-hq2-long-island-city-virginia.html).

Suttles, Gerald D. 1972. *The Social Construction of Communities.* Chicago: University of Chicago Press.

Swann, William B., Jr., and Jennifer K. Bosson. 2010. "Self and Identity." Pp. 589–628 in *Handbook of Social Psychology* (5th ed.), edited by S.T. Fiske, D.T. Gilbert, and G. Lindzey. New York: Wiley.

Tajfel, Henri, and John C. Turner. 1986. "The Social Identity Theory of Intergroup Behavior." Pp. 7–24 in *Psychology of Intergroup Relations*, edited by S. Worchel & W.G. Austin. Chicago: Nelson-Hall.

Thoits, Peggy A. 1989. "The Sociology of Emotions." *Annual Review of Sociology* 15: 317–42.

Tierney, Pamela. 2015. "An Identity Perspective on Creative Action in Organizations." Pp. 79–92 in *Oxford Handbook of Creativity, Innovation, and Entrepreneurship*, edited by C.E. Shalley, M.A. Hitt, and J. Zhou. New York: Oxford University Press.

Tiessen, James H. 1997. "Individualism, Collectivism, and Entrepreneurship: A Framework for International Comparative Research." *Journal of Business Venturing* 12(5): 367–84.

Tilly, Charles. 1973. "Do Communities Act?" *Sociological Inquiry* 43(3-4): 209–40.

Tönnies, Ferdinand. 1957 (1887). *Community and Society*, translated and edited by C.D. Loomis. London: Routledge and Kegan Paul.

Torpey, Elka, and Andrew Hogan. 2016. "Working in a Gig Economy." *Bureau of Labor Statistics.* May. Retrieved January 23, 2019 (https://www.bls.gov/careeroutlook/2016/article/what-is-the-gig-economy.htm?view_full).

Trades Union Congress. 2018. "Annual Commuting Time Is Up 18 Hours Compared to a Decade Ago, Finds TUC." *Trade Union Congress*. Retrieved June 3, 2019 (tuc.org.uk/news/annual-commuting-time-18-hours-compared-decade-ago-finds-tuc).

Tropical MBA. Retrieved January 15, 2019 (http://www.tropicalmba.com/dc/).

Turner, Victor. 1969. *The Ritual Process: Structure and Anti-Structure*. New York: Transaction Publishers.

Twenge, Jean M. 2006. *Generation Me: Why Today's Young Americans Are More Confident, Assertive, Entitled—and More Miserable Than Ever Before*. New York: Free Press.

Upton, Dell. 2007. "Sound as Landscape." *Landscape Journal* 26(1): 24–35.

Vallas, Steven P., and Emily R. Cummins. 2015. "Personal Branding and Identity Norms in the Popular Business Press: Enterprise Culture in an Age of Precarity." *Organization Studies (Journal of the European Group on Organization Studies)* 36(3): 293–319.

Van der Kroeff, Justus M. 1953. "Collectivism in Indonesian Society." *Social Research* 20(2): 193–209.

Veblen, Thorstein. 1899/1994. "The Theory of the Leisure Class." Pp. 1–404 in *The Collected Works of Thorstein Veblen*, Vol. 1. Reprint, London: Routledge.

Wellman, Barry. 1979. "The Community Question: The Intimate Networks of East Yorkers." *American Journal of Sociology* 84(5): 1201–31.

Wellman, Barry. 1988. "The Community Question Re-Evaluated." *Comparative Urban and Community Research* 1: 81–107.

Wellman, Barry. 1991. "Which Types of Ties and Networks Give What Kinds of Social Support?" Pp. 207–35 in *Advances in Group Processes*, Vol. 9, edited by E. Lawler and B. Markovsky. Greenwich, CT: JAI Press.

Wellman, Barry, and Scot Wortley. 1989. "Brothers' Keepers: Situating Kinship Relations in Broader Networks of Social Support." *Sociological Perspectives* 32(3): 273–306.

Wellman, Barry, and Scot Wortley. 1990. "Different Strokes from Different Folks: Community Ties and Social Support." *American Journal of Sociology* 96(3): 558–88.

Williams, Alex. 2019. "The New Sobriety." *New York Times*. Retrieved June 25, 2019 (https://www.nytimes.com/2019/06/15/style/sober-curious.html).

Williamson, Marianne. 1992. *A Return to Love: Reflections on the Principles of "A Course in Miracles."* New York: HarperCollins.

Wirth, Louis. 1938. "Urbanism as a Way of Life." *American Journal of Sociology* 44(1): 1–24.

Woldoff, Rachael A. 2011. *White Flight / Black Flight: The Dynamics of Racial Change in an American Neighborhood*. Ithaca, NY: Cornell University Press.

Woldoff, Rachael A., Travis Decola, and Robert C. Litchfield. 2011. "The Aspirational Creative Class: Urban Residential Preferences of College Students in Creative Majors." *City, Culture, and Society* 2(2): 75–83.

Woldoff, Rachael A., Dawn Marie Lozzi, and Lisa M. Dilks. 2013. "The Social Transformation of Coffee Houses: The Emergence of Chain Establishments and the Private Nature of Usage." *International Journal of Social Science Studies* 1(2): 205–18.

Woldoff, Rachael A., Lisa M. Morrison, and Michael Glass. 2016. *Priced Out: Stuyvesant Town and the Loss of Middle-Class Neighborhoods*. New York: New York University Press.

Wry, Tyler, and J.G. York. 2017. "An Identity-Based Approach to Social Enterprise." *Academy of Management Review*, 42(3): 437–60.

Yorks, Dayna M., Christopher A. Frothingham, and Mark Schuenke. 2017. "Effects of Group Fitness Classes on Stress and Quality of Life of Medical Students." *Journal of the American Osteopathic Association* 117(11): e17–e25.

Zhang, Ling Eleanor, and Vesa Peltokorpi. 2015. "Multifaceted Effects of Host Country Language Proficiency in Expatriate Cross-Cultural Adjustments: A Qualitative Study in China." *International Journal of Human Resource Management* 27(13): 1448–69.

Zhang, Raymond. 2017. "Southeast Asia's Ride-Hailing War Is Being Waged on Motorbikes." *New York Times*. Retrieved July 19, 2019 (https://www.nytimes.com/2017/12/08/technology/southeast-asia-ride-hailing.html).

INDEX

For the benefit of digital users, indexed terms that span two pages (e.g., 52–53) may, on occasion, appear on only one of those pages.

tattoos, 4–5, 54–55, 161–62
taxi cooperatives, 72–73
technology careers, 116, 142–43, 183
tech sabbath, 48–49
thirty-day visas, 66–67
Tirta Empul, 56
Tolle, Eckhart, 84
tourism, sustainability of, 189
tourist visit visas, 5, 205n19
travel costs, 66–67
tribes, 2, 186–87, 195n4
TripAdvisor, 65, 66–67
triple revolution, 77
trophy kids, use of term, 154
tropical diseases, 68–69

Ubud, Bali, 46, 58–59, 60, 61–62
underground economy, 138. *See also* work
    options and finances
Upwork.com, 118–19
urban subcultural theory (Fischer), 98

values. *See* core values, of digital nomads
virtual assistants (VAs), 118–19
visa agents, 70
visa runner stage
    explanation of, 5–6
    nomad stories, 161–71
visas, 5, 41–42, 66–67, 70, 138–40, 205n19
voluntary kinship (Fischer), 200n18

Wanderer bracelets, 135
water quality, 68, 199n50
water temples, 56
Wellman, Barry, 76
Western culture, pathological life/work
    aims, 8, 12–13, 22–23. *See also* creative
    class cities

WeWork, 128, 192
"What Community Supplies" (Sampson), 77
Who's Your City? (Florida), 16–18
Wi-Fi access, 60
Williamson, Marianne, 136–37
Winfrey, Oprah, 84
working holiday visas, 41–42
work options and finances, 113–51. *See also*
    coworking spaces
    coaching in personal development,
      116, 124–25
    dedicated remote employment
      contracts, 116–17
    employment markets, 138–41
    entrepreneurship, 119–21, 144–50,
      202n10, 204n41
    freelance work, 15–16, 117–19,
      140–41, 189–90
    functions of nomad hubs, 125–50
    funding creative passions, 122–23
    gig and project work, 121–22, 165
    income sources, 115–16
    masterminds, 145–47, 204n41
    negotiation of expertise, 141–43
    nomad stories, 113, 114–15, 116–17,
      119–24, 126, 128–29, 130–32, 133–
      35, 136–37, 138, 139–43, 144, 145,
      146–47, 149–51
    passive income streams, 123–24
    Startup Weekend events, 147–50
work tourism
    explanation of, 40–42
    as extractive industry, 70–73
    place branding for, 42–44

Yellow Flower, 153
Yoga Barn, The, 58–59, 163–64
yoga industry, 57–59, 61–62

JUL 2023